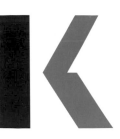

Kaplan Publishing are constantly finding new ways to make a difference to your studies and our exciting online resources really do offer something different to students looking for exam success.

This book comes with free MyKaplan online resources so that you can study anytime, anywhere

Having purchased this book, you have access to the following online study materials:

CONTENT	ACCA (including FFA,FAB,FMA)		FIA (excluding FFA,FAB,FMA)	
	Text	Kit	Text	Kit
iPaper version of the book	✓	✓	✓	✓
Interactive electronic version of the book	✓			
Progress tests with instant answers	✓			
Material updates	✓	✓	✓	✓
Latest official ACCA exam questions*		✓		
Extra question assistance using the signpost icon*		✓		
Timed questions with an online tutor debrief using the clock icon*		✓		
Interim assessment including questions and answers	✓		✓	
Technical articles	✓	✓	✓	✓

* Excludes F1, F2, F3, FFA, FAB, FMA

How to access your online resources

Kaplan Financial students will already have a MyKaplan account and these extra resources will be available to you online. You do not need to register again, as this process was completed when you enrolled. If you are having problems accessing online materials, please ask your course administrator.

If you are already a registered MyKaplan user go to www.MyKaplan.co.uk and log in. Select the 'add a book' feature and enter the ISBN number of this book and the unique pass key at the bottom of this card. Then click 'finished' or 'add another book'. You may add as many books as you have purchased from this screen.

If you purchased through Kaplan Flexible Learning or via the Kaplan Publishing website you will automatically receive an e-mail invitation to MyKaplan. Please register your details using this email to gain access to your content. If you do not receive the e-mail or book content, please contact Kaplan Flexible Learning.

If you are a new MyKaplan user register at www.MyKaplan.co.uk and click on the link contained in the email we sent you to activate your account. Then select the 'add a book' feature, enter the ISBN number of this book and the unique pass key at the bottom of this card. Then click 'finished' or 'add another book'.

Your Code and Information

This code can only be used once for the registration of one book online. This registration and your online content will expire when the final sittings for the examinations covered by this book have taken place. Please allow one hour from the time you submit your book details for us to process your request.

Please scratch the film to access your MyKaplan code.

Please be aware that this code is case-sensitive and
dashes within the passcode, but not when entering
support, please visit www.MyKaplan.co.uk

D1393073

PUBLISHING

BUSINESS TAX

Qualifications and Credit Framework

Level 4 Diploma in Accounting

Finance Act 2014

For assessments from 1 January to 31 December 2015

British Library Cataloguing-in-Publication Data

A catalogue record for this book is available from the British Library.

Published by
Kaplan Publishing UK
Unit 2, The Business Centre
Molly Millars Lane
Wokingham
Berkshire
RG41 2QZ

ISBN 978-0-85732-951-6

Printed and bound in Great Britain.

We are grateful to the Association of Accounting Technicians for permission to reproduce past assessment materials and example tasks based on the syllabus. The solutions to past answers and similar activities in the style of the syllabus have been prepared by Kaplan Publishing.

We are grateful to HM Revenue and Customs for the provision of tax forms, which are Crown Copyright and are reproduced here with kind permission from the Office of Public Sector Information.

CONTENTS

STUDY TEXT AND WORKBOOK

KAPLAN PUBLISHING

INTRODUCTION

HOW TO USE THESE MATERIALS

These Kaplan Publishing learning materials have been carefully designed to make your learning experience as easy as possible and to give you the best chance of success in your AAT assessments.

They contain a number of features to help you in the study process.

The sections on the Unit Guide, the Assessment and Study Skills should be read before you commence your studies.

They are designed to familiarise you with the nature and content of the assessment and to give you tips on how best to approach your studies.

STUDY TEXT

This study text has been specially prepared for the AAT AQ 2013 qualification.

It is written in a practical and interactive style:

- key terms and concepts are clearly defined
- all topics are illustrated with practical examples with clearly worked solutions based on sample tasks provided by the AAT in the new examining style
- frequent practice activities throughout the chapters ensure that what you have learnt is regularly reinforced
- 'pitfalls' and 'examination tips' help you avoid commonly made mistakes and help you focus on what is required to perform well in your examination.
- practice workbook activities can be completed at the end of each chapter

WORKBOOK

The workbook comprises:

Practice activities at the end of each chapter with solutions at the end of this text, to reinforce the work covered in each chapter.

Students may either attempt these questions as they work through the textbook, or leave some or all of these until they have completed the textbook as a final revision of what they have studied

ICONS

The study chapters include the following icons throughout.

They are designed to assist you in your studies by identifying key definitions and the points at which you can test yourself on the knowledge gained.

 Definition

These sections explain important areas of Knowledge which must be understood and reproduced in an assessment

 Example

The illustrative examples can be used to help develop an understanding of topics before attempting the activity exercises

 Activity

These are exercises which give the opportunity to assess your understanding of all the assessment areas.

Quality and accuracy are of the utmost importance to us so if you spot an error in any of our products, please send an email to mykaplanreporting@kaplan.com with full details, or follow the link to the feedback form in MyKaplan.

Our Quality Coordinator will work with our technical team to verify the error and take action to ensure it is corrected in future editions.

UNIT GUIDE

Principles of Business Tax (Knowledge)

3 credits

Calculating Business Tax (Skills)

3 credits

Purpose of the unit

The AAT has stated that this unit is to enable learners to understand the impact and significance of taxation on both unincorporated and incorporated businesses. By studying these taxes, learners can appreciate the tax implications of financial decisions made by such organisations.

Learning objectives

This unit will enable learners to:

- understand the impact of legislation and legislative changes
- understand tax law and its implications for unincorporated businesses
- understand tax law and its implications for incorporated businesses
- understand how to treat capital assets
- prepare the relevant pages of a tax return for an unincorporated business and accurately produce the computations to support this
- correctly complete corporation tax returns with all supporting computations for incorporated businesses.

Learning Outcomes and Assessment criteria

The unit consists of six learning outcomes testing Knowledge and Skills, which are further broken down into Assessment criteria. These are set out in the following table with Learning Outcomes in bold type and Assessment criteria listed underneath each Learning Outcome. Reference is also made to the relevant chapter within the text.

Knowledge (K) and Skills (S)

To perform this unit effectively you will need to know and understand the following:

		Chapter
1	**Prepare the relevant pages of a tax return for an unincorporated business and produce the computations to support this**	
1.1 S	Adjust trading profits and losses for tax purposes	11
1.2 S	Apply the basis of assessment for unincorporated businesses, including opening and closing years and overlap profits	13
1.3 S	Classify expenditure on capital assets in accordance with the statutory distinction between capital and revenue expenditure	4
1.4 S	Prepare computations of capital allowances	11
1.5 S	Make adjustments for private use of assets by owners	11
1.6 S	Divide profits and losses of partnerships amongst partners	12, 14
1.7 S	Prepare computations to show the changes in partnership structure for new partners and departing partners	12
1.8 S	Calculate national insurance contributions payable by self-employed persons	16

		Chapter
1.9 S	Identify and value any chargeable assets that have been disposed of; calculate the chargeable gain/or allowable loss and relevant reliefs as applicable under current tax law; and calculate any tax liability	20, 21, 22
1.10 S	Complete the self-employed or partnership supplementary pages of the tax return for individuals, and submit them within statutory time limits	11, 12, 15
2	**Complete corporation tax returns and supporting computations for incorporated businesses**	
2.1 S	Adjust trading profits and losses for tax purposes	3
2.2 S	Classify expenditure on capital assets in accordance with the statutory distinction between capital and revenue expenditure	3, 4
2.3 S	Prepare computations of capital allowances	4
2.4 S	Enter adjusted trading profits and losses, capital allowances, investment income and capital gains in the corporation tax computation	2, 3, 4, 5, 6, 7, 8
2.5 S	Calculate taxable total profits, and other relevant figures, as it applies to companies with periods longer than, shorter than and equal to 12 months	5, 7
2.6 S	Calculate corporation tax payable, taking account of marginal relief and associated companies	6, 7
2.7 S	Complete corporation tax returns and submit them within statutory time limits	5, 6, 9
2.8 S	Identify and value any chargeable assets that have been disposed of and calculate the chargeable gain/or allowable loss and relevant reliefs as applicable under current tax law	17, 18, 19, 22

		Chapter
3	**Understand the impact of legislation and legislative changes**	
3.1 K	Identify relevant tax authority legislation and guidance	Throughout
3.2 K	Explain the system of penalties and interest as it applies to income tax, corporation tax and capital gains tax	9, 15
3.3 K	Apply any changes that occur to taxation codes of practice, regulation or legislation	Implied throughout
4	**Understand tax law and its implications for unincorporated businesses**	
4.1 K	Describe the main regulations relating to disallowed expenditure	3, 11
4.2 K	Explain the basis of assessment for unincorporated businesses	13
4.3 K	Explain the availability and types of capital allowances	4, 11
4.4 K	Identify alternative loss reliefs, demonstrating how best to utilise that relief	14
4.5 K	Explain the basic allocation of trading profits between partners	12
4.6 K	Explain the self assessment process including payment of tax and filing of returns for unincorporated businesses	15, 16
4.7 K	Identify due dates of payments, including payments on account	15, 16
5	**Understand tax law and its implications for incorporated businesses**	
5.1 K	Explain the calculation of corporation tax payable by different sizes of companies including those with associated companies	2, 6, 7
5.2 K	Identify alternative loss reliefs for trading losses, describing how best to utilise that relief	8
5.3 K	Identify corporation tax payable and the due dates of payment, including instalments	6, 7, 9

		Chapter
6	**Understand how to treat capital assets**	
6.1 K	Identify capital gains exemptions and reliefs on assets	17, 20, 22
6.2 K	Identify methods by which chargeable assets can be disposed of	17, 18, 19, 21
6.3 K	Identify the rate of tax payable on gains on capital assets disposed of by individuals and entitlement to relevant reliefs	20, 22

Delivery guidance

The AAT have provided delivery guidance giving further details of the way in which the unit will be assessed.

Adjusted profits:

This is a vital area for all business types as it is the start to the tax computation. Learners can expect to receive information which has been prepared under accounting rules, and need to adjust or amend it appropriately for taxation rules. Such information could be for sole traders, partnerships or limited companies.

Students can expect questions on:

- the differences between capital and revenue expenses

- the impact of private usage on assets and expenses

- differences between the computation of profits and losses for unincorporated and incorporated businesses

- tax allowable and disallowable expenses.

Learners will mainly be required to complete computational style questions for this topic area, but some written tasks can be expected.

Capital allowances:

Always a complex area, learners must ensure that they are fully conversant with this topic. Not only must learners know how to do the calculations for plant and machinery, they must be able to explain these rules to tax payers. Capital allowances as they apply to opening, continuing and closing businesses must also be understood.

The key differences between the capital allowance computations under income tax rules and corporate tax rules must be understood, in particular the effect of private usage of assets.

Specifically included areas are:

- all allowances, such as annual investment allowance, first year allowance and writing down allowance

- rules from previous tax years as they would affect an accounting period ended during the relevant tax year

- capital allowances periods that straddle tax years

- computations of balancing allowances and balancing charges

- cessation of trade situations
- treatment of short life assets
- difference in capital allowance treatment for unincorporated and incorporated business.

Excluded topics

Periods which commence prior to 1 January 2013.

Partnerships and basis periods:

In relation to partnerships, there will be a maximum of three partners in any one scenario. Changes to partnerships will be assessed for changes to the partnership agreement and changes to the actual partners themselves.

The topic of basis periods could be for sole traders and/or partnerships. Therefore, learners can expect to see questions where the partnership has a new partner and/or a retiring partner, leading to computations of both the partnership profits and the profits assessable to tax under the basis periods rules.

Students can expect questions on:

- commencement of trade for a sole trader
- continuation of trade for a sole trader
- cessation of trade for a sole trader
- computation of, and impact of, overlap profits
- computation of partnership profits where the profit sharing ratio has changed, including salaries and interest on capital
- computation of partnership profits where the partners have changed
- impact of basis periods when there are changes to partners.

Whilst these tasks will be mainly of a computational nature, learners must be prepared to provide written information for clients.

Excluded topics

Change of accounting date.

Limited liability partnerships.

Incorporated businesses:

As the computation of trading profits, capital allowances and capital gains will be assessed in other tasks, learners will not be expected to calculate these figures again when tackling a task which combines these figures. Instead, learners will need to be able to show understanding of how all sources of income for incorporated businesses are used to compute the taxable total profits.

From there, learners will need to be able to calculate the corporation tax payable.

Specifically, learners can expect questions on:

- computation of taxable total profits from:
    - trading income
    - property income
    - investment income
    - capital gains
- qualifying charitable donations
- accounting periods less than, equal to, or longer than, twelve months
- computation of corporation tax payable including:
    - 31 March straddle
    - impact of associated companies
    - all corporation tax rates
    - due dates of payment for small and large companies.

These questions will mainly be of a computational nature.

National Insurance:

This is only in relation to self-employed persons. Therefore, only Class 2 and Class 4 will need to be understood.

Excluded topics

Class 1 or 3 NIC

Losses:

Losses for both unincorporated and incorporated businesses can be expected.

For unincorporated businesses, learners can expect questions on:

- carry forward of losses

- losses to be set against other income in the year of the loss and carry back to the previous year

- losses to be set against capital gains.

For incorporated businesses, learners can expect questions on:

- losses set against current profits

- losses set against profits from earlier years

- losses carried forward

- impact of losses on relief for qualifying charitable donations.

Both theory based questions and computational style questions can be expected within this topic area.

Excluded topics

Losses in the early years of trading.

Terminal loss relief.

Time limits for claiming loss relief.

Section numbers from the Acts.

Written advice to clients:

Badges of trade will feature so that learners can demonstrate understanding of how to decide if a trade is being carried on. Learners may need to be able to consider various situations and scenarios, and apply the rules under the badges of trade to determine how HMRC would consider the situation in the light of trading.

Other, theory based areas, that underpin the entire specific taxation topic will be assessable within this area.

Learners can expect questions that require them to:

- explain what taxation documentation individuals need to maintain and for how long

- explain implications of not providing full, accurate and timely tax information to HMRC

- explain how the various penalties and interest are applied by HMRC for:
  - late payment of both income tax and corporation tax
  - late filing of tax returns
  - filing of incorrect tax returns
  - failing to notify of chargeability
- explain the self-assessment process, including payments on account
- compute payments on account amounts, covering a number of years.

This topic area will be assessed via a free text written response from the learner. The questions will usually be client focussed so students will be expected to address their answers in a manner appropriate to such an audience.

Excluded topics

Complex computations such as daily interest.

Tax returns:

There are three tax returns which are assessable:

- Self-employment
- Partnerships
- CT600 short version

These are expected to be completed with accuracy and completed in conjunction with the learner's own figures, if appropriate.

Capital gains tax:

Learners must appreciate who and what is taxable under this heading. The impact that relationships between connected persons have on disposal of capital assets needs to be understood.

Computations can be expected on:

- chargeable assets being disposed of
- enhancement expenditure
- part disposals
- chattels
- share disposals, including matching rules, bonus issues and rights issues as they apply to both individuals and companies

- reliefs applicable to individuals, including:
  - Entrepreneurs' relief
  - rollover relief
  - gift relief
- capital gains tax payable by individuals
- annual exempt amount for individuals
- relief for capital losses
- indexation allowance for companies.

There are three questions that cover this large topic, one of which will only consider the gains and losses for shares. This question will be humanly marked.

Excluded topics

Takeovers and reorganisations.

Small part disposals of land.

Small part disposals rules as applicable to rights issues.

Reinvestment relief.

Computation of the indexation factor – this will be provided if appropriate

THE ASSESSMENT

The format of the assessment

The assessment has 11 tasks.

Task	Learning outcome	Assessment criteria	Maximum Marks	Title for topics within task range
1	1, 2, 4	1.1, 1.3, 1.5, 2.1, 2.2, 4.1	12	Computation of adjusted profits for sole traders, partnerships and limited companies
2	1, 2, 4	1.3, 1.4, 1.5, 2.2, 2.3, 4.3	14	Computation of capital allowances for sole traders, partnerships and limited companies
3	1, 4	1.2, 1.6, 1.7, 4.2, 4.5	12	Split of partnership profits for new, continuing and leaving partners. Basis periods for sole traders and partnerships
4	2, 5	2.4, 2.5, 2.6, 5.1, 5.3	12	Taxable total profits and corporation tax payable
5	1	1.8	4	National insurance contributions
6	4, 5	4.4, 5.2	6	Losses for sole traders, partnerships and limited companies
7	3, 4	3.1, 3.2, 3.3, 4.6, 4.7	10	Theory underpinning topic, payments on account and penalties
8	1, 2	1.10, 2.7	6	Tax returns
9	1, 2, 6	1.9, 2.8, 6.1, 6.2	8	Basics of capital gains tax
10	1, 2	1.9, 2.8	10	Taxation of shares
11	1, 2, 6	1.9, 2.8, 6.1, 6.3	6	Capital gains tax exemptions, losses, reliefs and tax payable

Time allowed

The time allowed for this assessment is **2 hours.**

Pass mark

The pass mark is 70%.

STUDY SKILLS

Preparing to study

Devise a study plan

Determine which times of the week you will study.

Split these times into sessions of at least one hour for study of new material. Any shorter periods could be used for revision or practice.

Put the times you plan to study onto a study plan for the weeks from now until the assessment and set yourself targets for each period of study – in your sessions make sure you cover the whole course, activities and the associated questions in the workbook at the back of the manual.

If you are studying more than one unit at a time, try to vary your subjects as this can help to keep you interested and see subjects as part of wider knowledge.

When working through your course, compare your progress with your plan and, if necessary, re-plan your work (perhaps including extra sessions) or, if you are ahead, do some extra revision / practice questions.

Effective studying

Active reading

You are not expected to learn the text by rote, rather, you must understand what you are reading and be able to use it to pass the assessment and develop good practice.

A good technique is to use SQ3Rs – Survey, Question, Read, Recall, Review:

1   **Survey the chapter**

    Look at the headings and read the introduction, knowledge, skills and content, so as to get an overview of what the chapter deals with.

2   **Question**

    Whilst undertaking the survey ask yourself the questions you hope the chapter will answer for you.

3   Read

Read through the chapter thoroughly working through the activities and, at the end, making sure that you can meet the learning objectives highlighted on the first page.

4   Recall

At the end of each section and at the end of the chapter, try to recall the main ideas of the section / chapter without referring to the text. This is best done after a short break of a couple of minutes after the reading stage.

5   Review

Check that your recall notes are correct.

You may also find it helpful to re-read the chapter to try and see the topic(s) it deals with as a whole.

Note taking

Taking notes is a useful way of learning, but do not simply copy out the text.

The notes must:

- be in your own words
- be concise
- cover the key points
- be well organised
- be modified as you study further chapters in this text or in related ones.

Trying to summarise a chapter without referring to the text can be a useful way of determining which areas you know and which you don't.

Three ways of taking notes

1   Summarise the key points of a chapter

2   Make linear notes

A list of headings, subdivided with sub-headings listing the key points.

If you use linear notes, you can use different colours to highlight key points and keep topic areas together.

Use plenty of space to make your notes easy to use.

3   Try a diagrammatic form

The most common of which is a mind map.

To make a mind map, put the main heading in the centre of the paper and put a circle around it.

Draw lines radiating from this to the main sub-headings which again have circles around them.

Continue the process from the sub-headings to sub-sub-headings.

Highlighting and underlining

You may find it useful to underline or highlight key points in your study text – but do be selective.

You may also wish to make notes in the margins.

Revision phase

Kaplan has produced material specifically designed for your final examination preparation for this unit.

These include pocket revision notes and a bank of revision questions specifically in the style of the syllabus.

Further guidance on how to approach the final stage of your studies is given in these materials.

Further reading

In addition to this text, you should also read the 'Student section' of the 'Accounting Technician' magazine every month to keep abreast of any guidance from the examiners.

TAX RATES AND ALLOWANCES

The tax rates and allowances that you need in the assessment will be given to you. These allowances are provided for use in this Study text.

Capital allowances

Annual investment allowance

From 1 January 2013	£250,000
From 1/6 April 2014	£500,000

Plant and machinery writing-down allowance	18%

Motor cars

CO_2 emissions up to 95 g/km	100%
CO_2 emissions between 96 and 130 g/km	18%
CO_2 emissions over 130 g/km	8%

Energy efficient and water saving plant

First year allowance	100%

Capital gains

Annual exempt amount	£11,000
Standard rate	18%
Higher rate (applicable where taxable income over £31,865)	28%
Entrepreneurs' relief rate	10%
Entrepreneurs' relief limit	£10,000,000

National Insurance rates

Class 2 contributions:	£2.75 per week
Small earnings exemption	£5,885 p.a.

Class 4 contributions:

Main rate	9%
Additional rate	2%
Lower earnings limit	£7,956
Upper earnings limit	£41,865

Corporation tax

Financial year	**2014**	**2013**
Small profits rate	20%	20%

Marginal relief:

Lower limit	£300,000	£300,000
Upper limit	£1,500,000	£1,500,000
Standard fraction	1/400	3/400

Main rate	21%	23%

Marginal relief formula: Fraction × (U – A) × N/A

Introduction to business tax

1

Introduction

This chapter presents an overview of business tax.

CONTENTS
1   Contents of the Study Text
2   Types of business entity

1 Contents of the Study Text

1.1 Three categories

The Study Text can be split into three specific categories:

		Chapters
•	Companies	2 – 9
•	Unincorporated traders (sole traders and partnerships)	10 – 16
•	Chargeable gains	17 – 22

The aim is to gradually consider each of the ways of taxing a business.

This will depend on whether an individual has decided to set up his business as a:

* company;
* sole trader; or
* partnership.

2 Types of business entity

2.1 Company

A company is a legal entity, separate from its owners and managers.

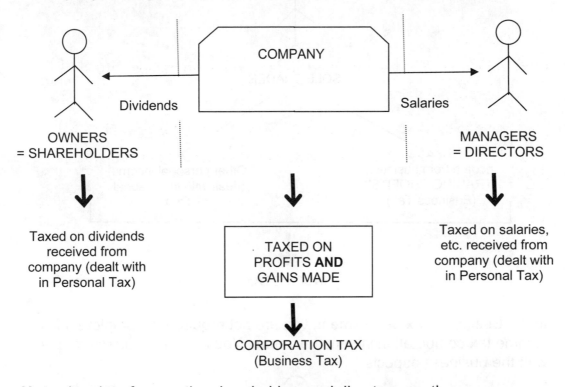

Note: In a lot of cases the shareholders and directors are the same people. However, this will have no effect on the Business Tax assessment.

2.2 Sole trader

An individual setting up an unincorporated business (i.e. not a company) on his/her own is known as a sole trader.

A sole trader is not a separate legal entity.

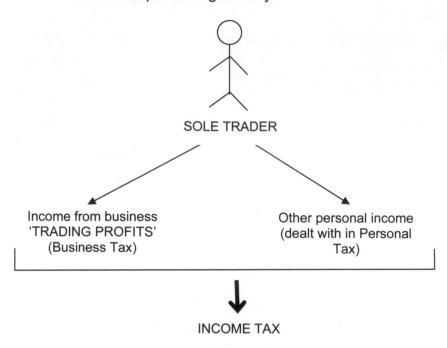

In the Business Tax assessment, you are not required to complete a full income tax computation/income tax return. You are only required to deal with the business aspects.

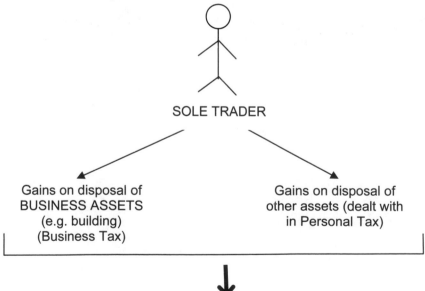

In the Business Tax assessment, you may be required to complete a capital gains tax computation. However, the sole trader will only have disposed of business assets.

2.3 Partnership

A partnership is another form of unincorporated business, but it is not a separate legal entity.

A partnership is formed when a number of individuals carry on a business together with a view of profit, i.e. a partnership is effectively a collection of sole traders working together.

Each partner pays his own income tax and capital gains tax on his share of the partnership's profits and gains.

3 Summary

There are three types of business entity to consider:

- company
- sole trader
- partnership.

Each has its own special rules for calculating profits, gains and tax.

Principles of corporation tax

2

Introduction

It is very likely that one of the 'tasks' in the assessment will include the preparation of a corporation tax computation. This chapter sets the scene.

KNOWLEDGE

Identify relevant tax authority legislation and guidance. (3.1 K)

Explain the calculation of corporation tax payable by different sizes of companies including those with associated companies. (5.1 K)

SKILLS

Enter adjusted trading profits and losses, capital allowances, investment income and capital gains in the corporation tax computation. (2.4 S)

CONTENTS

1   Introduction to corporation tax
2   The principle of chargeable accounting periods
3   Pro forma corporation tax computation

1 Introduction to corporation tax

1.1 Corporation tax

Corporation tax is paid by companies. A company can be recognised in the assessment because its name will end with:

- Ltd (which means limited company); or

- plc (which means public limited company).

Sole traders and partnerships do not pay corporation tax.

> ### Example
>
> Which of the following businesses pay corporation tax?
>
> (a) Amy's Motor Dealers Ltd
>
> (b) Bert & Sons
>
> (c) Christopher Diamond plc
>
> (d) Eric & Co
>
> **Solution**
>
> Corporation tax is paid by companies:
>
> (a) Amy's Motor Dealers Ltd (name ends in Ltd); and
>
> (c) Christopher Diamond plc (name ends in plc).

1.2 Corporation tax computation

Companies pay corporation tax on the total of their income and gains. Firstly, the period covered by the computation must be identified and then the income and gains to be included in the computation are calculated.

2 The principle of chargeable accounting periods

2.1 Chargeable accounting period

A company prepares a corporation tax computation for a 'chargeable accounting period' (CAP).

In a normal situation, a company prepares a 12 month set of financial accounts and has a matching CAP for corporation tax purposes.

 Example

Fred Ltd has prepared accounts for the year ended 31 December 2014. Gordon plc has prepared accounts for the year ended 31 March 2015.

For what period will the companies prepare their corporation tax computations?

Solution

Fred Ltd – computation for year ended 31 December 2014.

Gordon plc – computation for year ended 31 March 2015.

2.2 Accounts of less than 12 months

A CAP can be any length up to 12 months.

Where a company prepares a set of financial accounts of less than 12 months, there is a short CAP for corporation tax purposes.

 Example

Harry Ltd has previously prepared accounts to 31 December, until 31 December 2013. The company has now changed to preparing accounts to 30 September.

What is its first chargeable accounting period using the new date?

Solution

Harry Ltd has a CAP of 9 months ended 30 September 2014.

2.3 Accounts of more than 12 months

A CAP can never exceed 12 months.

Therefore, when a company prepares financial accounts for a period of more than 12 months, there must be two CAPs for corporation tax purposes.

The two CAPs are:

* CAP for the first 12 months; and

* a separate CAP for the balance period.

No other combination is acceptable.

A corporation tax computation is prepared for each CAP.

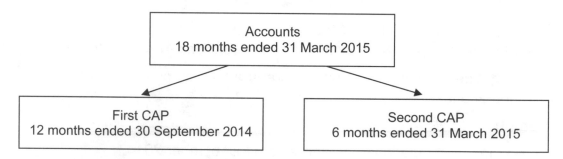

The method of allocating profits from the accounts between the two periods is covered in Chapter 7.

 Activity 1

Imogen Ltd has prepared accounts for the 15 months ended 31 July 2015.

What is/are the chargeable accounting period(s)?

A   15 months ended 31.7.15

B   3 months ended 31.7.14 and 12 months ended 31.7.15

C   12 months ended 30.4.15 and 3 months ended 31.7.15

D   11 months ended 31.3.15 and 4 months ended 31.7.15

---

3 Pro forma corporation tax computation

In the assessment you may be expected to prepare a corporation tax computation using a similar layout to the pro forma set out below.

The pro forma will become more familiar as you work through the chapters.

The pro forma includes references to the chapters in the textbook where each entry is considered in detail.

Company name

Corporation tax computation for XX months ended.......(the CAP)

	£	Chapter(s)
Trading profit	X	3, 4
Non-trade interest	X	5
Property income	X	5
Chargeable gains	X	5, 18
Total profits	X	
Less: Qualifying charitable donations	(X)	5
Taxable total profits (TTP)	X	
Corporation tax liability (at relevant rate)	X	6

Note that prior to the rewrite of the corporation tax legislation, 'Taxable total profits' (TTP) used to be called 'Profits chargeable to corporation tax' (PCTCT) and this term is still used on HMRC's corporation tax returns (see Chapter 5).

4 Summary

Identifying the correct chargeable accounting period(s) is an essential first step in correctly calculating corporation tax.

5 Test your knowledge

 ## Workbook Activity 2

Period of assessment

Read the following statements and state whether they are true or false.

1   Any business carrying on trading activities will pay corporation tax.

2   Corporation tax computations are prepared for a period of account.

3   The chargeable accounting period will always be the same as the period of account.

4   When a period of account exceeds 12 months there will be two chargeable accounting periods; the first 12 months and then the balance of the period.

 ## Workbook Activity 3

Harris Ltd

Harris Ltd started trading on 1 March 2014 and prepares its first set of accounts to 30 April 2015.

What is Harris Ltd's first chargeable accounting period?

A   2 months ended 30 April 2014

B   12 months ended 28 February 2015

C   13 months ended 31 March 2015

D   14 months ended 30 April 2015

Adjusted trading profits

Introduction

Task 1 in the assessment will involve the computation of adjusted profits for sole traders, partnerships and limited companies.

This chapter deals with adjustments for companies.

See Chapter 11 for further information on the taxation of trading profits for a sole trader or partnership.

KNOWLEDGE

Identify relevant tax authority legislation and guidance. (3.1 K)

Describe the main regulations relating to disallowed expenditure. (4.1 K)

SKILLS

Adjust trading profits and losses for tax purposes. (2.1 S)

Classify expenditure on capital assets in accordance with the statutory distinction between capital and revenue expenditure. (2.2 S)

Enter adjusted trading profits and losses, capital allowances, investment income and capital gains in the corporation tax computation. (2.4 S)

CONTENTS

1   Introduction to adjusted trading profits
2   Adjustment of profits calculation
3   Disallowable expenditure
4   Income included in the accounts but not taxable as trading profits
5   Detailed pro forma adjustment of profits

1 Introduction to adjusted trading profits

The first entry shown on the pro forma corporation tax computation is the adjusted trading profits of the company.

The starting point in determining the amount of adjusted trading profits is the net profit as shown in the accounts (i.e. the statement of profit or loss, formerly known as the income statement). However, the accounts may, for example, contain expenditure items which are not allowable for tax purposes.

The net profit shown in the accounts of the company must be adjusted for tax purposes to give the adjusted trading profit.

2 Adjustment of profits calculation

2.1 Pro forma adjustment of profits calculation

	£	Detail in:
Net profit as per accounts	X	
Add: Disallowable expenditure	X	Section 3
	——	
	X	
Less: Income included in the accounts but not taxable as trading profit	(X)	Section 4
	——	
Adjusted trading profit before capital allowances	X	
Less: Plant and machinery capital allowances	(X)	Chapter 4
	——	
Adjusted trading profit	X	
	——	

The three categories of adjustment are considered in turn, in the sections and chapters indicated above. In this chapter you will calculate the 'adjusted trading profit before capital allowances'.

An adjustment of profits will definitely be required in the assessment. It is essential that you understand the entries made.

3 Disallowable expenditure

3.1 The principle of disallowable expenditure

Expenditure included in the accounts has the effect of reducing the profits of the company.

However, some items of expenditure are acceptable deductions for financial accounting purposes but are not acceptable for corporation tax purposes.

As a result, the reduction that was made in the accounts must be reversed for corporation tax purposes (i.e. the expenditure must be added back).

This is known as 'disallowable expenditure'.

The general principle to be applied in relation to any particular item of expenditure is that it will only be allowable in arriving at the taxable trading profits if it has been incurred 'wholly and exclusively' for the purposes of the trade.

Example

Jack Limited has the following statement of profit or loss for its year ended 31 March 2015:

	£
Sales	100,000
Less: Cost of sales	(40,000)
Gross profit	60,000
Less: Expenditure (Note 1)	(35,000)
Net profit per accounts	25,000

Note 1: The expenditure can be analysed as follows:

	£
Wholly and exclusively for the purposes of the trade	33,000
Not wholly and exclusively for the purposes of the trade (i.e. disallowable expenditure)	2,000
	35,000

Calculate the adjusted trading profits of Jack Limited for the year ended 31 March 2015.

Solution

Jack Ltd – Adjusted trading profit – year ended 31 March 2015

	£
Net profit per accounts	25,000
Add: Disallowable expenditure	2,000
Adjusted trading profits	27,000

3.2 Examples of disallowable expenditure

The general principle of expenditure being incurred 'wholly and exclusively' for the purposes of the trade can be used in the assessment if you are in doubt.

However, there are many common examples of disallowable expenditure that tend to appear regularly in assessments. The common examples are set out in the remainder of Section 3.

3.3 Fines

Fines on the business should be disallowed as the business is expected to operate within the law. Typical examples are penalties for late payment of VAT or for breaking health and safety regulations.

In practice, however, HM Revenue and Customs usually allow a deduction for parking fines incurred by employees while on company business. This does not, however, apply to directors' parking fines.

Example

King plc is a chemical manufacturing company

King plc – Statement of profit or loss – year ended 31 March 2015

	£	£
Sales		700,000
Less: Cost of sales		(200,000)
Gross profit		500,000
Less: Expenditure		
Fine for polluting rivers	20,000	
Other allowable expenditure	200,000	
		(220,000)
Net profit per accounts		280,000

Calculate the adjusted trading profits for the year ended 31 March 2015.

Solution

King plc – Adjustment of profits – year ended 31 March 2015

	£
Net profit per accounts	280,000
Add: Disallowable expenditure	
Fine for polluting rivers	20,000
Adjusted trading profit	300,000

3.4 Fraud

Fraud undertaken by directors is disallowed. This is because the loss does not relate to the company's trading activities.

However, petty theft by non-senior employees which is not covered by insurance is generally allowable.

3.5 Donations

Donations to charity usually fail the wholly and exclusively test.

In practice, this means that there is no deduction for donations to national charities or political parties, unless there is some clear benefit to the trade.

However, small donations to local charities are allowable as they can effectively be classed as advertising.

Other charitable donations are always disallowed in the adjustment of profits computation.

These other charitable donations are however allowable for corporation tax purposes, but instead of allowing in the adjustment of profits, they are deducted in arriving at the company's taxable total profits as qualifying charitable donations. This is considered in detail at Chapter 5.

Example

Louise Ltd has net profit before tax of £123,000. In calculating this profit a deduction has been made for charitable donations as follows:

	£
To NSPCC – national charity	7,000
To local children's hospital	300
	7,300

Calculate the adjusted trading profit assuming all other expenses are allowable.

Solution

Louise Ltd – Adjusted trading profit

	£
Net profit per accounts	123,000
Add: Donation to national charity	7,000
Adjusted trading profit	130,000

3.6   Capital expenditure

As a rule, capital expenditure charged to the statement of profit or loss (e.g. depreciation, purchase of small capital items) is not an allowable expense for tax purposes.

For this reason, 'repairs' expenditure requires careful review, as it often contains items of a capital nature.

In general, repairs and redecoration are considered to be revenue expenditure and are therefore allowable. Improvements, however, are disallowable.

In practice, the distinction between a repair and an improvement is not clear-cut. Repairs usually involve restoring an asset to its original condition or replacing part of an asset with a modern equivalent. Improvements usually involve enhancing the asset in some way.

For example, the replacement of a single glazed window with a double glazed window would be a repair, whilst installing a new window in a brick wall would be an improvement.

Second-hand non-current assets

If a non-current asset (i.e. fixed asset) is purchased in a dilapidated state, and the purchase price reflects this, then initial 'repairs' expenditure to bring the asset to a fit state for use in the business will not be allowable.

Two cases illustrate the difficulty of applying this rule in practice.

In *Law Shipping Co Ltd v CIR (1923)* the company purchased a ship which was not in a seaworthy condition. Expenditure on making the ship seaworthy was held to be capital and therefore disallowed.

In *Odeon Associated Theatres Ltd v Jones (1971)* the company purchased some cinemas which were in a run-down condition. Expenditure incurred in renovating the cinemas was held to be revenue and therefore allowable.

These two cases can be distinguished. In the *Law Shipping* case, the ship was not usable until the repairs were undertaken and the purchase price reflected the condition it was in. By contrast, in the Odeon case, the cinemas were capable of being used for the purpose of the trade prior to their renovation. In addition, the repairs were to remedy normal wear and tear.

You do not need to remember the names of the legal cases mentioned but the principle of the decision made is important.

Legal expenses of a capital nature

The general rule to determine whether legal expenses are allowable is to look at the nature of the expense.

If they relate to a capital item, such as the purchase of a building, then the expenses will be disallowed.

Note that for tax purposes, leases are always treated as capital in this context, therefore legal expenses relating to leases will normally be disallowed (but see exception below).

If they relate to a revenue item, such as the collection of trade receivables or employee issues such as drawing up contracts of employment, then they will be allowable.

There are some exceptions to the capital rule.

The following expenses are allowable:

- the legal costs of renewing a short lease (i.e. 50 years or less).

- the legal costs of defending title to a non-current asset (e.g. disputes over land boundaries).

Depreciation

Depreciation, together with any loss on the sale of non-current assets, is disallowed and must be added back.

Relief for capital allowances may be given instead of depreciation (see Chapter 4).

 Activity 1

For each of the following items of expenditure, state if they would be treated as capital or revenue items for tax purposes.

1	Purchase of new office furniture	Revenue / Capital
2	Rates	Revenue / Capital
3	Repair to make asset usable after purchase	Revenue / Capital
4	Legal costs re purchase of new offices	Revenue / Capital
5	Legal costs re renewal of 20 year lease	Revenue / Capital

3.7 Irrecoverable debts (receivables)

The write off of a trade debt in the accounts as an irrecoverable debt is an allowable deduction from trading profits. Consequently the recovery of a trade debt previously written off is taxable.

The write off of a non-trade debt (e.g. a loan to a former employee or a supplier), is not an allowable deduction from trading profits.

Note that 'irrecoverable debts' are also sometimes referred to as 'impaired debts' or 'bad debts'.

A provision for bad debts, which is calculated in accordance with International Financial Reporting Standards (IFRS), is allowable when computing adjusted trading profits.

As a company's accounts are required to be drawn up using IFRS and these standards require objective evidence of impairment in a debt, a bad debt provision in a company's accounts will be specific in nature and allowable for tax purposes.

It is possible that a company's accounts could include a provision relating to matters other than receivables (e.g. inventory provision). Any movement in a provision described as general should be disallowed for tax purposes.

Example

The impaired debts account of Greenidge Ltd for the year ended 30 April 2015 appears as follows:

	£		£
		Provision for irrecoverable debts b/f	445
Written off:			
– Trade debts	274		
– Former employee	80	Recoveries – trade debts	23
Provision for irrecoverable debts c/f	419	Statement of profit or loss	305
	———		———
	773		773
	———		———

Show any adjustments required for tax purposes.

Solution

In this example, the information is presented in the form of a 'T' account.

The first stage is to establish a breakdown of the statement of profit or loss charge of £305.

Remember that this figure comprises amounts written off and recovered, and movements in provisions.

Statement of profit or loss charge:

	£	Allowable?
Decrease in provision for irrecoverable debts (£445 – £419)	(26)	✓
Amounts written off:		
Trade debt	274	✓
Former employee	80	✗
Recoveries – trade	(23)	✓
	———	
	305	
	———	

The write off of the debt owed by the former employee is disallowed.

The recovery of the trade debts is taxable.

The *decrease* in the provision for irrecoverable debts will be specific in nature and is therefore not adjusted for.

The adjustment to the trading profits for tax purposes is therefore:

Add: Former employee debt written off   £80
                                                        ─────

Write-offs of non-trading loans (such as here to the former employee) are not allowable deductions from trading profits, however they are allowed as a deduction from non-trade related interest income – take care, as it is easy to miss this point (see Chapter 5).

3.8 Interest payable

For the purpose of computing a company's adjusted trading profits you need to distinguish between trading and non-trading payments.

Interest payable on trading loans is an allowable expense in calculating trading profits. For example, interest payable on bank overdrafts or loan notes (also referred to as debentures) used for trading purposes.

Interest payable on non-trading loans is not an allowable expense in calculating trading profits. A loan to purchase an investment would be an example of a non-trading loan. Interest on such a loan should be added back in the adjustment to profits computation.

However, interest in respect of non-trading loans is allowable as a deduction from non-trade related interest income (see Chapter 5).

3.9 Other miscellaneous adjustments

Pre-trading expenditure

Expenditure incurred up to seven years before a trade commences is allowed as an expense of the first CAP of trading, provided it would have been allowable had the trade existed at the time the expenditure was incurred.

Entertaining

The cost of entertaining customers and suppliers is disallowed. However, the cost of entertaining staff is allowable.

Gifts

Gifts to employees are allowable.

Other gifts, for example gifts to customers, are only allowable if they fulfil the following three conditions:

- They incorporate a conspicuous advertisement for the business.

- The total cost per donee is not more than £50 per annum.

- The gift is not food, drink (alcoholic or otherwise) or tobacco or a voucher.

Note that if the cost exceeds the £50 limit, the whole amount is disallowed.

Therefore desk diaries or pens embossed with the company name usually qualify but a bottle of whisky carrying an advert for the company would not.

Trade samples

Trade samples which are not for resale are allowable.

Hire or lease charges

The rules for disallowing part of the leasing charges for cars are based on the level of CO_2 emissions.

Leasing charges for cars with CO_2 emissions of 130 g/km or less are allowed in full.

There is a standard disallowance of 15% of the leasing charges for a lease on a car with CO_2 emissions over 130 g/km.

 Example

BSG Ltd starts to lease two cars on 1 May 2014. The details of the leased cars are as follows:

(1)   The first car has a retail price of £21,000 and CO_2 emissions of 145 g/km. The leasing charges up to 31 December 2014 are £6,400.

(2)   The other car has a retail price of £15,000 and CO_2 emissions of 120 g/km. The leasing charges up to 31 December 2014 are £4,700.

Show the amount disallowed for the purposes of calculating the adjusted trading profits in the year ended 31 December 2014.

Solution

The only disallowance is for the first car as the CO_2 emissions exceed 130 g/km.

The disallowed amount is (15% of £6,400) = £960

3.10   Dividends

Dividends are paid out of profits after they have been subjected to tax. They are not expenses incurred in earning those profits. They are therefore not allowable expenditure.

However, there is normally no adjustment required as the computation starts with the 'net profit' which for a company is before the deduction of dividends paid. In a correctly drawn up statement of profit or loss dividends have not been deducted from net profit and so do not need to be added back.

An adjustment is only required if a question specifically tells you that the net profit given is after dividends have been deducted.

3.11   Summary

Common items of allowable and disallowable expenditure are summarised below.

Expenditure	Allowable	Disallowable
Fines	Employee parking fines	Other fines and penalties
Fraud	Petty theft by non-senior employees	By directors
Donations	Small donations to local charities	Other donations
In relation to non-current assets	Capital allowances on plant and machinery	Depreciation Profit or loss on sale
Repairs	Revenue expenditure Repairs and redecoration	Capital expenditure Improvements Work required on a newly-purchased asset to make it fit for use
Legal expenses	Relate to revenue matters – debt collection, employee contracts	Relate to capital matters – but note exceptions
Irrecoverable debts	Trade debts	Non-trade debts
Interest payable	On trading loans	On non-trading loans
Entertaining	Staff	Customers and suppliers
Gifts	To employees Other gifts provided conditions satisfied	All other gifts
Car leasing	CO_2 emissions of 130 g/km or less	Other cars – disallow 15% of leasing costs

Activity 2

1   Jamelia Ltd operates a business selling high quality second hand clothes.

Which of the following costs is NOT deductible in arriving at the tax adjusted trading profits?

A   Repairs to shop premises, carried out two weeks after the shop opened.

B   Advertising in the local paper.

C   Parking fine incurred by the Managing Director for parking outside the shop.

D   Cost of writing off stock that wouldn't sell.

2   Bakers R Us Ltd incurred the following expenses for the year ended 31 March 2015, but is unsure of their treatment for tax purposes.

Which of the following is NOT deductible in arriving at Bakers R Us Ltd's tax adjusted trading profit?

A   The cost of new plant and machinery that is used in the bread making process.

B   The write off of a trade debt owed by a customer.

C   Legal fees in chasing the debt owed by a customer.

D   A provision against the debt owed by a customer.

4   Income included in the accounts but not taxable as trading profits

4.1   Types of income

The following are examples of income which may be included in the statement of profit or loss, but which are not taxable as trading profits.

- Income taxed in another way, for example rental income (property income), interest receivable.

- Dividends received.

- Profits on sales of non-current (i.e. capital) assets.

4.2 Effect

As these types of income are not taxable as trading profits, they must be deducted to arrive at the correct adjusted trading profits.

5 Detailed pro forma adjustment of profits

5.1 Pro forma for a company

	+ £	− £
Net profit per accounts	X	
Add: Disallowable expenditure:		
Depreciation	X	
Loss on sale of non-current assets	X	
Capital expenditure	X	
Legal expenses of capital nature	X	
Fines and penalties	X	
Donations (unless small and to local charity)	X	
Entertaining (other than staff)	X	
Gifts to customers	X	
Proportion of car leasing costs	X	
Less: Income in accounts but not trading profits:		
Rental income		X
Profit on sale of non-current assets		X
Interest receivable		X
Dividend income		X
	X	X
	(X)	
Adjusted trading profit before capital allowances	X	

Example

The statement of profit or loss of STD Ltd for the year ended 31 March 2015 showed a profit of £42,000 after accounting for the following items:

Expenditure:	£	Income:	£
Depreciation	9,500	Insurance recovery	
Loan note interest (Note 1)	8,000	re flood damage to	
Irrecoverable debts:		trading inventory	6,500
Trade debts written off	4,000	Profit on sale of plant	3,200
– Increase in provision	1,000		
Entertainment expenses			
(Note 2)	2,700		
Legal fees re new lease	3,200		
General expenses (Note 3)	1,800		

Notes:

(1) The loan note was issued to raise finance to purchase plant and machinery for the purpose of the trade.

(2) Entertainment consists of expenditure on:

	£
Entertaining customers	1,200
Staff dance (30 people)	900
Gifts to customers of food hampers	600

(3) General expenses comprises:

	£
Parking fines	
(relating to employees on company business)	300
Fees for employees attending courses	1,500

Compute the adjusted trading profit for the above period.

Solution

Step 1: Start your solution with the company's net profit:

	+ £	– £
Net profit		42,000

Step 2: Add back any disallowable items of expenditure

Go through each expense in turn and decide whether or not it needs to be added back. If it does require adding back, add the figure to the plus column of your pro forma.

If you do not know how to treat a particular item, guess. You have a good chance of getting the right answer.

Step 3: Deduct income in accounts which is not taxable as trading profits

Deal with any income in the order in which it appears in the accounts. For each item, ask yourself whether it relates to the company's trade.

If it does, no action is required. If it does not, include the figure in the minus column.

Step 4: Finish by totalling the pro forma

Note that it is not essential for you to put headings such as 'disallowable expenditure' on your pro forma. You could simply state 'add' and 'less'.

You do, however, need to list each adjusted item in words as well as figures.

Approach in CBT

You might be given a pro forma and will not have to type in expense headings and numbers. Instead you may have to select correct headings and numbers from drop down menus.

Alternatively, the task in the assessment may require you to drag and drop each item which needs adjustment into the appropriate part of the computation.

STD Ltd – Adjustment of profit for the year ended 31 March 2015

	+ £	– £
Net profit	42,000	
Depreciation	9,500	
Entertainment expenses	1,800	
Legal fees	3,200	
General expenses	—	
Profit on sale of plant		3,200
	56,500	(3,200)
	(3,200)	
Adjusted trading profit	53,300	

Explanation

1   Depreciation (capital expenditure) is not an allowable deduction.

2   Loan note interest is allowable (assuming the loan note proceeds were used for trading purposes).

3   Write-offs of trade debts and provisions in a company's accounts are allowable.

4   Expenditure on entertaining customers is not allowable. Expenditure on entertaining staff is allowable. The cost of the hampers is not allowable as they contain food.

5   The legal fees in respect of the new lease are a capital item, and are therefore not allowable.

6   Parking fines incurred by employees will generally be allowed. Course fees are also allowable, assuming the course relates to the company's trade.

7   The insurance recovery is in respect of trading inventory. It is therefore taxable as trading profits, and no adjustment needs to be made.

8   Profits on the sale of non-current assets are effectively negative depreciation and are therefore not taxable.

In an assessment you should try to work methodically through the statement of profit or loss and ensure you deal with all relevant items.

Example

The statement of profit or loss of DTS Ltd for the year ended 31 March 2015 showed a profit of £53,000 after accounting for the following items:

Expenditure:	£	Income:	£
Depreciation	8,300	Rents received	8,400
Loss on sale of lorry	6,000	Profit on sale of plant	7,400
Legal fees re employees' service contracts	600		
Penalty for late VAT return	2,200		
Repairs (Note 1)	6,400		

Note:

(1) Included in the figure for repairs is an amount of £5,000 incurred in installing new windows in a recently acquired second-hand warehouse.

This building had suffered fire damage resulting in all of its windows being blown out shortly before being acquired by DTS Ltd. Other repairs were of a routine nature.

Compute the adjusted trading profit for the above period.

Solution

DTS Ltd – Adjustment of profit for the year ended 31 March 2015

	+ £	– £
Net profit	53,000	
Depreciation	8,300	
Loss on sale of lorry	6,000	
Legal fees re employees' service contracts	—	
Penalty for late VAT return	2,200	
Repairs	5,000	
Rents received		(8,400)
Profit on sale of plant		(7,400)
	74,500	(15,800)
	(15,800)	
Adjusted trading profit	58,700	

Explanation

1   Depreciation (capital expenditure) is not an allowable deduction.

2   Losses on the sale of non-current assets are treated in the same way as depreciation – they are added back. Conversely, profits on the sale of non-current assets are deducted.

3   Legal fees in connection with the service contracts are wholly and exclusively for the trade and are therefore allowable.

4   VAT penalties are not allowable.

5   The cost of new windows is not allowable. It is capital expenditure required to put a new asset into a usable state (*Law Shipping* case).

6   Rents received are taxable as property income and not trading profits, therefore deduct.

In an assessment you should try to work methodically through the information given and ensure you deal with all relevant items.

 Activity 3

Brazil Ltd

The following is the statement of profit or loss of Brazil Ltd, an established company, for the year ended 30 April 2015:

	£	£
Sales		240,458
Less: Cost of sales		(183,942)
Gross profit		56,516
Other income		5,000
Salaries and wages	24,174	
Rent and rates	8,560	
Legal and professional charges	3,436	
General expenses	1,211	
Depreciation	3,047	
		(40,428)
Net profit		21,088

The following further information is given:

(1) **Other income**

This comprises bank deposit interest for the year received on 30 April 2015.

(2) **Legal and professional charges**

This item includes the following:

	£
Legal fees in connection with new lease	325
Legal fees in connection with action by employee for unfair dismissal	830
Payment to employee for unfair dismissal	1,200
Accountancy charges	1,081

(3) **General expenses**

These include a payment of £200 to the Friends of the Local Hospital, and a donation of £25 to Save the Children.

Required:

Calculate the adjusted trading profit for the year for tax purposes.

 Activity 4

Cashew Ltd

The following is the statement of profit or loss of Cashew Ltd, an established company, for the year ended 31 March 2015:

	£	£
Gross profit		47,214
Other income		4,000
Salaries and wages	20,509	
Repairs to premises	3,263	
Travelling and entertaining expenses	1,964	
Irrecoverable debts	(630)	
Depreciation	2,120	
		(27,226)
Net profit		23,988

The following further information is given:

(1) **Other income**

This comprises bank deposit interest for the year received on 31 March 2015.

(2) **Repairs to premises**

Included in this item is £1,450 incurred in fitting a new shop-front to a former office and £250 for the initial repainting of a new shop.

(3) **Travelling and entertaining expenses**

These include expenses of entertaining UK customers of £326 and gifts to customers of Christmas hampers costing £528 (cost £48 each).

(4) **Irrecoverable debts**

The figure in the accounts is made up as follows:

	£
Trade debt recoveries	(232)
Decrease in provision for irrecoverable trade debts	(398)
	(630)

Required:

Calculate the adjusted trading profit for the year for tax purposes.

6 Summary

You should now be able to successfully attempt questions requiring you to calculate the adjusted trading profit for corporation tax purposes.

The starting point for computing adjusted trading profits is the net profit shown in the company's accounts. This must be adjusted in respect of the following items:

- Disallowable expenditure.

  The main types of disallowable expenditure are:

  - expenditure not wholly and exclusively for the purpose of the trade

  - expenditure disallowed under the detailed rules.

- Income included in the accounts but not taxable as trading profits. For example:

  - rents and interest

  - profits on the sale of capital assets.

When writing out answers on paper, it is advisable to use a '+' and '–' column and deal with each adjustment as you work methodically through the question. There is no need to arrange your answer into the two types of adjustment shown above. Either presentation may be seen in the assessment.

7 Test your knowledge

Workbook Activity 5

Katrina Ltd

Katrina Ltd incurred the following costs for the year ended 31 March 2015. For each item of expenditure state the tax treatment in arriving at Katrina Ltd's trading profits.

Choice of treatment is 'Deductible' or 'Not deductible'.

1. Fees incurred in chasing a debt which was over 6 months old.

2. Legal fees incurred in acquiring a 5 year lease over new shop premises.

3. Qualifying charitable donation to a national charity.

4. Small donation to a local charity.

5. Costs of purchasing computer equipment.

Workbook Activity 6

Adjustment of profits

What adjustment, if any, should you make for the following items included in a company's statement of profit or loss when calculating adjusted trading profits?

State 'add back' or 'no adjustment'.

1. Managing director's salary (he owns 99% of the shares)

2. Overdraft interest

3. Interest on a loan to purchase an investment property

4. Gifts of diaries to customers, costing £5 each and embossed with the company's name

5. Gifts of bottles of wine to customers, costing £5 each and embossed with the company's name

Workbook Activity 7

Tricks Ltd

Tricks Ltd's statement of profit or loss for the year ended 31 March 2015 was as follows:

	£	£
Sales		370,150
Loan note interest receivable		4,100
UK dividends received (net of tax credit)		12,000
Profit on the sale of an investment		2,750
		————
		389,000
Allowable trading expenses	125,750	
Disallowable trading expenses	5,900	
Loan note interest payable (Note)	8,100	
	————	(139,750)
		————
Net profit		249,250
		————

Note: The funds raised by the issue of the loan note were used to purchase machinery for use in the business.

Required:

Calculate Tricks Ltd's adjusted trading profits for the year ended 31 March 2015.

Workbook Activity 8

Cricket Limited

Cricket Limited has the following results for the year ended 31 December 2014:

	£		£
Salaries, wages	20,041	Gross trading profit	802,350
Legal charges (Note 1)	2,436		
Impaired debts (Note 2)	480		
Depreciation – Factory	20,000		
– Plant	10,000		
Repairs (Note 3)	7,800		
Sundry expenses (allowable)	3,492		
Net profit	738,101		
	802,350		802,350

Notes:

(1) **Legal charges**

	£
Debt collection	1,136
Staff service agreements	300
In connection with lease of new office premises	1,000
	2,436

(2) **Impaired debts**

	£
Loan to former employee written off	200
Increase in provision for impaired debts	280
	480

(3) **Repairs**

	£
Repainting	200
New office furniture	7,600
	7,800

Required:

Show Cricket Limited's adjusted trading profits for the year ended 31 December 2014.

Workbook Activity 9

Uranus Ltd

The following items are charged against profit in the accounts of Uranus Ltd for the year ended 31 March 2015:

1   Running expenses of the managing director's BMW totalling £10,000 (including depreciation of £6,000). His total mileage in the year was 12,000 of which 6,000 was private. The car was owned by Uranus Ltd.

2   Entertainment expenditure totalling £25,000 of which £10,000 was incurred on overseas customers, £11,000 on UK customers and £4,000 on the annual company dinner for 200 employees.

3   Lease rental of £6,000 on sales director's car costing £20,000. The lease commenced on 1 April 2014. The car has CO_2 emissions of 145 g/km.

Required:

State how you would deal with each of the above items when preparing the company's computation of adjusted trading profits for the year ended 31 March 2015.

 Workbook Activity 10

Saturn Ltd

The following items are charged against profit in the accounts of Saturn Ltd for the year ended 31 March 2015:

1   A payment of £616 to the Royal National Lifeboat Institution (a registered national charity).

2   The write off of £8,000 against a trade debt of the company, being 80% of the debt. The liquidator of the debtor company had advised Saturn Ltd of this figure but in the event £5,000 of the debt was paid in May 2015.

3   Trade samples costing £7,000 in total which are put through the letter boxes of 2,000 homes in the East Midlands.

Required:

State how you would deal with each of the above items when preparing the company's computation of adjusted trading profits for the year ended 31 March 2015.

Capital allowances – plant and machinery

Introduction

In the assessment there will be tasks relating to the calculation of trading profits.

These will include a task testing adjusting of profits (as per Chapter 3) and a task to calculate the plant and machinery capital allowances.

Capital allowances are a very important topic.

KNOWLEDGE

Identify relevant tax authority legislation and guidance. (3.1 K)

Explain the availability and types of capital allowances. (4.3 K)

SKILLS

Classify expenditure on capital assets in accordance with the statutory distinction between capital and revenue expenditure. (1.3 S) / (2.2 S)

Prepare computations of capital allowances. (2.3 S)

Enter adjusted trading profits and losses, capital allowances, investment income and capital gains in the corporation tax computation. (2.4 S)

CONTENTS

1   Introduction to capital allowances
2   Qualifying expenditure
3   The allowances
4   Calculating the allowances
5   Capital allowances treatment of cars
6   Short life assets
7   Pro forma computation for capital allowances on plant and machinery
8   Impact of the length of the accounting period
9   Business cessation

1 Introduction to capital allowances

1.1 Capital allowances

Capital allowances are a form of depreciation that is allowable for tax purposes. The allowances are only given on certain items of capital expenditure.

This syllabus includes plant and machinery capital allowances only.

1.2 Capital allowances v depreciation

Each business can decide its own rate of depreciation for accounting purposes. In theory, identical businesses with the same assets could have different amounts of depreciation.

In order for everyone to be treated the same, HMRC use a standard calculation of capital allowances for tax purposes.

The capital allowances are deducted instead of depreciation, to arrive at the adjusted trading profit.

 Example

Marcus Ltd and Nigel Ltd are two companies making the same products.

In the year ended 31 December 2015, both companies made profits before depreciation/capital allowances of £200,000. Both have only one piece of machinery that they bought in the year for £150,000.

The companies have different methods of calculating depreciation, giving the following amounts:

Marcus Ltd	£25,000
Nigel Ltd	£35,000

For tax purposes, both companies would have capital allowances of £150,000.

Compare the accounting profits and adjusted trading profits of both companies.

Solution

	Marcus Ltd £	Nigel Ltd £
Profit before depreciation	200,000	200,000
Less: Depreciation	(25,000)	(35,000)
Accounting profits	175,000	165,000
Adjustment of profits computation		
Accounting profits	175,000	165,000
Add: Depreciation	25,000	35,000
Adjusted profit before capital allowances	200,000	200,000
Less: Capital allowances	(150,000)	(150,000)
Adjusted trading profit	50,000	50,000

In reality there are likely to be many more adjustments that could give rise to different adjusted trading profits for tax purposes (as per Chapter 3).

However, this example illustrates that identical businesses could have different accounting profits, but have the same adjusted trading profits on which their tax is calculated.

2 Qualifying expenditure

2.1 What qualifies as plant and machinery?

There is no automatic right to tax relief for capital expenditure.

In order to qualify for capital allowances, expenditure must usually be in respect of plant or machinery.

The most common types of capital expenditure found in a set of financial accounts that are treated as 'plant and machinery' for tax purposes are:

- plant and machinery including moveable partitioning
- fixtures and fittings
- motor vehicles including cars, vans and lorries
- computer equipment and software

In addition, the cost of alterations to buildings needed for the installation of plant qualifies as plant and machinery.

3 The allowances

3.1 Main types of capital allowances

The following are the main types of capital allowances that may be available to a company in respect of plant and machinery.

(a) Writing-down allowance (WDA)

- given at 18% on a reducing balance basis on most assets
- given at 8% on a reducing balance basis for cars with CO_2 emissions exceeding 130 g/km (see section 5 below)

(b) Annual investment allowance (AIA)

- a 100% allowance for the first £500,000 (£250,000 prior to 1 April 2014) of expenditure incurred by a company on plant and machinery
- where a company has a year-end straddling 1 April 2014, the maximum AIA is found via time apportionment.

  for example, the maximum AIA for the year ended 31 December 2014 is £437,500 ((£250,000 × 3/12) + (£500,000 × 9/12)).

- where a company spends more than the maximum AIA the excess expenditure may qualify for a WDA.

(c) First year allowance (FYA)

– a 100% allowance is available on:

- low emission cars with CO_2 emissions of 95 g/km or less (see section 5 below)

- energy efficient and water saving technologies that are environmentally friendly (see section 4.8 below)

– additions qualifying for the FYA are added into the capital allowances computation after the deduction of WDAs.

 Example

Olivia Ltd purchased a machine costing £510,000 on 1 May 2014 in its year ended 31 March 2015. This is its only capital item.

Calculate the capital allowances for the first three years of ownership.

Solution

Olivia Ltd – Capital allowances

	£	Allowances £
Year ended 31 March 2015		
Cost	510,000	
AIA (max)	(500,000)	500,000
	10,000	
WDA (18% × £10,000)	(1,800)	1,800
	8,200	501,800
Year ended 31 March 2016		
WDA (18% × £8,200)	(1,476)	1,476
	6,724	
Year ended 31 March 2017		
WDA (18% × £6,724)	(1,210)	1,210
	5,514	

4 Calculating the allowances

4.1 Expenditure not pooled

As companies may have many assets, it would be extremely time-consuming to calculate allowances separately for each asset. Therefore, all qualifying expenditure is added to the main pool, apart from:

- cars with CO_2 emissions exceeding 130 g/km; and

- assets for which a short life asset election has been made.

4.2 General pool (or main pool)

Most items of plant and machinery go into the general pool (also known as the main pool). Once an asset enters the pool, it loses its identity. This means that the writing down allowance (WDA) is calculated on the balance of the whole pool of assets, rather than on the individual assets.

When a new asset is acquired, the purchase price increases the value of the pool. When an asset is disposed of, the pool value is reduced by the lower of the sale proceeds or the original cost of the asset (see section 4.6 below).

Allowances are given for chargeable accounting periods. Allowances commence in the year in which the expenditure is incurred. A full WDA is given in the year of purchase irrespective of the date of purchase within that year.

4.3 Annual investment allowance (AIA)

The AIA is a 100% allowance for the first £500,000 (£250,000 prior to 1 April 2014) of expenditure incurred by a company on plant and machinery in a 12-month period.

The AIA:

- is not available for expenditure on cars.

- applies for a 12 month accounting period. The allowance is pro-rated for short accounting periods.

Where expenditure on plant and machinery in a 12 month period exceeds the maximum the excess is added to the pool balance on which a WDA can be claimed.

4.4   First year allowance (FYA)

A first year allowance is given in the year that a qualifying asset is purchased.

A 100% FYA is given for expenditure on low emission cars (see section 5) and energy efficient and water saving technologies (see section 4.8).

 Example

Marble Ltd commenced trading on 1 October 2013. In its first year of trading the company made the following purchases:

- plant and machinery (purchased 1 May 2014)   £400,000
- a car for the office manager (CO_2 emissions 120 g/km)   £11,000

Required:

(a)   Calculate how much of Marble Ltd's capital expenditure is eligible for writing down allowances after deduction of the AIA.

(b)   What would your answer to part (a) be if the plant and machinery had cost £180,000?

Solution

(a)   **Year ended 30 September 2014**

	£	General pool £
Additions:		
Not qualifying for AIA:		
Car		11,000
Qualifying for AIA:		
Plant and machinery	400,000	
Less AIA (note)	(375,000)	
Balance eligible for 18% WDA	25,000	25,000
Eligible for WDA		36,000

Note: The maximum AIA for the year ended 30 September 2014 is £375,000 ((£250,000 × 6/12) + (£500,000 × 6/12)).

(b) If the plant and machinery had cost £180,000

	£	General pool £
Additions:		
Not qualifying for AIA:		
Car		11,000
Qualifying for AIA:		
Plant and machinery	180,000	
Less AIA (Note)	(180,000)	
	————	Nil
Eligible for WDA		11,000
		————

Note: The unused AIA of £195,000 (£375,000 – £180,000) is lost.

4.5 Writing down allowances (WDA)

An annual WDA of 18% is given on a reducing balance basis.

It is given on:

- the unrelieved expenditure in the pool brought forward at the beginning of the accounting period (known as the tax written down value (TWDV))

- plus any additions eligible for WDAs

- less disposals of plant and machinery.

The TWDV brought forward includes all prior period expenditure, less capital allowances already claimed.

 Example

Plaster Ltd commenced trading on 1 November 2013 preparing accounts to 31 October each year.

On 1 May 2014 the company purchased £420,000 of plant and machinery and on 1 August 2014 it purchased a car costing £22,000 with CO_2 emissions of 125 g/km.

Calculate the capital allowances available to Plaster Ltd for the year ended 31 October 2014.

Plaster Ltd – Capital allowances computation

	£	General pool £	Allowances £
Addition not qualifying for AIA			
Car		22,000	
Addition qualifying for AIA	420,000		
Less AIA (note 1)	(395,833)		395,833
	———		
Balance expenditure	24,167	24,167	
	———		
		46,167	
WDA (18% × £46,167)		(8,310)	8,310
		———	
TWDV c/f		37,857	
		———	
Total allowances			404,143
			———

Note: The maximum AIA for the year ended 31 October 2014 is £395,833 ((£250,000 × 5/12) + (£500,000 × 7/12)).

4.6 Disposal in the general pool

When a pool item is sold, the sale proceeds are deducted from the pool. However, this deduction cannot exceed the asset's original cost.

The following example illustrates the working of the general pool, including disposals.

Example

Apple Ltd prepares accounts to 31 March each year.

On 1 May 2014 Apple Ltd incurred expenditure of £10,000 on the purchase of shop fittings and machinery. On 1 June 2014 the company sold some machinery for £6,000 (cost £4,000).

On 5 May 2015 the company sold equipment for £2,395 which had cost £11,200 in May 2010.

The tax written down value of the pool at 1 April 2014 was £8,260.

Compute the capital allowances for the years ended 31 March 2015 and 31 March 2016.

Assume the rates of allowances for the year ended 31 March 2015 continue into the future.

Solution

Step 1: **Identify the balance brought forward at the beginning of the accounting period**

This is the *tax written down value* (Tax WDV or TWDV).

	Pool £
Year ended 31 March 2015	
TWDV brought forward	8,260

Step 2: **Identify the accounting periods in which the additions and disposals occur**

In the year ended 31 March 2015, Apple Ltd acquired plant costing £10,000 and sold plant for £6,000 (cost £4,000).

The second disposal occurs in the second accounting period.

Step 3: **Identify any additions on which the AIA can be claimed**

The plant acquired on 1 May 2014 qualifies for the AIA.

Deal with this addition *before* calculating the WDA for that year on the other items in the general pool.

Step 4: **Prepare the capital allowances computation**

Deal with one accounting period at a time.

	£	General pool £	Allowances £
Year ended 31 March 2015			
TWDV b/f		8,260	
Additions qualifying for AIA	10,000		
Less: AIA (max £500,000)	(10,000)		10,000
		Nil	
Disposals			
1 June 2014 (proceeds restricted to cost)		(4,000)	
		4,260	
WDA at 18%		(767)	767
TWDV c/f		3,493	
Total allowances			10,767

	£	General pool £	Allowances £
Year ended 31 March 2016			
TWDV b/f		3,493	
Disposals			
5 May 2015		(2,395)	
		1,098	
WDA at 18%		(198)	198
TWDV c/f		900	
Total allowances			198

4.7 Balancing charges

If on the disposal of an asset in the main pool, the disposal proceeds exceed the pool balance (after additions to the pool in the year have been added) a negative balance will be left on the pool.

This gives rise to a 'balancing charge'.

A balancing charge is added to the pool to bring the pool balance back to £Nil.

A balancing charge is treated as a negative capital allowance (i.e. added to the adjusted trading profit).

4.8 Energy efficient and water saving technologies

A first year allowance (FYA) of 100% is available on purchases of plant and machinery which is energy efficient, reduces water use or improves water quality.

100% FYA also applies to new (not second hand) electric vans.

The additions qualifying for FYA are included in the capital allowances computation after the deduction of the WDAs.

First year allowances are given in full in the period of purchase, **regardless** of the length of the accounting period (i.e. the FYA is never time apportioned).

5 Capital allowances treatment of cars

5.1 Motor vehicles v motor cars

In financial accounts we tend to group all motor vehicles together. For example, we include cars, vans, lorries, motor bikes, etc. together as motor vehicles.

For tax purposes, vans, lorries and motorbikes are treated like all other plant and machinery. They are included in the general pool and qualify for:

- AIA in the accounting period of purchase

- WDA.

However, motor cars have a different treatment.

5.2 Capital allowances treatment of motor cars

The capital allowances available in respect of motor cars depend on the level of their CO_2 emissions.

- Motor cars with CO_2 emissions between 96 and 130 g/km are added to the general pool and attract a WDA of 18%.

- If the car has emissions exceeding 130 g/km then it must be put into the special rate pool where the WDA is only 8%.

- New low emission motor cars are however eligible for a first year allowance (FYA) in the year of purchase.

  The rate of the FYA is 100% and it is only for cars with low CO_2 emissions (95 g/km or less).

  Very few cars are low emission cars.

You will be told the level of CO_2 emissions for each car in the assessment. Remember also that motor cars **never** qualify for the 100% AIA.

5.3 Disposals of cars

(a) *Main pool cars*

Deduct lower of disposal proceeds or original cost from main pool balance before WDA is calculated (i.e. like normal pool disposals)

(b) *Low emission cars*

As for (a)

(c) *Special rate pool cars*

Deduct lower of disposal proceeds or original cost from special rate pool balance.

If a positive balance remains – give WDA at 18% (main pool cars) or 8% (special rate pool cars) (Note this applies **even if there are no cars left** in the special rate pool).

If a negative balance remains – a balancing charge applies (see 4.7 above).

 Example

Patrick Ltd has a year ended 31 March 2015. Its general pool had a TWDV brought forward of £31,000 at 1 April 2014.

In the year ended 31 March 2015, it has purchased two assets:

(a) a car (CO_2 emissions 120 g/km) costing £9,000; and

(b) a van (not zero emission) costing £4,000 (on 1 February 2015).

There were no disposals in the year.

Required:

(a) Calculate the capital allowances for the year.

(b) What would your answer be to (a) if the car was low emission.

Solution

(a)   **Patrick Ltd – Capital allowances – year ended 31 March 2015**

	£	General pool £	Allowances £
TWDV b/f		31,000	
Additions not qualifying for AIA		9,000	
Additions qualifying for AIA			
Van	4,000		
AIA	(4,000)		4,000
		Nil	
Disposals		Nil	
		40,000	
WDA (£40,000 × 18%)		(7,200)	7,200
TWDV c/f		32,800	
Total capital allowances			11,200

(b)   **Patrick Ltd – Capital allowances – year ended 31 March 2015**

	£	General pool £	Allowances £
TWDV b/f		31,000	
Addition qualifying for AIA			
Van	4,000		
Less: AIA	(4,000)		4,000
		Nil	
Disposals		Nil	
		31,000	
WDA (£31,000 × 18%)		(5,580)	5,580
Addition qualifying for FYA			
Car	9,000		
Less: FYA (100%)	(9,000)		9,000
		Nil	
TWDV c/f		25,420	
Total capital allowances			18,580

Example

Joist Ltd prepares accounts to 31 March each year.

In the year ended 31 March 2015 it purchased the following cars:

(1)　Car costing £16,000 with CO_2 emissions of 118 g/km

(2)　Car costing £20,000 with CO_2 emissions of 180 g/km

The tax WDV brought forward on the general pool was £21,480.

Calculate Joist Ltd's capital allowances for the year ended 31 March 2015.

Solution

Joist Ltd – Capital allowances – year ended 31 March 2015

	General pool £	Special rate pool £	Allowances £
TWDV b/f	21,480		
Additions not qualifying for AIA			
Car – CO_2 96–130 g/km	16,000		
Car – CO_2 >130 g/km		20,000	
	37,480		
WDA at 18%	(6,746)		6,746
WDA at 8%		(1,600)	1,600
TWDV c/f	30,734	18,400	
Total capital allowances			8,346

Example

Grin Ltd prepares accounts to 31 March each year.

At 1 April 2014 the tax written down values brought forward were:

General pool £15,400
Special rate pool £17,000

During the year ended 31 March 2014 the company purchased plant for £20,000 and two cars with CO_2 emissions of 170 g/km costing £20,000 each.

There were no additions in the year ended 31 March 2016.

There were no disposals in the year ended 31 March 2015 but in the year ended 31 March 2016, one of the cars purchased in the previous year was sold for £13,500.

Required:

Calculate Grin Ltd's capital allowances for the years ended 31 March 2015 and 2016.

Assume the rates of allowances for the year ended 31 March 2015 continue into the future.

Solution

The first task is to decide how many columns are needed to answer this question. There are two balances brought forward which require their own columns and a column is required on the left to deduct the AIA.

A pro forma can then be set up as below

		General pool	Special rate pool	Allowances
	£	£	£	£
Year ended 31 March 2015				
TWDV b/f		15,400	17,000	

Now the additions can be put into the appropriate column and the allowances calculated.

Grin Ltd – Capital allowances

	£	General pool £	Special rate pool £	Allowances £
Year ended 31 March 2015				
TWDV b/f		15,400	17,000	
Additions:				
Not qualifying for AIA or FYA				
Cars over 130 g/km			40,000	
			———	
Qualifying for AIA			57,000	
Plant	20,000			
AIA	(20,000)			20,000
	———			
WDA at 18%		(2,772)		2,772
WDA at 8%			(4,560)	4,560
		———	———	
Tax WDV c/f		12,628	52,440	———
Total allowances				27,332
				———
Year ended 31 March 2016				
Disposals			(13,500)	
			———	
			38,940	
WDA at 18%		(2,273)		2,273
WDA at 8%			(3,115)	3,115
		———	———	
Tax WDV c/f		10,355	35,825	
		———	———	
Total allowances				5,388
				———

The example below demonstrates the full capital allowances working.

 Example

JNN Ltd started trading on 1 April 2014, preparing accounts to 31 March each year.

The following assets have been purchased since the company began trading.

Date of purchase	Asset	Cost
		£
9 November 2014	Used car	1,472
10 February 2015	Used car	928
1 March 2015	Plant and machinery	502,800
8 June 2015	New car	19,500
20 October 2016	New car	18,071

The cars acquired on 9 November 2014 and 10 February 2015 have CO_2 emissions between 96 – 130 g/km.

The new car acquired on 8 June 2015 has CO_2 emissions of 180 g/km; the one acquired on 20 October 2016 has CO_2 emissions of 90 g/km.

All the cars are used by employees 60% for business and 40% privately.

Calculate the capital allowances due for the three years ending 31 March 2017.

Assume the rates of allowances for the year ended 31 March 2015 continue into the future.

Solution

The approach is as follows:

*   Allocate additions and disposals to the relevant accounting periods. Any acquisitions made prior to the commencement of trading are treated as if made on the first day of trading.

*   Identify which additions qualify for AIA and FYA.

*   Ignore information about private use as this is not relevant to companies.

JNN Ltd – Capital allowances computation

	General pool £	Special rate pool £	Total allowances £
Y/e 31 March 2015			
TWDV b/f			
Additions: No AIA:			
Cars (£1,472 + £928)	2,400		
Qualifying for AIA			
Plant and machinery	502,800		
Less AIA (max 250,000)	(500,000)		500,000
	2,800		
	5,200		
WDA (18% × £5,200)	(936)		936
TWDV c/f	4,264		
Total allowances			500,936
Y/e 31 March 2016			
Additions: No AIA:			
Car – CO_2 > 130 g/km		19,500	
WDA @ 18%/8%	(768)	(1,560)	2,328
TWDV c/f	3,496	17,940	
Total allowances			2,328
Y/e 31 March 2017			
WDA @ 18%/8%	(629)	(1,435)	2,064
Additions qualifying for FYA			
Low emission car	18,071		
Less FYA @ 100%	(18,071)		18,071
	Nil		
TWDV c/f	2,867	16,505	
Total allowances			20,135

Activity 1

ENT Ltd prepares accounts to 31 December annually.

On 1 January 2014 the tax written down value of plant and machinery brought forward on the general pool was £24,000.

The following transactions took place in the year to 31 December 2014.

15 April 2014	Purchased car for £12,600 (emissions 180 g/km)
30 April 2014	Sold plant for £3,200 (original cost £4,800)
16 July 2014	Purchased car for £9,200 (emissions 120 g/km)
17 August 2014	Purchased car for £9,400 (emissions 125 g/km)
12 December 2014	Purchased energy saving plant for £2,615

In the following year to 31 December 2015, ENT Ltd sold for £7,900 the car originally purchased on 17 August 2014. The car originally purchased on 15 April 2014 was sold for £9,400 on 9 November 2015. There were no other transactions.

Required:

Compute the capital allowances and balancing adjustments for the years ended 31 December 2014 and 31 December 2015.

Assume the rates of allowances for the year ended 31 March 2015 continue into the future.

6 Short life assets

6.1 Short life asset treatment

Where an asset is expected to have a life of approximately nine years or less, it may be beneficial to remove it from the general pool and treat it as a short life asset.

Capital allowances are calculated separately for each short life asset. When the asset is sold there will be a balancing adjustment.

- Where it is sold for less than its TWDV there will be a tax deductible balancing allowance equal to the excess of the TWDV over the sales proceeds.

- Where it is sold for more than its TWDV there will be a taxable balancing charge equal to the excess of the sales proceeds over the TWDV.

A short life asset election will be advantageous if it is anticipated that the asset will be sold for less than its TWDV, such that a balancing allowance will arise, within the following eight accounting periods.

The following conditions apply:

- Short life asset treatment is not available for cars.

- If a short life asset is not sold within eight years of the end of the accounting period in which it was purchased, its TWDV will be transferred back into the general pool.

- A short life asset election must be made within two years of the end of the accounting period in which the expenditure was incurred.

However, note that the AIA is available against short life assets and the business can choose the expenditure against which the AIA is matched.

If eligible for the AIA, there may be no expenditure left to 'de-pool' and the short life asset election will not be made.

If there is expenditure in excess of the maximum AIA on assets eligible for the AIA, it may be advantageous for the AIA to be allocated against the general pool expenditure rather than a short life asset and for the short life asset election to be made.

 Example

View Ltd prepares accounts to 31 March each year.

On 1 May 2013 the company purchased a lathe for £20,000. The lathe was required for an 18-month contract and was sold on 30 November 2014 for £7,000. View Ltd claimed to treat the lathe as a short life asset.

The company purchased other machinery in the year ended 31 March 2014 such that the AIA limit was exceeded. The AIA was not claimed in respect of the lathe.

Required:

Calculate the capital allowances available in respect of the lathe for the years ended 31 March 2014 and 2015.

Solution

Capital allowances are calculated separately for the lathe and it is not included in the general pool.

View Ltd – Capital allowances

	Short life asset £	Allowances £
Year ended 31 March 2014		
Additions:		
Not qualifying for AIA or FYA		
Lathe	20,000	
WDA at 18%	(3,600)	3,600
	————	————
Tax WDV c/f	16,400	
Year ended 31 March 2015		
Disposals	(7,000)	
	————	
	9,400	
Balancing allowance	(9,400)	9,400
	————	————
Tax WDV c/f	–	
	————	

View Ltd has accelerated the capital allowances in respect of the lathe by treating it as a short life asset. If no short life asset claim had been made, the tax written down value would have remained in the general pool and View Ltd would have continued to claim WDAs in respect of it.

Note that if the lathe had been sold for more than £16,400, the claim would not have been beneficial as it would have resulted in a balancing charge.

6.2 Approach to assessment questions

Note that in the assessment you will not have to prepare computations involving short life assets. However you are expected to know the treatment of short life assets and may be asked to write a brief description of short life asset treatment.

7 Pro forma computation for capital allowances on plant and machinery

7.1 Plant and machinery allowances

Capital allowances are an important element of the syllabus. To answer capital allowances questions successfully, it is vital to use a methodical approach to work through the information in the question.

The following approach to computational questions together with the following pro forma will help you to deal with the information in the correct order.

7.2 Approach to computational questions

For plant and machinery capital allowances, adopt the following step-by-step approach:

1   Read the information in the question and decide how many columns you will require.

2   Draft the layout and insert the TWDV b/f (does not apply in a new trade).

3   Insert additions not eligible for the AIA or FYA into the appropriate column.

4   Insert additions eligible for the AIA in the first column, and then allocate the AIA to the additions. If additions exceed the maximum AIA available (watch out for year ends straddling 1 April 2014) then the remaining expenditure is added to the general pool and eligible for the WDA.

5   Deal with any disposal by deducting the lower of cost or sale proceeds.

6   Calculate the WDA at the appropriate rate on each of the pools.

7   Insert additions qualifying for 100% FYA in the first column and give the FYA.

8   Calculate the TWDV to carry forward to the next accounting period and add the 'total allowances' column.

9   Deduct the total allowances from the tax adjusted trading profits.

Pro forma capital allowances computation

	£	General pool £	Special rate pool £	Allowances £
TWDV b/f		X	X	
Additions:				
Not qualifying for AIA or FYA:				
Cars (96 – 130 g/km)		X		
Cars (over 130 g/km)			X	
Qualifying for AIA:				
Plant and machinery purchased	X			
Less AIA (do not exceed maximum)	(X)			X
	——			
Balance of AIA qualifying expenditure to general pool		X		
Disposals (lower of original cost or sale proceeds)		(X)	(X)	
		——	——	
		X	X	
WDAs at appropriate rates		(X)	(X)	X
Qualifying for FYA:				
Low emission cars (up to 95 g/km) and other qualifying assets	X			
Less FYA at 100%	(X)			X
	——	Nil		
		——	——	
TWDV c/f		X	X	
		——	——	
Total allowances				X
				——

7.3 Approach to assessment questions

In the CBT you will be given a blank grid to enter capital allowance figures.

It will not be necessary to enter lines dividing totals and subtotals, but otherwise you should be able to produce a computation that is the same as that which you would draw up on paper.

It is recommended that you prepare the computation on the paper provided before entering it on screen.

This activity will be manually marked.

8 Impact of the length of the accounting period

8.1 Short chargeable accounting periods

Capital allowances are computed for chargeable accounting periods and deducted in calculating trading profits.

The allowances calculated so far were all for 12 month accounting periods.

Where the accounting period is less than 12 months long, the AIA and WDA must be scaled down accordingly. You must perform this calculation to the nearest month.

If the period for which accounts are drawn up exceeds 12 months, the capital allowances are computed in two stages – the first 12 months, then the balance (see Chapter 2, Section 2.3).

Note that first year allowances are never time apportioned.

Therefore expenditure on low emission cars, energy efficient and water saving plant and machinery are always given the FYA in full, even if the length of the accounting period is less than 12 months.

Example

KNN Ltd started to trade on 1 April 2014 and, on that day, purchased a machine costing £505,000.

Calculate the capital allowances due for the first period of account on the assumption that accounts are prepared to

(i)   31 March 2015

(ii)   31 January 2015

(iii)   31 August 2015

Solution

	(i) 31 March 2015 (12 months) £	(ii) 31 January 2015 (10 months) £	(iii) 31 August 2015 (17 months) £
First period of account:			
First CAP (max 12 months)			
Addition:			
Qualifying for AIA:			
Plant and machinery	505,000	505,000	505,000
Less AIA: max	(500,000)		(500,000)
(10/12 × £500,000)		(416,667)	
	_____	_____	_____
	5,000	88,333	5,000
WDA (18%)	(900)		(900)
WDA (18%) × 10/12		(13,250)	
	_____	_____	_____
TWDV c/f	4,100	75,083	4,100
Second CAP			
(balance of period of account)			
WDA (18% × 5/12)	n/a	n/a	(308)
	_____	_____	_____
TWDV c/f	4,100	75,083	3,792
	_____	_____	_____

Note that in example (iii) corporation tax is charged separately on an accounting period of 12 months ending on 31 March 2015 and on an accounting period of 5 months ending on 31 August 2015 (see Chapter 2).

 Activity 2

ABC Ltd buys a car costing £16,000 in its accounting period of nine months to 31 December 2014. The car has CO_2 emissions of 120 g/km.

What capital allowances are available?

A £2,880

B £1,280

C £960

D £2,160

9 Business cessation

9.1 Final accounting period

In the accounting period of cessation no allowances are given other than balancing adjustments.

Any additions and disposals in the final period are allocated to the appropriate columns in the capital allowances working.

At the end of the period there will be no tax WDV carried forward, so there must be a balancing adjustment on all categories in the capital allowances working.

- If there is a positive balance remaining, a balancing allowance is given.
- If there is a negative balance remaining, a balancing charge arises.

 Example

DRN Ltd, a medium-sized company that had been trading for many years preparing accounts to 31 March, ceased trading on 30 September 2015.

The tax written down value of the pool at 1 April 2014 was £12,600. On 1 October 2014, DRN Ltd purchased some plant for £4,600.

All items of plant were sold on 30 September 2015 for £8,000 (no item was sold for more than cost).

Calculate the capital allowances due for the year ended 31 March 2015 and the six months ended 30 September 2015.

Solution

DRN Ltd – Capital allowances computation

	£	General pool £	Allowances £
Year ended 31 March 2015			
TWDV b/f		12,600	
Addition qualifying for AIA			
1 October 2014	4,600		
Less: AIA	(4,600)		4,600
		Nil	
Less: WDA (18%)		(2,268)	2,268
TWDV c/f		10,332	
Total allowances			6,868
6 months ended 30 September 2015			
Disposal		(8,000)	
		2,332	
Balancing allowance		(2,332)	2,332

Note: If plant is not sold until after the date of cessation, the proceeds eventually realised are used as the market value on cessation.

In effect it is treated as if sold on cessation for market value.

Activity 3

JKL Ltd ceased trading on 31 March 2015 and sold all of its plant and machinery on that date. The tax written down value of the pool at 1 April 2014 was £2,000.

What capital allowances are due based on the disposal proceeds below?

Please tick whether it is a balancing allowance or balancing charge and complete the amount.

Disposal proceeds	Balancing allowance	Balancing charge	Amount £
Scrapped for no proceeds			
Sold for £500			
Sold for £2,200			

10 Summary

Capital allowances are granted, instead of depreciation, to give tax relief for the cost of capital assets over the life of the assets.

A tabular layout is essential for computing capital allowances on plant and machinery.

The table should have separate columns for each of the following:

- general pool

- special rate pool

When an asset is expected to have a short life and to be sold for less than its written down value, it may be beneficial to exclude it from the general pool and treat it as a short life asset, however, this will not be tested in a full capital allowance computation.

When an accounting period is less than 12 months long, the maximum annual investment allowance and writing down allowances must be scaled down accordingly.

First year allowances are never scaled down.

11 Test your knowledge

 Workbook Activity 4

Plant and machinery allowances

Which one of the following statements is false?

A   The cost of alterations to buildings needed for the installation of plant is specifically eligible for plant and machinery capital allowances

B   The AIA is not available on cars, unless it is a low emission car

C   If the period of account of a business is less than 12 months, the AIA and WDA are scaled down proportionately

D   A short life asset election cannot be made in respect of a car

 Workbook Activity 5

Annual Investment Allowance

Which of the following acquisitions will qualify for the annual investment allowance?

A   A warehouse

B   Display equipment in a shop

C   A car used partly for business purposes by an employee

D   A pool car used exclusively for business use

Workbook Activity 6

Banks Ltd

Banks Ltd prepared accounts for the three month period ended 31 March 2015.

On 1 February 2015 a car with CO_2 emissions of 162 g/km was purchased for the sales director at a cost of £16,000. It is used by him 60% for business purposes.

What are the capital allowances available on this car for the three months ended 31 March 2015?

 Workbook Activity 7

Faraday Ltd

Faraday Ltd has the following fixed asset information for the year ended 31 March 2015.

Balances brought forward at 1 April 2014:	£
General pool	398,100
Special rate pool	28,060
Additions:	
Machinery	493,345
Energy saving plant	20,850
Office furniture	33,610
Managing Director's car (CO_2 emissions 178 g/km)	48,150
Disposals:	
Machinery (Cost £25,000)	16,875
Director's car (CO_2 emissions 198 g/km, cost £31,000))	23,100

Required:

Calculate Faraday Ltd's total capital allowances and show the balances to carry forward to the next accounting period.

Workbook Activity 8

Deni Ltd

Deni Ltd is a manufacturing business preparing accounts to 30 September each year.

At 1 October 2013, the written-down value of plant and machinery in the general pool was £25,000.

During the year ended 30 September 2014, the following transactions were undertaken:

Purchases		£
1 January 2014	Machinery	376,250
15 March 2014	Second-hand machinery	10,000
20 June 2014	MD's car with CO_2 emissions of 120 g/km (used 80% for business)	19,600
Sales		
30 July 2014	Machinery (cost £6,000)	1,750

Required:

Compute Deni Ltd's capital allowances for the accounting period ended 30 September 2014.

Workbook Activity 9

TEN Ltd

TEN Ltd prepares accounts to 31 December annually. On 1 January 2014, the balance of plant and machinery brought forward was £16,000.

The following transactions took place in the year to 31 December 2014.

15 April 2014   Purchased car for £15,000 (CO_2 emissions 125 g/km)

30 April 2014   Sold plant for £2,000 (original cost £1,600)

26 July 2014   Purchased two new cars for £9,300 each. Both of these cars qualify as low-emission cars.

In the following year to 31 December 2015, TEN Ltd sold for £7,600 one of the cars originally purchased on 26 July 2014.

The car originally purchased on 15 April 2014 was sold for £8,000 on 9 May 2015. There were no other transactions.

Required:

Compute the capital allowances for the years ended 31 December 2014 and 31 December 2015.

Assume the rates of allowances for the year ended 31 March 2015 continue into the future.

 Workbook Activity 10

Booker Ltd

Booker Ltd trades as a manufacturer in York and prepares accounts to 31 March each year. In 2014 it decided to change its year end and prepared accounts for the 9 month period to 31 December 2014.

The balance on the general pool was £18,150 at 1 April 2014. In July 2014, the company sold for £4,900 a car bought in 2010 for £7,800 (the car was purchased for £11,000 and had CO_2 emissions of 117 g/km). The company also purchased a second-hand car with CO_2 emissions of 125 g/km for £5,750 in July 2014. There was 10% private use of both cars by employees.

In December 2014 it also purchased plant for £378,750.

Required:

Calculate Booker Ltd's capital allowances for the 9 m/e 31 December 2014 and show the tax written-down values carried forward.

Calculation of taxable total profits

5

Introduction

In Chapters 2 – 4 we have been working towards calculating the adjusted trading profit of a company, the major source of income found on most corporation tax computations.

In this chapter we add to that knowledge to enable a full computation of the taxable total profits of a company.

KNOWLEDGE

Identify the relevant tax authority legislation and guidance. (3.1 K)

SKILLS

Enter adjusted trading profits and losses, capital allowances, investment income and capital gains in the corporation tax computation. (2.4 S)

Calculate taxable total profits, and other relevant figures, as it applies to companies with periods longer than, shorter than and equal to 12 months (2.5 S)

Complete corporation tax returns and submit them within statutory time limits. (2.7 S)

CONTENTS

1 Pro forma corporation tax computation
2 Taxable total profits
3 Corporation tax return (part 1)

1 Pro forma corporation tax computation

1.1 Pro forma

The first stage of a single company computation is to ascertain the company's taxable total profits. This comprises income and gains, less qualifying charitable donations.

The pro forma that was set out in Chapter 2 is set out again below. It will be referred to throughout this chapter.

Company name

Corporation tax computation for XX months ended…(the CAP)

	£
Trading profit	X
Non-trade interest	X
Property income	X
Chargeable gains	X
Total profits	X
Less: Qualifying charitable donations	(X)
Taxable total profits	X
Corporation tax liability at relevant rate (to be considered in Chapter 6)	X

2 Taxable total profits

2.1 Adjusted trading profit

The adjusted trading profit and capital allowances have been covered in the previous chapters, so you can now compute the trading profit that is entered in the computation of taxable total profits.

	Chapter	£
Adjusted trading profit	3	X
Less: Capital allowances		
Plant and machinery	4	(X)
Trading profit		X

2.2 Interest income (the loan relationship rules)

We consider the loan relationship rules at this point because of their relevance to the computation of trading profit and non-trade interest.

The loan relationship rules apply when a company pays or receives interest, or incurs any cost relating to a loan.

The legislation distinguishes between trading purposes and non-trading purposes, in relation to the interest.

For assessment purposes:

If a company **receives** interest you can normally assume that it is for non-trading purposes.

For example:

- interest received on a building society account.
- interest received on a bank deposit account.

If a company **pays** interest you can normally assume that it is for trading purposes.

For example:

- interest paid on a bank overdraft.
- interest paid on a loan to purchase new machinery.

You will, however, need to read the question carefully to make sure that these assumptions are not contradicted.

Net or gross?

Most interest paid by or received by a company is paid or received gross (with the exception of interest paid to individuals).

All amounts shown on corporation tax computations must be shown gross.

If interest is paid to an individual by a company it is paid net of 20% tax. Hence, the interest must be grossed up.

The gross interest is calculated as follows:

Interest paid to individual × 100/80

Example

Rye Ltd pays and receives the following amounts of interest.

		£
(a)	Interest received on deposit account with Bat East Bank plc	5,000
(b)	Interest paid on overdrawn business bank account	(2,000)
(c)	Interest paid on loan made to the company by Mr Smith	(2,000)

Compute the gross figures to be used in the corporation tax computation.

Solution

Gross amounts to be included in calculation of taxable total profits:

		£
(a)	Interest received	5,000
(b)	Interest paid on overdraft	(2,000)
(c)	Interest paid on loan by Mr Smith (£2,000 × 100/80)	(2,500)

Trading loans

Interest paid

All interest on trading loans deducted in the statement of profit or loss is an allowable deduction from trading profits.

This means you will not need to make any adjustments in converting the accounting profit into the adjusted trading profit.

Interest received

You are unlikely to see any interest received for trading purposes.

However, if you do, such interest is included in the trading profit and therefore needs no adjustment.

Non-trading loans

Interest paid

Interest deducted in the statement of profit or loss in relation to non-trading loans is disallowed in computing adjusted trading profits (i.e. add it back in the adjustment of profit computation).

Instead, the interest is an allowable deduction from non-trade interest income.

The main example of this type of interest will be interest paid on a loan to buy an investment property or shares.

Interest received

Interest income shown in the statement of profit or loss (e.g. interest on a deposit account) will be from a non-trade loan and therefore must be deducted from net profit in the adjustment of trading profit computation and instead treated as non-trade interest income.

Other costs incurred in respect of loan relationships

All other costs in relation to non-trading loan relationships are disallowed in computing adjusted trading profits, but are allowed as a deduction from non-trade interest income instead.

The main example of this will be loans to former employees, customers or suppliers which have been written off.

Accruals basis

All interest in corporation tax computations must be dealt with on an accruals basis (not received and paid basis).

The accruals basis means the amount due within the accounting period.

> ### 💡 Example
>
> Sam Limited has received the following interest on its bank deposit account that was opened on 1 April 2014:
>
> | Date received | £ |
> |---|---|
> | 30 June 2014 | 1,000 |
> | 31 December 2014 | 3,000 |
> | 30 June 2015 | 4,000 |
>
> Assuming interest accrues evenly between each date; calculate the non-trade interest income to be shown in the corporation tax computation for year ended 31 March 2015.

Solution

1 April 2014 account opened	30 June 2014 received £1,000	31 December 2014 received £3,000	30 June 2015 received £4,000

31 March 2015

Interest accrued

£1,000   £3,000 $\frac{3}{6}$ × £4,000

Non-trade interest for year ended 31 March 2015
= (£1,000 + £3,000 + £2,000) = £6,000

The figure shown in the accounts will normally be the accrued amount. You are therefore unlikely to have to calculate this.

 Activity 1

The statement of profit or loss of ABC Ltd includes interest received on an investment in Government securities.

How should this be dealt with in the computation of the taxable total profits?

A   Deducted from net profit

B   Included as non-trading income

C   Deducted from net profit and included as non-trading income

D   No adjustment

2.3 Patent royalties

Patent royalties paid or received by companies are dealt with for tax purposes on an accruals basis.

Royalties payable

Royalties are relieved as a trading expense against trading profits on a normal accruals basis. So if they have been correctly charged through the accounts no adjustment should be needed.

Royalties receivable

Royalties receivable on patents are taxed as trading profits. Again, if the income has been correctly shown on an accruals basis no adjustment should be needed.

Royalties subject to income tax deductions

Patent royalties are usually received gross, except that patent royalties received from individuals are received net of 20% tax.

Similarly, all patent royalties are usually paid gross, except that patent royalties paid to individuals are paid net of basic rate tax.

All amounts shown in corporation tax computations must be shown gross.

Therefore, patent royalties paid to/received from an individual must be grossed up. The gross patent royalties are calculated as follows:

Patent royalties (cash amount) × 100/80

Example

Tom Ltd receives the following patent royalties.

What are the gross figures to be used in the corporation tax computation?

(a)	Received from Rye Ltd	£3,000
(b)	Received from Eric	£3,900

Solution

Gross amounts to be used:

(a)	From Rye Ltd	£3,000
(b)	From Eric (£3,900 × 100/80)	£4,875

2.4 Dividend income

Dividend income received by companies is not chargeable to corporation tax. In a correctly prepared set of financial statements, dividends are not included in arriving at net income. If dividend income is included in the net income, it must be deducted when computing the adjusted trading profits.

This is because dividend income is paid out of after-tax profits of another company (i.e. the profits generating the dividend have already been subject to UK corporation tax in that other company).

2.5 Property income

The calculation of property income is not in the Business Tax syllabus.

If a company has property income you will be given the figure to use in calculating the taxable total profits.

2.6 Chargeable gains

A company's taxable total profits include chargeable gains as well as income.

The calculation of the chargeable gain or loss on the disposal of capital assets is covered in a later chapter.

For the purpose of this chapter, all individual gains and losses are already computed. You will, however, need to be able to produce a summary of the position for the purpose of calculating taxable total profits.

This is shown as follows:

	£
Gain (transaction 1)	X
Gain (transaction 2)	X
Loss (transaction 3)	(X)
	X
Less: Capital losses brought forward	(X)
Net chargeable gains	X

Current period gains and losses are netted off automatically.

Excess capital losses are covered in Chapter 8.

 Activity 2

1 GHI Ltd made a capital gain on the disposal of shares during 2014 of £60,000. It had capital losses brought forward of £25,000.

How much should be included in taxable total profits?

2 How would your answer differ if capital losses brought forward had amounted to £75,000?

2.7 Qualifying charitable donations

The final component in calculating taxable total profits is to deduct from the total profits (income and gains) any qualifying charitable donations. These are paid gross by companies.

The gross amount deductible for a CAP is the amount *paid* in that CAP. This may be a different figure from the amount accrued in the accounts.

A qualifying charitable donation is basically any donation made by a company to a charity unless it already qualifies as a business expense. Only donations that are 'small' and 'local in effect' will normally be allowed as a trading expense. It is therefore usually donations made to national charities which are treated as qualifying charitable donations.

Note that in the corporation tax return submitted to HMRC, qualifying charitable donations are referred to as 'charges paid' (see Chapter 5).

Note also that in the past it was necessary for a donation to be made under Gift Aid to be allowable. However this requirement no longer applies to company donations (but is still required for donations by individuals).

Activity 3

Laserjet Ltd (1)

Laserjet Ltd provided you with the following information for its year to 31 March 2015.

	£
Adjusted trading profit before capital allowances	500,600
Capital allowances	16,000
Rental income (net of expenses)	32,000
Bank loan interest payable on a loan to purchase rental property (accrued)	4,000
Building society interest receivable (accrued)	20,000
10% loan note interest receivable (accrued)	6,000
Donation paid to national charity	14,000

Required:

Calculate the taxable total profits for the year ended 31 March 2015.

Approach to the question

You need a methodical approach to calculate taxable total profits.

Step 1: Set up a skeleton CT computation pro forma (this may be given in the assessment).

	£
Trading profit (W1)	
Non-trade interest (W2)	
Property income	
	———
Less: Qualifying charitable donations	
	———
Taxable total profits	
	———

Note that the labels in the computation are not required to be in any particular order, but it is accepted best practice to put the trading profit first.

Step 2: Prepare any necessary workings separately from the pro forma

Work through the information methodically. The figure for trading profit often (though not in this example) requires more than one working for the component parts of:

- adjusted trading profit.

- capital allowances on plant and machinery.

As you complete each working, slot the result into the pro forma.

3 Corporation tax return (part 1)

3.1 The short return

The corporation tax return, CT600, must be completed for the chargeable accounting period. The return can either be:

- the short form (4 pages); or

- the long form (8 pages).

In an assessment you would only be required to complete part of the short form.

The first page includes details of the company and the chargeable accounting period, and whether any supplementary pages are required.

Page 3 requires details of capital allowances and losses

The last page requires details of the company's bank account if a repayment is due, and contains a declaration that the return is complete and correct.

The computation of taxable total profits and the corporation tax payable is required on page 2.

In the assessment you will only be required to complete either the top or bottom of page 2 of the return. This page is reproduced below.

3.2 The return – up to the calculation of taxable total profits

This chapter covers the calculation of taxable total profits. However, you should note that HMRC's corporation tax return still uses old terminology and refers to this figure as 'profits chargeable to corporation tax'.

It also refers to 'charges paid' which is the old terminology for qualifying charitable donations.

We have not dealt with entries to go in all boxes. However, the main ones considered are:

	Boxes
Trading profit	3
Non-trade interest	6
Property income	11
Chargeable gains	16 – 18
Charges paid (i.e. qualifying charitable donations)	35

There are gaps in the numbering of the boxes so that the numbers correspond with those used on the long form, which includes additional boxes.

The remainder of the short form dealing with calculation of the tax will be dealt with in Chapter 6.

In the assessment you will be given most of the information to enter into the form but you may have to calculate some of the figures such as totals and subtotals.

The following is important in connection with the completion of forms in the exam.

- When completing the form in the exam, figures must be entered in the correct boxes.

- You will only be asked to complete one page of the form.

- Commas need not be entered for numbers of four digits or more.

- You do not need to fill in every box, only the relevant ones.

Page 2

Company tax calculation

Turnover

| 1 | Total turnover from trade or profession | | **1** £ |

Income

3	Trading and professional profits	**3** £	
4	Trading losses brought forward claimed against profits	**4** £	
5	Net trading and professional profits		box 3 minus box 4 **5** £
6	Bank, building society or other interest, and profits and gains from non-trading loan relationships		**6** £
11	Income from UK land and buildings		**11** £
14	Annual profits and gains not falling under any other heading		**14** £

Chargeable gains

16	Gross chargeable gains	**16** £	
17	Allowable losses including losses brought forward	**17** £	
18	Net chargeable gains		box 16 minus box 17 **18** £
21	**Profits before other deductions and reliefs**		sum of boxes 5, 6, 11, 14 & 18 **21** £

Deductions and Reliefs

24	Management expenses under S75 ICTA 1988	**24** £	
30	Trading losses of this or a later accounting period under S393A ICTA 1988	**30** £	
31	*Put an 'X' in box 31 if amounts carried back from later accounting periods are included in box 30*	**31**	
32	Non-trade capital allowances	**32** £	
35	Charges paid	**35** £	
37	**Profits chargeable to corporation tax**		box 21 minus boxes 24, 30, 32 and 35 **37** £

Tax calculation

38	Franked investment income	**38** £
39	Number of associated companies in this period or	**39**
40	Associated companies in the first financial year	**40**
41	Associated companies in the second financial year	**41**
42	*Put an 'X' in box 42 if the company claims to be charged at the starting rate or the small companies' rate on any part of its profits, or is claiming marginal rate relief*	**42**

Enter how much profit has to be charged and at what rate of tax

Financial year *(yyyy)*	Amount of profit	Rate of tax	Tax
43	**44** £	**45**	**46** £ p
53	**54** £	**55**	**56** £ p

63	Corporation tax		total of boxes 46 and 56 **63** £ p
64	Marginal rate relief	**64** £ p	
65	Corporation tax net of marginal rate relief	**65** £ p	
66	Underlying rate of corporation tax	**66** • %	
67	Profits matched with non-corporate distributions	**67**	
68	Tax at non-corporate distributions rate	**68** £ p	
69	Tax at underlying rate on remaining profits	**69** £ p	
70	**Corporation tax chargeable**		See note for box 70 in CT600 Guide **70** £ p

CT600 (Short) (2008) Version 2

Example

Victor Ltd has the following results for its year ended 31 March 2015.

Enter the figures for the computation of taxable total profits on the short form CT600 as indicated.

	£	£	CT 600 box
Trading profit		100,000	3
Non-trade interest income		20,000	6
Property income		5,000	11
Chargeable gains	8,000		16
Less: Capital losses	(3,000)		17
	———		
		5,000	18
		———	
		130,000	
Less: Qualifying charitable donations		(8,000)	35
		———	
Taxable total profits		122,000	
		———	

Don't forget to include sub-totals and totals in an assessment (i.e. boxes 5, 21, and 37).

Solution

Company tax calculation

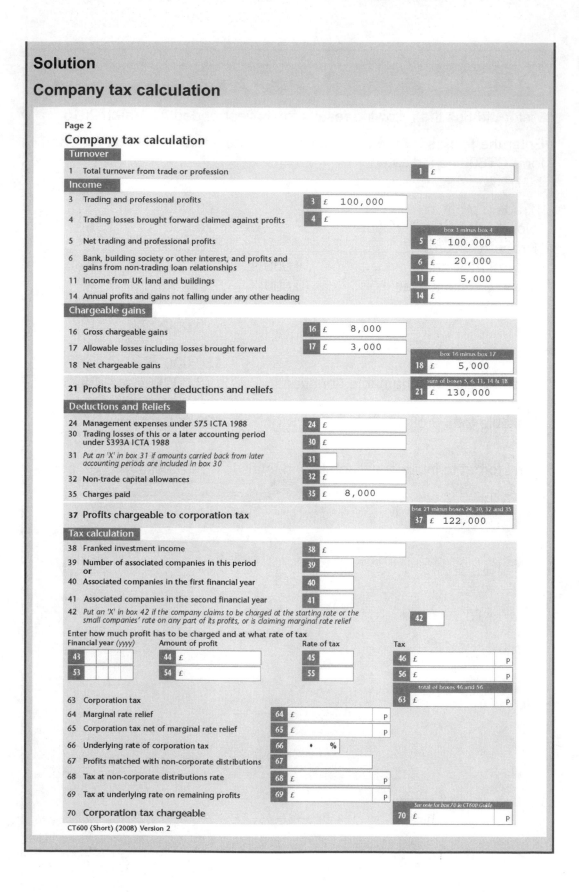

Page 2
Company tax calculation

Turnover

1	Total turnover from trade or profession	**1** £

Income

3	Trading and professional profits	**3** £ 100,000
4	Trading losses brought forward claimed against profits	**4** £
5	Net trading and professional profits	*box 3 minus box 4* **5** £ 100,000
6	Bank, building society or other interest, and profits and gains from non-trading loan relationships	**6** £ 20,000
11	Income from UK land and buildings	**11** £ 5,000
14	Annual profits and gains not falling under any other heading	**14** £

Chargeable gains

16	Gross chargeable gains	**16** £ 8,000
17	Allowable losses including losses brought forward	**17** £ 3,000
18	Net chargeable gains	*box 16 minus box 17* **18** £ 5,000

21	**Profits before other deductions and reliefs**	*sum of boxes 5, 6, 11, 14 & 18* **21** £ 130,000

Deductions and Reliefs

24	Management expenses under S75 ICTA 1988	**24** £
30	Trading losses of this or a later accounting period under S393A ICTA 1988	**30** £
31	*Put an 'X' in box 31 if amounts carried back from later accounting periods are included in box 30*	**31**
32	Non-trade capital allowances	**32** £
35	Charges paid	**35** £ 8,000

37	**Profits chargeable to corporation tax**	*box 21 minus boxes 24, 30, 32 and 35* **37** £ 122,000

Tax calculation

38	Franked investment income	**38** £
39	Number of associated companies in this period or	**39**
40	Associated companies in the first financial year	**40**
41	Associated companies in the second financial year	**41**
42	*Put an 'X' in box 42 if the company claims to be charged at the starting rate or the small companies' rate on any part of its profits, or is claiming marginal rate relief*	**42**

Enter how much profit has to be charged and at what rate of tax

Financial year *(yyyy)*	Amount of profit	Rate of tax	Tax	
43	**44** £	**45**	**46** £	p
53	**54** £	**55**	**56** £	p

63	Corporation tax	*total of boxes 46 and 56* **63** £ p
64	Marginal rate relief	**64** £ p
65	Corporation tax net of marginal rate relief	**65** £ p
66	Underlying rate of corporation tax	**66** • %
67	Profits matched with non-corporate distributions	**67**
68	Tax at non-corporate distributions rate	**68** £ p
69	Tax at underlying rate on remaining profits	**69** £ p
70	**Corporation tax chargeable**	*See note for box 70 in CT600 Guide* **70** £ p

CT600 (Short) (2008) Version 2

Activity 4

Complete the extract (see below) of the short form CT600 for Laserjet Ltd in Activity 3.

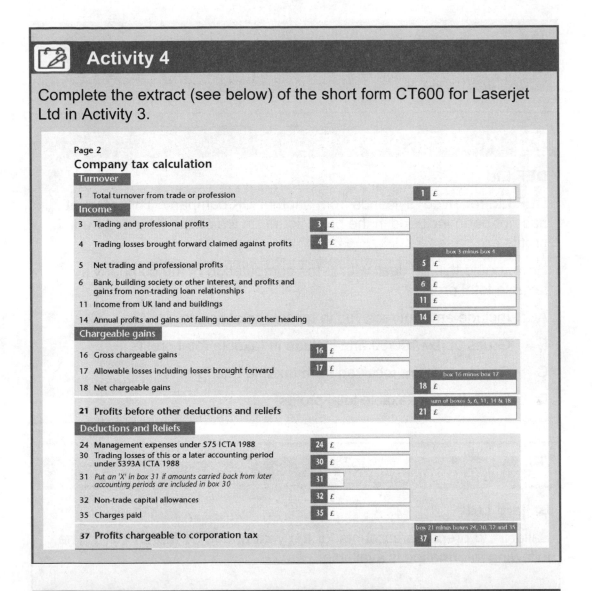

Page 2

Company tax calculation

Turnover

1   Total turnover from trade or profession   1 £

Income

3   Trading and professional profits   3 £

4   Trading losses brought forward claimed against profits   4 £

                                                                    box 3 minus box 4
5   Net trading and professional profits   5 £

6   Bank, building society or other interest, and profits and   6 £
    gains from non-trading loan relationships

11 Income from UK land and buildings   11 £

14 Annual profits and gains not falling under any other heading   14 £

Chargeable gains

16 Gross chargeable gains   16 £

17 Allowable losses including losses brought forward   17 £

                                                                    box 16 minus box 17
18 Net chargeable gains   18 £

21 **Profits before other deductions and reliefs**   *sum of boxes 5, 6, 11, 14 & 18*
                                                                                21 £

Deductions and Reliefs

24 Management expenses under S75 ICTA 1988   24 £

30 Trading losses of this or a later accounting period   30 £
    under S393A ICTA 1988

31 Put an 'X' in box 31 if amounts carried back from later   31
    accounting periods are included in box 30

32 Non-trade capital allowances   32 £

35 Charges paid   35 £

                                                                    box 21 minus boxes 24, 30, 32 and 35
37 **Profits chargeable to corporation tax**   37 £

4   Summary

Make sure you are very familiar with the pro forma corporation tax computation.

Setting out your computations as shown in the pro forma will help to ensure that your computations and submissions to HM Revenue and Customs (HMRC) are always made in accordance with the current law and take account of current HMRC practice.

The short return CT600 is set out in a similar manner to the pro forma.

5 Test your knowledge

 Workbook Activity 5

DEF Ltd

DEF Ltd received dividends from another UK company. This amount has not been included in the profit figure on which the adjusted trading profits are based.

How should this be dealt with in the computation of the company's taxable total profits?

A   Include amount received in taxable total profits

B   Gross up by 100/90 and include in taxable total profits

C   Deduct amount received from taxable total profits

D   Exclude from taxable total profits

 Workbook Activity 6

Ballard Ltd

Ballard Ltd prepares accounts for the year ended 31 March 2015. The following information is available:

	£
Adjusted trading profits before capital allowances	56,000
Bank interest receivable	3,000
UK dividends received	9,000

The tax written down value of the general pool was £24,000 on 1 April 2014 and on 1 January 2015 the company purchased a lorry for £14,000.

What are Ballard Ltd's taxable total profits for the year ended 31 March 2015?

A   £40,680

B   £41,430

C   £49,680

D   £50,430

Workbook Activity 7

Pitch Ltd (1)

Pitch Ltd has the following results for the year ended 31 March 2015:

	£
Adjusted trading profits (before capital allowances)	766,801
Capital allowances	24,688
Rents receivable	3,500
Bank deposit interest receivable	2,400
Dividends received from UK companies (including tax credit)	4,800
Qualifying charitable donation paid	(1,000)

Required:

Show Pitch Ltd's taxable total profits for the year ended 31 March 2015.

 Workbook Activity 8

Pitch Ltd (2)

You are required to complete the following extract of the short form for Pitch Ltd for the year to 31 March 2015 (see below).

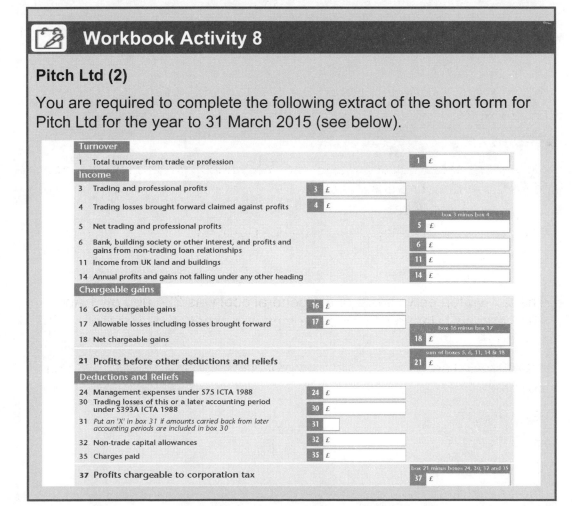

Calculation of corporation tax liability

Introduction

This chapter follows on from the previous chapter.

Having completed the calculation of taxable total profits it is possible to calculate the corporation tax liability.

The calculation of the corporation tax liability could also form a standalone task in the assessment.

KNOWLEDGE
Identify relevant tax authority legislation and guidance. (3.1 K)
Explain the calculation of corporation tax payable by different sizes of companies including those with associated companies. (5.1 K)
Identify corporation tax payable and the due dates of payment, including instalments. (5.3 K)

SKILLS
Enter adjusted trading profits and losses, capital allowances, investment income and capital gains in the corporation tax computation. (2.4 S)
Calculate corporation tax payable, taking account of marginal relief and associated companies. (2.6 S)
Complete corporation tax returns and submit them within statutory time limits. (2.7)

CONTENTS

1 The corporation tax liability
2 Rates of corporation tax
3 Marginal relief
4 Corporation tax return (part 2)

1 The corporation tax liability

1.1 Calculating the corporation tax liability

Once you have computed a company's taxable total profits, the next stage of the computation is to calculate the corporation tax liability. This is essentially divided into two steps.

- Determining 'augmented profits'' (A), a term which is used to determine the tax rates that will apply.

- Applying relevant tax rates to calculate the liability.

Step 1: Determining 'augmented profits'

	£	
Taxable total profits	X	'N'
Add: Current FII	X	
	___	
Augmented profits	X	'A'
	___	

FII is franked investment income. Current FII is the term used to describe dividends received in the current period, grossed up by the tax credit of 100/90.

If you recall from Chapter 5, dividends received by a company are not taxed under corporation tax. However, they are used to determine the tax rate to apply to its taxable profits.

Taxable total profits (N) are charged to corporation tax, but the figure of augmented profit (A) is used to determine the rate of tax.

Step 2: Apply the relevant tax rates

The tax calculation is based on two main factors:

- Augmented profits (A) (from Step 1).

- The Financial Year (FY) which matches the CAP.

A Financial Year (FY) runs from 1 April to the following 31 March.

FY2014 is the period from 1 April 2014 to 31 March 2015 (note it tells you in which year the period starts).

For each FY the following information may be provided:

	FY2013	FY2014
Small profits rate (SPR)	20%	20%
Main rate (MR)	23%	21%
Small profits rate		
– Lower limit	£300,000	£300,000
– Upper limit	£1,500,000	£1,500,000
– Standard fraction	3/400	1/400

Each of the rates will be considered in turn, so that we can see how the rates and the limits are used.

2 Rates of corporation tax

2.1 The rates of tax

As noted above, in FY2014 the rates of corporation tax are based on the level of augmented profits.

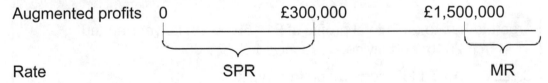

2.2 Small profits rate

If a company has augmented profits (A) of up to £300,000 in FY2014 then its taxable total profits are taxed at 20%.

Example

Zachary Ltd has taxable total profits of £148,000 in its year ended 31 March 2015, and dividends received of £4,500.

Calculate Zachary Ltd's corporation tax liability.

Solution

	£
Taxable total profits (N)	148,000
Plus: FII (£4,500 × $\frac{100}{90}$)	5,000
Augmented profits (A)	153,000

As 'A' is less than £300,000, then 'N' is taxed at 20%.

Corporation tax liability (£148,000 × 20%) = £29,600.

2.3 Main rate

If a company has 'A' of at least £1,500,000 in FY2014 then 'N' is taxed at 21%.

 Example

Argo Ltd has taxable total profits of £1,450,000 in its year ended 31 March 2015, and dividends received of £72,000.

Calculate Argo Ltd's corporation tax liability.

Solution

	£
Taxable total profits (N)	1,450,000
Plus: FII (£72,000 × $\frac{100}{90}$)	80,000
Augmented profits (A)	1,530,000

As 'A' is at least £1,500,000, 'N' is taxed at 21%.

Corporation tax liability (£1,450,000 × 21%) = £304,500.

'N' is below the limit of £1,500,000 but this is irrelevant. 'A' determines the tax rate to be applied to taxable total profits ('N').

3 Marginal relief

3.1 The marginal band

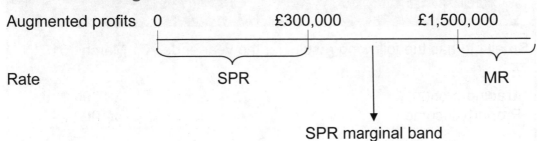

SPR marginal band

3.2 SPR marginal band

Where a company's augmented profits are between £300,000 and £1,500,000 in FY2014, corporation tax is first calculated at the main rate of 21%.

Marginal relief is then deducted. Marginal relief reduces the actual rate of tax paid to a rate between the small profits rate of 20% and the main rate of 21%.

The calculation is set out below.

	£
Taxable total profits at main rate (21% in FY2014)	X
Less: Marginal relief	(X)
Corporation tax liability	X

Marginal relief is found by using the formula:

$$\text{Fraction} \times (U - A) \times \frac{N}{A}$$

Where:

U = Upper limit

A = Augmented profits

N = Taxable total profits

As noted in 1.1 above, for the SPR marginal band, the fraction is $^1/_{400}$ and U is £1,500,000.

Note that in the assessment you may be required to show pence when calculating the corporation tax liability; read the instructions carefully.

The following examples illustrate the calculation of the corporation tax liability.

> **Example**
>
> Small Ltd has the following results for the year ended 31 March 2015.
>
> | | £ |
> |---|---|
> | Trading profit | 260,000 |
> | Property income | 40,000 |
> | | 300,000 |
> | Less: Qualifying charitable donations | (10,000) |
> | Taxable total profits | 290,000 |
>
> Calculate Small Ltd's corporation tax liability if:
>
> (a) no dividends are received from UK companies.
>
> (b) £9,000 of dividends are received from UK companies.
>
> (c) £45,000 of dividends are received from UK companies.
>
> **Solution**
>
> (a) **No dividends received**
>
> | | £ |
> |---|---|
> | Taxable total profits (N) | 290,000 |
> | Plus: FII | Nil |
> | Augmented profits (A) | 290,000 |
>
> Identify the Financial Year(s) which applies and determine the tax rate.
>
> FY2014 applies to the year ended 31 March 2015 and therefore to the whole of the accounting period.
>
> 'A' is below the lower limit therefore 'N' is taxed at 20%
>
> Corporation tax liability (£290,000 × 20%)   £58,000

(b) **£9,000 dividends received**

	£
Taxable total profits (N)	290,000
Plus: FII (£9,000 × $\frac{100}{90}$)	10,000
Augmented profits (A)	300,000

FY2014 applies and 'A' is equal to the lower limit therefore 'N' is taxed at 20%.

Corporation tax liability (£290,000 × 20%)	£58,000

The increase in the level of augmented profits has not altered the outcome; the corporation tax liability is as before.

(c) **£45,000 dividends received**

	£
Taxable total profits (N)	290,000
Plus: FII (£45,000 × $\frac{100}{90}$)	50,000
Augmented profits (A)	340,000

'A' is above £300,000 but below £1,500,000; marginal relief is available.

	£
£290,000 × 21%	60,900.00
Less: Marginal relief	
$\frac{1}{400}$ × (£1,500,000 – £340,000) × $\dfrac{£290,000}{£340,000}$	(2,473.53)
Corporation tax liability	58,426.47

Activity 1

Walton Ltd (1)

Walton Ltd's statement of profit or loss for the year ended 31 March 2015 was as follows:

	£	£
Sales		486,280
Bank interest receivable		2,900
UK dividends received (net of tax credit)		13,365
Profit on the sale of an investment		3,054
		———
		505,599
Allowable trading expenses	109,756	
Disallowable trading expenses	6,344	
Overdraft interest payable	6,000	
	———	
		(122,100)
		———
Net profit		383,499
		———

Capital allowances have been calculated at £4,800.

All dividends were received in July 2014.

The capital gain on the sale of the investment has been calculated at £1,538.

Required:

Calculate Walton Ltd's corporation tax liability for the year ended 31 March 2015.

4 Corporation tax return (part 2)

4.1 The return – the calculation of the tax liability

In the previous chapter we saw the short form CT600.

We can now complete the tax calculation on the bottom of page 2.

The boxes likely to be completed in an assessment are as follows:

Box	Detail
38	Franked investment income – gross amount of dividends received.
39	Number of associated companies in this period – likely to be NIL (see Chapter 7).
40 and 41	See Chapter 7.
42	Check box to indicate if the SPR or marginal relief apply.
43 – 46	Shows the Financial Year, the taxable total profits and tax at 20% / 21%.
53 – 56	See Chapter 7.
64 – 65	Shows the result of the marginal relief calculation.
66 – 69	Will not be used in the assessment.
70	Shows the corporation tax payable. This will be the figure from box 63 or 65.

Example

Small Ltd in the previous example (part (c)) has the following results:

Year ended 31 March 2015

	£	Box
Taxable total profits	290,000	44
Plus: FII	50,000	38
Augmented profits	340,000	
It has no associated companies		39
£290,000 × 21%	60,900.00	46
Less: Marginal relief		
$\frac{1}{400} \times (£1,500,000 - £340,000) \times \frac{£290,000}{£340,000}$	(2,473.53)	64
Corporation tax liability	58,426.47	65, 70

Complete the tax calculation on Form CT600.

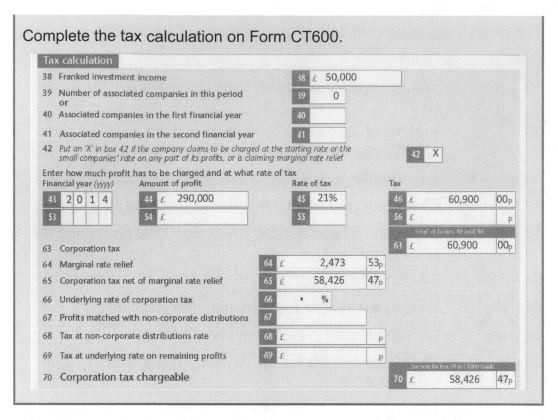

Activity 2

Walton Ltd (2)

Complete the tax calculation on the short Form CT600 (see below) for Activity 1.

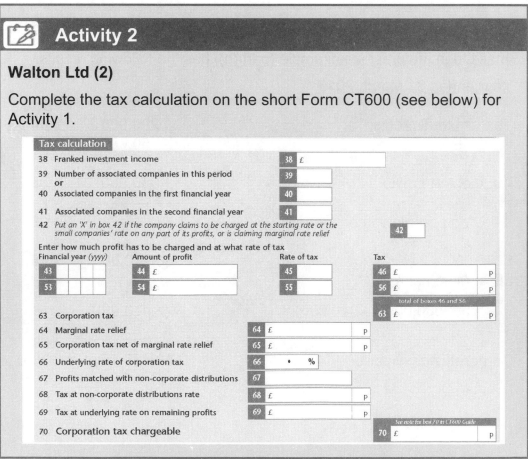

5 Summary

There are two rates of corporation tax in FY2014:

- Small profits rate   20%
- Main rate   21%

Between these rates there is a marginal band to gradually move between the rates.

The rate applying in a Financial Year is determined by:

- Augmented profits (Taxable total profits plus FII)

but the rate is applied to:

- Taxable total profits

Marginal relief is calculated using the formula:

$$\text{Fraction} \times (U - A) \times \frac{N}{A}$$

Where:

U = Upper limit

A = Augmented profits

N = Taxable total profits

6 Test your knowledge

Workbook Activity 3

G Ltd

The following details relate to the corporation tax computation of G Ltd for the 12 month accounting period ended 31 March 2015:

	£
Tax adjusted trading profit (after disallowing the write off of a loan to a customer of £600 and a national charity donation of £1,800)	677,500
Bank interest receivable	2,800
Loan interest received	22,000
UK dividends received	36,000

Required:

Calculate G Ltd's corporation tax liability for the year ended 31 March 2015.

Workbook Activity 4

Osmond Ltd

Osmond Ltd had the following results for the year ended 31 March 2015:

	£
Trading profit	510,000
Loan note (debenture) interest receivable	8,000
UK dividends received (net of tax credit)	18,000
Capital gain on the sale of an investment	7,500

Required:

Calculate Osmond Ltd's corporation tax liability for the year ended 31 March 2015.

Workbook Activity 5

Tar Ltd

The taxable total profits for Tar Ltd for the year to 31 March 2015 were £747,013. Dividends received amounted to £4,800.

Required:

(a) Calculate the corporation tax liability for the year to 31 March 2015.

(b) Complete the tax calculation on the extract of form CT600 (see below).

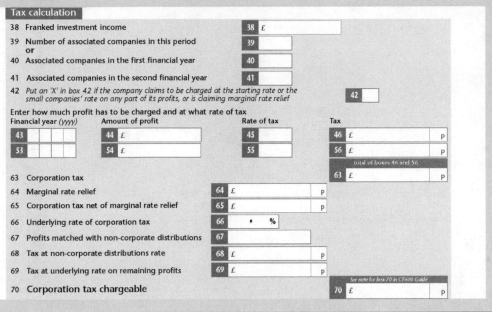

7

Corporation tax – special scenarios

Introduction

There are a number of issues that can make the calculation of corporation tax slightly more complex.

These include short and long periods of account and accounting periods which straddle 31 March, as well as the effect of associated companies.

These issues are considered in this chapter.

KNOWLEDGE	CONTENTS
Identify relevant tax authority legislation and guidance. (3.1 K)	1 Associated companies 2 Short accounting periods 3 Non 31 March year ends 4 Long periods of account
Explain the calculation of corporation tax payable by different sizes of companies including those with associated companies. (5.1 K)	
Identify corporation tax payable and the due dates of payment, including instalments. (5.3 K)	

SKILLS

Enter adjusted trading profits and losses, capital allowances, investment income and capital gains in the corporation tax computation. (2.4 S)

Calculate taxable total profits, and other relevant figures, as it applies to companies with periods longer than, shorter than and equal to 12 months. (2.5 S)

Calculate corporation tax payable, taking account of marginal relief and associated companies. (2.6 S)

1 Associated companies

1.1 The principle of associated companies

Two companies are associated if:

- One controls the other; or

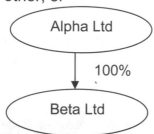

Alpha Ltd owns all of the shares in Beta Ltd, hence they are associated

- both are controlled by the same person(s)

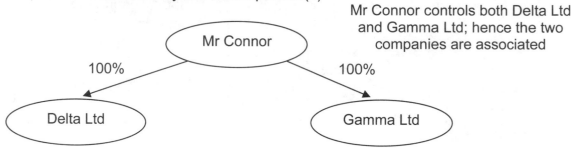

Mr Connor controls both Delta Ltd and Gamma Ltd; hence the two companies are associated

- Combining both of these rules:

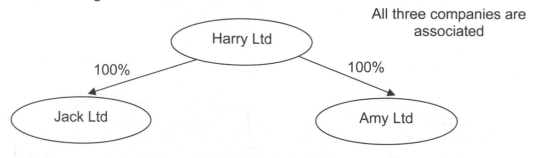

All three companies are associated

Essentially control means that more than 50% of the shares are owned by a 'person'. A 'person' means an individual or a company.

Note that Mr Connor in the second example is not an associate of Delta Ltd or Gamma Ltd. Only companies can count as associates.

1.2 The effect of being associated companies

The profit limits used for determining corporation tax rates are divided by the total number of associated companies.

Hence, for the Harry Ltd group of companies shown in 1.1 above, each company will have profit limits of:

- £1,500,000 ÷ 3 = £500,000
- £300,000 ÷ 3 = £100,000

Example

Andrew Ltd has one wholly owned subsidiary, Beckham Ltd (i.e. Andrew Ltd owns 100% of the shares in Beckham Ltd).

Andrew Ltd has the following results for its year ended 31 March 2015:

	£
Trading profit	600,000
Rental profits	100,000
Bank interest income	30,000
Dividends received (not from Beckham Ltd)	27,000

Calculate the corporation tax liability of Andrew Ltd for its year ended 31 March 2015.

Solution

Step 1: Calculate taxable total profits and augmented profits.

Andrew Ltd

Corporation tax computation – year ended 31 March 2015

	£
Trading profit	600,000
Property income	100,000
Non-trade interest	30,000
Taxable total profits	730,000

	£
Taxable total profits (N)	730,000
Plus: FII (£27,000 × $\frac{100}{90}$)	30,000
Augmented profits (A)	760,000

Step 2: Draw a diagram of the group. Identify the associated companies.

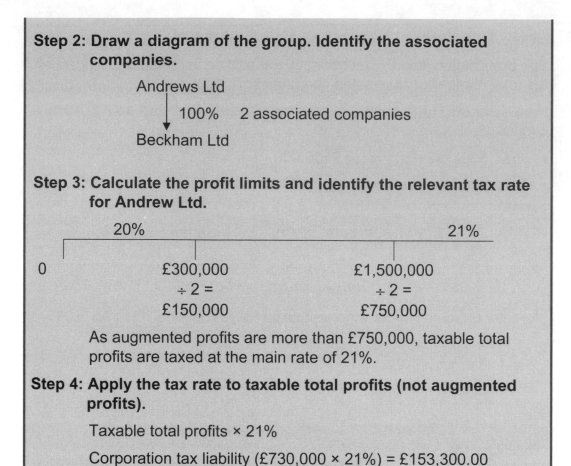

Andrews Ltd

100%   2 associated companies

Beckham Ltd

Step 3: Calculate the profit limits and identify the relevant tax rate for Andrew Ltd.

20%		21%

0   £300,000   £1,500,000
                 ÷ 2 =   ÷ 2 =
                 £150,000   £750,000

As augmented profits are more than £750,000, taxable total profits are taxed at the main rate of 21%.

Step 4: Apply the tax rate to taxable total profits (not augmented profits).

Taxable total profits × 21%

Corporation tax liability (£730,000 × 21%) = £153,300.00

If the augmented profits are between the lower and upper limits then the company is marginal. When calculating the small profits rate marginal relief, the upper limit to be used is the normal limit divided by the number of associates.

Example

The facts are as the previous example except that Andrew Ltd has trading profits of £300,000, reducing the taxable total profits to £430,000.

Calculate the corporation tax liability of Andrew Ltd for its year ended 31 March 2015.

Solution

Step 1: Calculate taxable total profits and augmented profits.

Andrew Ltd

Corporation tax computation – year ended 31 March 2015

	£
Taxable total profits (N)	430,000
Plus: FII (£27,000 × $^{100}/_{90}$)	30,000
	———
Augmented profits (A)	460,000
	———

Steps 2 and 3 are the same as in the previous example, so the limits are £150,000 to £750,000.

As 'A' is between the upper and lower limits the company is marginal.

Step 4: Calculate corporation tax liability

£430,000 × 21%	90,300.00
Less: Marginal relief	
$^{1}/_{400}$ × (£750,000 – £460,000) × $\frac{£430,000}{£460,000}$	(677.72)
	———
Corporation tax liability	89,622.28
	———

Activity 1

Swan Ltd prepares accounts for the year ended 31 March 2015.

Swan Ltd has for many years owned 60% of the shares of Goose Ltd and 75% of the shares of Duck Ltd.

Swan Ltd has taxable total profits of £140,000 for the year ended 31 March 2015, and also received franked investment income of £10,000 from unconnected companies during the year.

What is Swan Ltd's corporation tax liability for the year ended 31 March 2015?

A   £28,000.00

B   £29,400.00

C   £28,583.33

D   £31,500.00

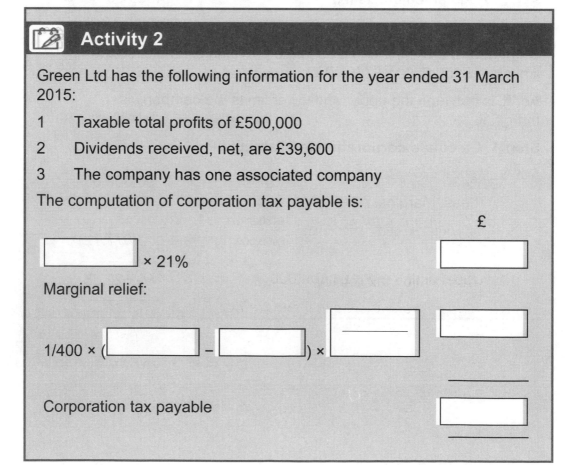 **Activity 2**

Green Ltd has the following information for the year ended 31 March 2015:

1   Taxable total profits of £500,000

2   Dividends received, net, are £39,600

3   The company has one associated company

The computation of corporation tax payable is:

£

[   ] × 21%   [   ]

Marginal relief:

1/400 × ([   ] − [   ]) × [—]   [   ]

Corporation tax payable   [   ]

2 Short accounting periods

2.1 Changing the profit limits

Short accounting periods (i.e. those of less than 12 months) can have an impact on the calculation of the corporation tax liability.

This is because the lower and upper profits limits are annual limits and have to be time apportioned to match the length of the accounting period.

 Example

June Ltd had a nine month accounting period to 31 March 2015. It received a dividend of £18,000 and its taxable total profits were £290,000.

Calculate June Ltd's corporation tax liability for the period to 31 March 2015.

Solution

Step 1: Calculate profits and compare to limits

	£
Taxable total profits (N)	290,000
Plus: FII	20,000
	————
Augmented profits (A)	310,000
	————

FY2014 applies, but to a nine month period therefore:

Lower limit = $\frac{9}{12}$ × £300,000	£225,000
Upper limit = $\frac{9}{12}$ × £1,500,000	£1,125,000

'A' is between the limits therefore marginal relief applies.

Step 2: Calculate the tax liability

	£
£290,000 × 21%	60,900.00
Less: Marginal relief	
$\frac{1}{400} \times (£1,125,000 - £310,000) \times \frac{£290,000}{£310,000}$	(1,906.05)
Corporation tax liability	58,993.95

Make sure you calculate tax on taxable total profits and not on augmented profits.

Note that 'U' in the formula is the time apportioned upper limit.

3 Non 31 March year ends

3.1 The principle of different Financial Years and tax rates

The rates of corporation tax are set for financial years. A Financial Year runs from 1 April to the following 31 March. Financial Year 2014 is the period from 1 April 2014 to 31 March 2015.

The CAP of a company with a year end of 31 December 2014 falls into two Financial Years as follows:

- three months of the year (1 January 2014 to 31 March 2014) falls into FY2013

- nine months of the year (1 April 2014 to 31 December 2014) falls into FY2014.

The following rates apply:

	FY2013 1 January 2014 – 31 March 2014	FY2014 1 April 2014 – 31 December 2014
Small profits rate	20%	20%
Main rate	23%	21%
Marginal relief fraction	3/400	1/400
Lower limit	£300,000	£300,000
Upper limit	1,500,000	£1,500,000

As the corporation tax rates change from FY2013 to FY2014, it is necessary to time apportion the taxable total profits and the augmented profits and compute the corporation tax for each Financial Year separately as set out below.

Step 1

Determine augmented profits as before and identify the appropriate rate of tax (i.e. small profits, main, or marginal).

Step 2

Time apportion taxable total profits between the Financial Years and proceed as before taking the number of months into account.

If the augmented profits exceed the upper limit, a proportion of the taxable total profits will be taxed at each of the two rates of tax. For example, for the year ended 31 December 2014 the corporation tax liability would be calculated as follows:

		£
FY2013	Taxable total profits × 3/12 × 23%	X
FY2014	Taxable total profits × 9/12 × 21%	X
		X

In the Business tax assessment, any accounting period with a non 31 March year end is likely to fall within Financial Years 2013 and 2014. Accordingly, it will be necessary to carry out the calculations set out above.

Where there is no change in the rates and limits between Financial Years there is no need to time apportion. The corporation tax return form provides space to split the calculation over two Financial Years; however, it is acceptable not to split the calculation on the form if the rates have not changed over the two years.

If the company is marginal the calculations of marginal relief must also be time apportioned. This is shown in the following example.

Example

Marginal Ltd had taxable total profits of £295,000 for the year ended 30 September 2014 and received a dividend of £32,400 on 15 May 2014.

Calculate Marginal Ltd's corporation tax liability for the year ended 30 September 2014 and complete the calculation on the Form CT600 below.

Solution

	£
Taxable total profits (N)	295,000
Plus: FII (£32,400 × 100/90)	36,000
Augmented profits (A)	331,000

Therefore marginal relief applies.

Calculate the tax for each Financial Year separately. Six months of the CAP fall into FY2013 and the remaining six months fall into FY2014.

	FY2013 6/12 £	FY2014 6/12 £
Taxable total profits (6/12:6/12)	147,500	147,500
Augmented profits (6/12:6/12)	165,500	165,500
Apportioned upper limit (6/12:6/12)	750,000	750,000

Corporation tax:

	£ p
FY2013 (1 October 2013 – 31 March 2014)	
(£147,500 × 23%)	33,925.00
Less: Marginal relief	
3/400 × (£750,000 – £165,500) × £147,500/£165,500	(3,906.97)
	30,018.03
FY2014 (1 April 2014 – 30 September 2014)	
£147,500 × 21%	30,975.00
Less: Marginal relief	
1/400 × (£750,000 – £165,500) × £147,500/£165,500	(1,302.32)
Corporation tax liability	59,690.71

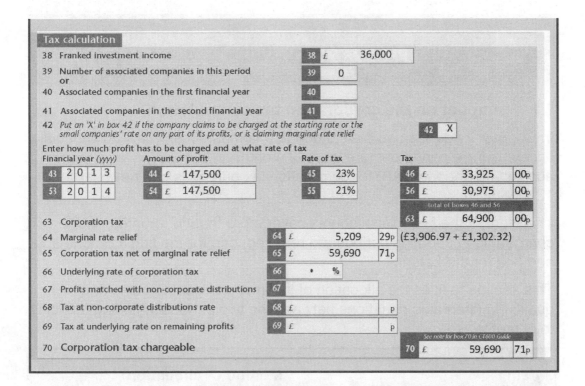

Tax calculation

38	Franked investment income	38 £	36,000	
39	Number of associated companies in this period or	39	0	
40	Associated companies in the first financial year	40		
41	Associated companies in the second financial year	41		
42	Put an 'X' in box 42 if the company claims to be charged at the starting rate or the small companies' rate on any part of its profits, or is claiming marginal rate relief		42 X	

Enter how much profit has to be charged and at what rate of tax

Financial year (yyyy)	Amount of profit	Rate of tax	Tax
43 2013	44 £ 147,500	45 23%	46 £ 33,925 00p
53 2014	54 £ 147,500	55 21%	56 £ 30,975 00p
			total of boxes 46 and 56

63	Corporation tax	63 £	64,900 00p
64	Marginal rate relief	64 £ 5,209 29p	(£3,906.97 + £1,302.32)
65	Corporation tax net of marginal rate relief	65 £ 59,690 71p	
66	Underlying rate of corporation tax	66 • %	
67	Profits matched with non-corporate distributions	67	
68	Tax at non-corporate distributions rate	68 £ p	
69	Tax at underlying rate on remaining profits	69 £ p	
		See note for box 70 in CT600 Guide	
70	**Corporation tax chargeable**	70 £ 59,690 71p	

 Activity 3

Rhos Ltd

Rhos Ltd had taxable total profits of £740,000 for the year ended 31 December 2014 and received a dividend of £39,600 on 15 November 2014.

Required:

Calculate Rhos Ltd's corporation tax liability for the year ended 31 December 2014 for inclusion on the corporation tax return form.

4 Long periods of account

4.1 Impact on the corporation tax computation

In Chapter 2 you learned that, although a company can draw up financial accounts for a period of more than 12 months, a company's 'chargeable accounting period' (CAP) for corporation tax purposes can never exceed 12 months.

Therefore, if the financial accounts cover more than 12 months, two chargeable accounting periods are required; one for the first 12 months and one for the balance.

This section tackles the allocation of income, chargeable gains and qualifying charitable donations between the two periods in finding taxable total profits.

Item	Method of allocation
Trading profit before deducting capital allowances	Time apportioned
Capital allowances (see Chapter 4)	Separate computation for each CAP
Property income	Time apportioned
Non-trade interest	Period in which accrued (Note)
Chargeable gains	Period of disposal
Qualifying charitable donation	Period in which paid
Franked investment income	Period dividend received

Note: If information to apply the strict accruals basis is not available, then time apportion.

Be very careful when calculating the number of months in the second period – double check it – as it is crucial for time apportioning calculations and easy to get wrong.

Example

Printer Ltd has prepared accounts for the 16 months to 31 August 2014, with the following information.

	£
Adjusted trading profit before capital allowances	365,000
Building society interest	
Received 30 June 2013 (of which £1,950 related to year ended 30 April 2013)	2,450
Received 30 June 2014	2,675
Accrued on 31 August 2014	200
Rents from property	26,010
Chargeable gains	
Disposal on 31 March 2014	25,700
Disposal on 1 May 2014	49,760
Dividend received from UK company	
(gross amount) on 1 February 2014	10,000
Qualifying charitable donations:	
Paid 31 July 2013	6,000
Paid 31 January 2014	6,000

Capital allowances for the two CAPs derived from the 16 month period of account are £20,000 and £6,250 respectively.

Show how the company's period of account will be divided into CAPs and compute the taxable total profits for each CAP assuming, where relevant, that all income is deemed to accrue evenly.

Solution

The procedure to be followed is exactly the same as for a 12 month period, but incorporating the allocation rules.

	12 months to 30 April 2014 £	4 months to 31 August 2014 £
Trading profit (W1)	253,750	85,000
Non-trade interest (W2)	2,531	844
Property income (W3)	19,507	6,503
Chargeable gains	25,700	49,760
	301,488	142,107
Less: Qualifying charitable donations (W4)	(12,000)	Nil
Taxable total profits	289,488	142,107

Note: The dividend received is not relevant for taxable total profits. The chargeable gains are allocated according to the date of the transaction.

Workings:

(W1) Trading profit

	Total £	12m £	4m £
Adjusted profit (see note)	365,000	273,750	91,250
Less: Capital allowances		(20,000)	(6,250)
Trading profit		253,750	85,000

Note: The adjusted trading profit before capital allowances is time **apportioned** (it is acceptable to apportion on a monthly basis in the assessment).

(W2) Non-trade interest – Building society interest

As the accrual at 30 April 2014 is not given, the total amount which would be included in the statement of profit or loss for the 16 month period on the accruals basis is calculated, then time apportioned:

		Total £	12m £	4m £
Received	30 June 2013	2,450		
	30 June 2014	2,675		
Add	Closing accrual	200		
Less	Opening accrual	(1,950)		
		3,375	2,531	844

(W3) Property income

Rental income is assessable as property income, which is assessed on an accruals basis for the 16 months and then time apportioned into the two CAPs:

	Total £	12m £	4m £
Property income	26,010	19,507	6,503

(W4) Qualifying charitable donations

	£
31 July 2013	6,000
31 January 2014	6,000
	12,000

In y/e 30 April 2014

Nil in 4 months to 31 August 2014 as none paid.

The procedure for finding the corporation tax liability now follows the rules outlined earlier, except that you have *two* calculations.

The point to watch, however, is that as the second computation is the 'balance' of the accounts it will always be a *short* period.

The profits limits of £300,000 and £1,500,000 therefore need to be reduced proportionately when considering the tax rate to apply.

Example

Calculate the corporation tax liability for Printer Ltd for its two chargeable accounting periods.

Solution

Step 1: Calculation of augmented profits

	12 months to 30 April 2014 £	4 months to 31 August 2014 £
Taxable total profits (as above)	289,488	142,107
Plus: FII (received Feb 2014)	10,000	Nil
Augmented profits	299,488	142,107

Step 2: Compare with the limits for the appropriate Financial Years

	12 months to 30 April 2014		4 months to 31 August 2014
	FY2013 11 months	FY2014 1 month	FY2014 4 months
Lower limit			
– Full limit	£300,000		
– 4 months limit (£300,000 × $^4/_{12}$)			£100,000
Upper limit			
– Full limit	£1,500,000		
– 4 months limit (£1,500,000 × $^4/_{12}$)			£500,000
Rates to apply	small profits rate		Marginal relief applies
	20%	20%	21%

Step 3: Calculate the corporation tax liability

	£ p
12 months to 30 April 2014	
(no change in small profits tax rate)	
FY2013 and 2014	
(£289,488 × 20%)	57,897.60

	£ p
4 months to 31 August 2014	
(£142,107 × 21%)	29,842.47
Less: Marginal relief	
¹⁄₄₀₀ × (£500,000 – £142,107)	(894.73)
Corporation tax liability	28,947.74

As you can see, it is possible to have different tax rates applying even though the information is generated from the same set of accounts.

 Activity 4

Chinny Ltd

Chinny Ltd has for many years prepared accounts to 30 September, but changes its accounting date to 31 December by preparing accounts for the 15 months ended 31 December 2014.

The accounts show a profit, as adjusted for tax purposes (but before deducting capital allowances), of £250,000.

Capital allowances for the two CAPs based on the 15 month period of account were £13,450 and £5,818 respectively.

The company also had income in the period as follows:

		£
Building society interest receivable	1 Oct 2013 – 30 Sept 2014	4,420
	1 Oct 2014 – 31 Dec 2014	780
Chargeable gains	Disposal 15 Dec 2014	55,000
Rents received	31 July 2014	8,000

The rents accrued at 30 September 2013 and 31 December 2014 were £3,000 and £5,000 respectively.

Required:

Calculate the amounts of corporation tax payable for this 15 month period of account.

5 Summary

If the CAP is less than 12 months long and/or there are associated companies, the small profits limits must be apportioned.

If marginal relief applies, U in the formula is the adjusted upper limit.

If you are given a period of account of more than 12 months, the first step is to split it into the two CAPs and compile the two separate taxable total profits / augmented profits figures using the apportioning rules.

Each CAP is then dealt with separately.

If a CAP straddles 31 March 2014, taxable total profits and augmented profits are time apportioned between the two Financial Years in order to calculate the corporation tax liability. However, there is only one amount of corporation tax payable – it is merely calculated in two parts.

6 Test your knowledge

Workbook Activity 5

Corporation tax

1   What are the small profit limits for a company with two associated companies?

Lower limit: [   ]

Upper limit: [   ]

2   What would your answer be if the same company had a CAP which was 9 months long?

Lower limit: [   ]

Upper limit: [   ]

3   If a company has a period of account of longer than 15 months, the trading profits before capital allowances are time apportioned.

True or False?

4   If a CAP straddles Financial Years 2013 and 2014 you should apportion the taxable total profits between the two financial years.

True or False?

Workbook Activity 6

Long period of account

When a company has a period of account that exceeds 12 months, how are the following apportioned:

	Time apportioned	Separate computation	Period in which arises
Adjusted trading profits			
Capital allowances			
Rental income			
Interest income			
Chargeable gains			
Qualifying charitable donation paid			

Tick the appropriate treatment.

 Workbook Activity 7

Wolf Ltd

Wolf Ltd has for many years prepared accounts to 30 September, but changes its accounting date to 31 December by preparing accounts for the 15 months ended 31 December 2014.

The accounts show a profit, as adjusted for tax purposes (but before deducting capital allowances) of £300,000.

Capital allowances for the two CAPs based on the 15 month period of account were £17,000 and £8,000 respectively.

The company also had income and chargeable gains in the period as follows:

Chargeable gains (disposal 15 December 2014)   £25,000

Rents receivable   £20,000

Required:

Calculate the amounts of corporation tax payable for this 15 month period of account.

Workbook Activity 8

Unbelievable Upshots Ltd

Unbelievable Upshots Ltd is a UK resident company which manufactures industrial springs. It has one associated company. For many years it had prepared accounts to 31 May, but it decided to change its accounting date to 28 February.

The company's results for the 9 months ended 28 February 2015 are summarised below:

	£
Adjusted trading profit before capital allowances	643,675
Dividend received from non-associated company	45,000
Interest receivable	13,000
Chargeable gains	30,000

On 1 June 2014 the tax WDVs of plant and machinery were:

	£
General pool	102,000
Special rate pool	7,000

On 1 January 2015 the company purchased machinery for £396,250.

Required:

(a) Calculate the capital allowances for the 9 months ended 28 February 2015.

(b) Calculate the taxable total profits for the 9 months ended 28 February 2015.

(c) Calculate the corporation tax payable for the 9 months ended 28 February 2015.

Workbook Activity 9

Unpredictably Uptown Limited

Unpredictably Uptown Limited (UUL) is a UK resident company which makes fashionable ladies clothing. It has no associated companies. The company has previously prepared accounts to 31 March but has now changed its accounting date to 30 September.

In the 18 months period to 30 September 2015 the company had the following results:

	£
Adjusted trading profits (Note 1)	990,000
Donation to charity (Note 2)	(20,000)
Bank interest receivable (Note 3)	12,500
Dividend received (net) on 28.2.2015	17,500

Note 1: Adjusted trading profits

No capital allowances are due.

Note 2: Donation

On 31 December 2014 the company made a payment of £20,000 to a national charity.

Note 3: Bank interest

	£
30.09.14 received	5,000
31.03.15 received	4,000
30.09.15 received	3,500
	———
	12,500
	———

The interest is non-trading interest. The amounts received were the amounts accrued to date.

Required:

Calculate the corporation tax liability of UUL for the period ended 30 September 2015.

Assume the FY2014 rates continue to apply in the future.

Relief for company losses

Introduction

This chapter covers the various reliefs available for losses within a company.

KNOWLEDGE	CONTENTS
Identify relevant tax authority legislation and guidance. (3.1 K)	1 Trading losses
Identify alternative loss reliefs for trading losses, describing how best to utilise that relief (5.2 K)	2 Capital losses
SKILLS	
Enter adjusted trading profits and losses, capital allowances, investment income and capital gains in the corporation tax computation. (2.4 S)	

1 Trading losses

1.1 Adjusted trading losses

In Chapter 3 we considered how to calculate an adjusted trading profit.

An adjusted trading loss is computed in the same way. However, when a company makes an adjusted trading loss, its trading profit assessment for the accounting period is nil.

Example

Carlos Ltd has had the following results for its year ended 31 March 2015:

	£	£
Gross profit		30,000
Less: Depreciation	5,000	
Allowable expenses	12,000	
	———	(17,000)
Net profit per accounts		13,000
		———

The capital allowances for the year amount to £21,000.

Calculate the adjusted trading profit/ (loss) for the year.

Solution

Step 1: Set up an adjustment of profits pro forma as in Chapter 3.

Step 2: Calculate the adjusted trading profit/(loss)

Work through the statement of profit or loss line by line as previously to calculate the adjusted trading profit/ (loss).

Carlos Ltd

Adjustment of profit/(loss) – year ended 31 March 2015

	£
Net profit per accounts	13,000
Add: Disallowable expenses	
Depreciation	5,000
	18,000
Less: Capital allowances	(21,000)
Adjusted trading loss	(3,000)
Trading profit assessment	Nil

The trading profit figure to be entered onto the pro forma corporation tax computation is nil.

The accounts may show a net **loss** to be adjusted. If this is the case, adding disallowable expenses will REDUCE the loss.

Example

Assume Carlos Ltd in the previous example had a net loss per accounts of (£10,000). Calculate the adjusted trading loss.

Solution

	£
Net loss per accounts	(10,000)
Add: Depreciation	5,000
	(5,000)
Less: Capital allowances	(21,000)
Adjusted trading loss	(26,000)

1.2 Summary of trading loss reliefs

There are three forms of relief available to a company which makes a trading loss:

- Current year relief
- Carry back relief
- Carry forward relief

1.3 Current year relief

A trading loss can be relieved against total profits of the loss making accounting period. The set off is against profits before the deduction of qualifying charitable donations.

A claim for current year (or carry back) relief must be made within two years of the end of the loss making accounting period.

 Example

Sage Ltd had the following results for the year ended 31 March 2015.

	£
Adjusted trading loss	(40,000)
Property income	10,000
Chargeable gain	50,000
Qualifying charitable donations	10,000

Show how relief would be obtained for the loss in the current period.

Approach to the example

It is *essential* once a loss has been identified to set up a loss memorandum as a working and allocate the loss to it, so that the relief for the loss does not exceed the actual amount of loss available.

Even where there is a trading loss, this does not alter the basic approach to a question.

- Present the CT computation in the standard pro forma.
- Support it with workings where necessary (one of which will be the loss memorandum).

Solution

Sage Ltd – Corporation tax computation – y/e 31 March 2015

	£
Trading profit	Nil
Property income	10,000
Chargeable gains	50,000
Total profits	60,000
Less: Loss relief – Current year	(40,000)
	20,000
Less: Qualifying charitable donations	(10,000)
Taxable total profits	10,000

Working:

(W1) Loss memorandum

	£
Year ended 31 March 2015	
Current period loss	(40,000)
Relieved in current period	40,000
Loss c/f	Nil

Setting off the loss before the deduction of qualifying charitable donations (QCDs) may result in the QCDs becoming unrelieved. Excess amounts of QCDs are lost.

Example

What if Sage Ltd in the previous example made a loss of £60,000?

Solution

	£
Total profits before QCDs (as before)	60,000
Less: Loss relief – Current year	(60,000)
	Nil
Less Qualifying charitable donations	Wasted
Taxable total profits	Nil

> The QCD is unrelieved. It has not been used as there are insufficient profits to set it against.
>
> It is an important principle in the use of most loss reliefs that, where there is an available loss, no restriction in set off is permitted.
>
> This means that it would *not* have been possible here to restrict the loss relief to (£50,000) so as to then relieve a QCD of (£10,000), and find an alternative use for the remaining (£10,000) loss.

Unused qualifying charitable donations cannot be carried forward or back and are therefore wasted.

1.4 Carry back relief

A trading loss may be carried back for relief against total profits in the preceding 12 months, but only *after* the loss has first been relieved against any available current period profits.

The loss is set off against total profits *before* deducting QCDs.

In other words, the order in which the loss is applied is as follows:

- First, against total profits of the current year *(before* QCDs).

- Second, against total profits of the previous 12 months (again, *before* the deduction of QCDs).

In questions this is often referred to as 'setting off the loss as soon as possible'.

When a company ceases to trade, it can carry back the loss for 36 months rather than 12. This rule is not examinable.

Approach to losses questions

A longer style task in the assessment may involve utilising company losses over several years; a methodical approach is very important for these tasks.

- Lay out the years side by side in a table, leaving space to insert any loss reliefs.

- Keep a separate working for the trading loss – the memorandum.

- Firstly set the loss against the total profits (before QCDs) of the year of loss.

- Then carry the balance of the loss back against total profits (before QCDs) of the previous 12 months.

- State whether there is any unrelieved loss remaining.

- Keep a running tally in the loss memorandum working.

Here is a pro forma. The loss has been incurred in 2015.

Pro forma corporation tax loss computation

	2014	2015
	£	£
Trading profit	X	Nil
Non-trade interest	X	X
Property income	X	X
Chargeable gains	X	X
Total profits	X	X
Less: Loss relief		
– Current period		(X)
– Carry back	(X)	
	Nil	Nil
Less: Qualifying charitable donations	Wasted	Wasted
Taxable total profits	Nil	Nil

Loss memorandum:

	£
Current year loss (2015)	X
Less: Current year relief	(X)
Carry back relief	(X)
Loss still available	X

Example

Marjoram Ltd has the following results for the three accounting periods to 31 December 2015.

Year ended 31 December	2013	2014	2015
	£	£	£
Trading profits/(loss)	11,000	9,000	(45,000)
Building society interest	500	500	500
Chargeable gains	–	–	4,000
Qualifying charitable donations	250	250	250

Show the taxable total profits for all periods affected, assuming that loss relief is taken as soon as possible.

Solution

Marjoram Ltd

Corporation tax computations

Year ended 31 December	2014 £	2015 £
Trading profit	9,000	Nil
Non-trade interest	500	500
Chargeable gain	Nil	4,000
Total profits	9,500	4,500
Less: Loss relief		
– Current loss relief		(4,500)
– Carry back relief	(9,500)	
	Nil	Nil
Less: Qualifying charitable donations	Wasted	Wasted
Taxable total profits	Nil	Nil

Note: The year ended 31 December 2013 is not affected; the loss cannot be carried back that far.

Loss working

	£
Loss for the year ended 31 December 2015	45,000
Less: Current year relief	(4,500)
	40,500
Less: Carry back 12 months	(9,500)
Loss still available at 1 January 2016	31,000

Activity 1

Banks Ltd has the following results:

Year ended 31 March	2014	2015
	£	£
Adjusted trading profit/(loss)	50,000	(120,000)
Bank interest	2,000	3,000
Qualifying charitable donation	1,000	500

On the assumption that Banks Ltd uses its loss as early as possible, what is the trading loss carried forward to the year ended 31 March 2016?

A   £117,000

B   £68,000

C   £66,500

D   £65,000

Short previous accounting period

Losses can be carried back 12 months. This usually means the loss can be deducted from the profits of the previous accounting period. However, if the previous accounting period is less than 12 months long, it will be possible to carry the loss back to cover a proportion of the profits for the period preceding that.

Example

Amla Ltd has the following results for the three accounting periods to 31 December 2014.

	12m to 30 April 2013	8m to 31 Dec 2013	12m to 31 Dec 2014
	£	£	£
Trading profits/(loss)	40,000	18,000	(100,000)
Bank interest	2,000	1,500	1,700
Qualifying charitable donation	1,000	1,000	1,000

Show the taxable total profits for all periods affected, assuming that loss relief is taken as soon as possible.

Solution

Amla Ltd

Corporation tax computations

	12m to 30 April 2013 £	8m to 31 Dec 2013 £	12m to 31 Dec 2014 £
Trading profits	40,000	18,000	Nil
Bank interest	2,000	1,500	1,700
Total profits	42,000	19,500	1,700
Less: Loss relief			
– Current loss relief			(1,700)
– c/b relief		(19,500)	
(max 4/12 × £42,000)	(14,000)		
	28,000	Nil	Nil
Qualifying charitable donations	(1,000)	Wasted	Wasted
Taxable total profits	27,000	Nil	Nil

Note: The loss can be carried back 12 months. This covers the whole of the 8 months to 31 December 2013 and 4 months of the year ended 30 April 2013. The maximum loss that can be deducted for the year ended 30 April 2013 is equal to 4/12 of the total profits i.e. £14,000

Loss working

	£
Loss for the year ended 31 December 2014	100,000
Less: Current year relief	(1,700)
	98,300
Less: Carry back 8m to 31 Dec 2013	(19,500)
	78,800
Carry back to year ended 30 April 2013	(14,000)
Loss still available at 1 January 2015	64,800

1.5 Carry forward relief

Where any loss remains unrelieved after the current year and carry back claims have been made, the carry forward of the remaining loss is automatic. This also applies where no current year and carry back claims are made, as there is no compulsory requirement to use such reliefs.

The carry forward relief automatically allows trading losses to be set against future trading profits of the same trade as soon as they arise.

They cannot be relieved against any other profits. Such losses have to be used against the first available trading profits.

> ### Example
>
> Mint Limited began trading on 1 April 2012 and has the following results:
>
> | Year ended 31 March | 2013 | 2014 | 2015 |
> |---|---|---|---|
> | | £ | £ | £ |
> | Adjusted trading profit/(loss) | 15,000 | (100,000) | 40,000 |
> | Non-trade interest | 5,000 | 10,000 | 10,000 |
> | Chargeable gain | – | 40,000 | – |
>
> Show how the loss relief would be claimed where relief is required as soon as possible.
>
> **Solution**
>
> **Mint Ltd – Corporation tax computations**
>
> | Year ended 31 March | 2013 | 2014 | 2015 |
> |---|---|---|---|
> | | £ | £ | £ |
> | Trading profit | 15,000 | Nil | 40,000 |
> | Less: Loss relief b/f | | | (30,000) |
> | | | | 10,000 |
> | Non-trade interest | 5,000 | 10,000 | 10,000 |
> | Chargeable gain | – | 40,000 | – |
> | Total profits | 20,000 | 50,000 | 20,000 |
> | Less: Loss relief | | | |
> | – Current year | | (50,000) | |
> | – Carry back | (20,000) | | |
> | Taxable total profits | Nil | Nil | 20,000 |

> **Working: Loss memorandum**
>
> | | £ |
> |---|---|
> | Loss for the year ended 31 March 2014 | 100,000 |
> | Less: Current year relief | (50,000) |
> | Carry back relief | |
> | – Year ended 31 March 2013 | (20,000) |
> | | ———— |
> | | 30,000 |
> | Less: Used in year ended 31 March 2015 | (30,000) |
> | | ———— |
> | Loss left to c/f | Nil |
> | | ———— |

1.6   Factors to be considered when choosing loss relief

Companies have the following choices when considering loss relief:

- Current year claim then carry back claim then carry forward the remaining loss or,

- Current year claim then carry forward the remaining loss or,

- Carry forward all the loss.

When deciding which choice to make there are two main considerations:

(1) **Cash flow**

Where the company wants earliest relief a current and carry back claim would be preferred.

This enables the company to claim tax repayments for the previous year which is a useful cash flow for a company suffering losses.

(2) **Rate of relief**

Where the company wants to obtain the highest possible tax saving then the rate of tax saved is important.

A company would prefer to claim relief in the periods when it is paying tax at the highest rate of tax.

For example, it would prefer to carry forward a loss if it expects to pay tax at the main rate next year but is paying tax at the small profits rate in the current year.

You may have to make a choice of relief in the assessment and / or may be asked to select what factors a company should take into account when choosing the best relief.

2 Capital losses

Both trading and capital losses may be examined in the assessment.

Capital losses may occur in questions in isolation, but where a mixture of losses appear it is essential to distinguish the reliefs available.

The treatment of capital losses will be covered in detail in Chapter 18. However, in summary:

- A capital loss incurred in the current period is automatically relieved against current period gains. Any excess is then carried forward for relief against gains in future accounting periods.

- There is no carry back facility and a capital loss cannot be used against any other profit.

Activity 2

Coriander Ltd

Coriander Ltd began trading on 1 January 2012 and has the following results:

	Trading profit or (loss) £	Non-trade interest £	Qualifying charitable donation £	Capital gains or (losses) £
Year ended 31 Dec:				
2012	37,450	1,300	3,000	(5,000)
2013	(81,550)	1,400	3,000	
2014	20,000	1,600	3,000	12,000

Required:

Calculate taxable total profits for all years, assuming all reliefs are claimed at the earliest opportunity. State the amounts of losses carried forward.

Approach to the question

- Set up CT pro formas for all years leaving space to enter any loss reliefs.

- Set up a loss memorandum for the loss for the year ended 31 December 2013.

- There is also a capital loss to deal with which has more restrictive use than a trading loss.

Activity 3

Read the following statements and state whether they are true or false.

1   Trading losses can be relieved by carry back before being offset in the year of loss.

2   Trading losses are deducted from other income after deducting qualifying charitable donations.

3   Trading losses carried forward can only be set against trading profits from the same trade.

4   Capital losses can be offset against other income in the year of the loss, but only against capital gains in future years.

3   Summary

Losses often appear in assessments.

The rules depend on the type of loss:

*   Trading losses – current year and carry back relief against total profits before qualifying charitable donations, carry forward against trading profits only.

*   Capital losses – current year against chargeable gains only, carry forward against chargeable gains only.

4 Test your knowledge

 Workbook Activity 4

AB Ltd

The following details relate to AB Ltd.

Year ended	31.12.13	31.12.14
	£	£
Adjusted trading profit/(loss)	19,000	(67,000)
Bank interest received	2,000	1,000
Chargeable gains	4,000	4,000
Qualifying charitable donation	10,000	

Required:

Assuming AB Ltd uses its loss as early as possible, what is the amount of loss carried forward at 31 December 2014?

A   £62,000

B   £47,000

C   £42,000

D   £37,000

 Workbook Activity 5

Eldorado (Birmingham) Limited

Eldorado (Birmingham) Limited prepares accounts annually to 31 August in each year. The company commenced to trade on 1 September 2012.

The results for the first few years were as follows:

	2013	2014	2015
	£	£	£
Trading profits/(loss)	18,000	(81,000)	(6,000)
Chargeable gain	3,000		
Property income	22,000	22,000	22,000

Required:

Show how relief is obtained for the trading losses, assuming that relief is claimed as soon as possible.

Workbook Activity 6

Read the following statements and state whether they are true or false.

1   Capital losses can only be offset against chargeable gains in the year of the loss, and then against chargeable gains in future years.

2   Trading losses carried forward can be set against trading profits from the same trade in any future year in which it is beneficial to do so.

3   Trading losses can be deducted from other income and chargeable gains of the current accounting period.

4   Where trading losses have been relieved against the total profits of the loss making period, any losses remaining must then be offset against the total profits of the previous 12 months.

 Workbook Activity 7

Potter Limited

The following is the income of Potter Limited which commenced to trade on 1 October 2013.

Year ended 30 September	2014	2015
	£	£
Adjusted trading profit (loss)	(35,000)	94,000
Bank interest receivable	11,400	8,400
Rents receivable (after deducting expenses)	21,300	21,400
Donation to national charity paid 30 Sept	500	500

Required:

Calculate the taxable total profits for the years ending 30 September 2014 and 2015, indicating how you would obtain relief as soon as possible for the loss.

Workbook Activity 8

Uncut Undergrowth Ltd

Uncut Undergrowth Ltd is a UK resident company that began trading on 1 July 2012. The company's results are summarised as follows:

	Year ended 30.6.13 £	6 months to 31.12.13 £	Year ended 31.12.14 £
Trading profit/(loss)	35,000	25,000	(350,000)
Non-trade loan interest receivable	–	15,000	22,000
Property income	25,000	–	–
Chargeable gains/(loss)	(40,000)	–	30,000
Donation to national charity	1,000	1,000	1,000

Required:

Calculate the taxable total profits for all of the years in the question after giving maximum relief at the earliest time for the trading losses sustained and any other reliefs.

Also show any balance of losses carried forward.

Payment and administration – companies

Introduction

This chapter looks at the payment and administration aspects of corporation tax (see Chapter 15 for sole traders and partnerships).

KNOWLEDGE

Identify relevant tax authority legislation and guidance. (3.1 K)

Explain the system of penalties and interest as it applies to income tax, corporation tax and capital gains tax. (3.2 K)

Identify corporation tax payable and the due dates of payment, including instalments. (5.3 K)

SKILLS

Complete corporation tax returns and submit them within statutory time limits. (2.7 S)

CONTENTS

1 Corporation tax self assessment (CTSA)
2 HM Revenue and Customs' (HMRC) compliance checks
3 Record keeping requirements
4 Payment of corporation tax
5 Approach to preparing written answers

1 Corporation tax self assessment (CTSA)

1.1 Scope

Corporation tax self assessment (CTSA) requires companies to submit a tax return for each CAP and a self assessment of any tax payable.

1.2 Filing the return

A company is required to file a return (form CT600) when it receives a notice requiring it to do so.

All companies must file their returns online.

A company which is chargeable to tax, but which does not receive a notice requesting a return, must notify HMRC within 12 months of the end of the accounting period.

Failure to notify may result in a penalty. The penalty is calculated in broadly the same way as penalties for incorrect returns (see below) and is a maximum of 100% of the tax outstanding.

The return must include a calculation (self assessment) of the corporation tax payable for the accounting period covered by the return.

The return must be made within:

- 12 months of the end of the period of account or, if later,

- three months from the date of the notice requiring the return.

Long periods of account

The return date is based on the period of account (which may be more than 12 months long).

For a set of accounts of more than 12 months long, there will be two CAPs, two corporation tax computations and therefore two returns to file.

However, both returns will have the same filing date; 12 months after the end of the period of account.

Example

Edgar Ltd has prepared a set of accounts for the 15 months ended 31 March 2015.

Identify the period(s) for which return(s) must be completed and the filing date(s).

Solution

The period of account is the period for which accounts are drawn up (i.e. 15 months to 31 March 2015).

	Periods for returns	Filing date
(i)	First 12 months	
	– 12 months ended 31 December 2014	31 March 2016
(ii)	Balance	
	– 3 months ended 31 March 2015	31 March 2016

Penalties for late filing

Failure to submit a return by the due date will result in a penalty.

The system operates as follows:

•	Immediate penalty	£100
•	Delay of more than three months	an additional £10 per day (maximum 90 days = £900)
•	Delay of more than six months	an additional 5% of tax due
•	Delay of more than 12 months, the penalties above, plus:	

No deliberate withholding of information	5% of tax due
Deliberate withholding of information	70% of tax due
Deliberate withholding of information with concealment	100% of tax due

The penalties based on the tax due are each subject to a minimum of £300.

A penalty will not be charged if the taxpayer has a reasonable excuse for the late filing, for example a serious illness. A lack of knowledge of the tax system is not a reasonable excuse.

Example

Flat Ltd received a notice to file Form CT600 for the year ended 30 June 2013 on 31 August 2013. The company submitted the corporation tax return on 28 February 2015 and paid its corporation tax liability of £35,000.

What penalties will be charged in respect of the late filing of the return?

Solution

The corporation tax return was due to be filed on 30 June 2014, 12 months after the end of the period of account. The return was filed more than six months but less than 12 months late.

There will be an immediate penalty of £100.

Because the return is more than three months late there will also be a penalty of £10 per day for up to 90 days.

Because the return is more than six months late there will be a further penalty of 5% of the corporation tax due, i.e. £1,750.

The total penalty charged will be £2,750 (£100 + £900 + £1,750).

1.3 Amending the return

A company can amend a return within 12 months of the filing due date.

HMRC can amend a return to correct obvious errors within:

* nine months of the date it was filed, or

* nine months of the filing of an amendment.

If the company disagrees with HMRC's amendment it may reject it.

This rejection should be made within:

* the normal time limit for amendments or,

* if this time limit has expired, within three months of the date of correction.

1.4 Recovery of overpaid tax

A company may claim a repayment of tax within four years of the end of an accounting period. An appeal against HMRC's decision on such a claim must be made within 30 days.

A company is not allowed to make such a claim if its return was made in accordance with a generally accepted accounting practice which prevailed at the time.

1.5 Interest on late payments of corporation tax

Interest is charged automatically on late paid corporation tax:

- from the due date

- to the date of payment.

Where there is an amendment to the self assessment interest runs:

- from the date the tax would have been payable had it been correctly self assessed in the first place.

Interest paid on late payments of corporation tax is allowable as a deduction from non-trade interest income.

1.6 Interest on overpaid corporation tax

If corporation tax is overpaid HMRC will pay interest:

- from the later of the normal due date (see below) and the date of overpayment

- to the date it is refunded.

Interest received on overpaid corporation tax is assessable as non-trade interest income.

Detailed computations of interest will not be required in the assessment (such as daily calculations), but the principles must be understood.

1.7 Penalties for incorrect returns

A penalty will be charged where:

- an inaccurate return is submitted to HMRC or

- the company fails to notify HMRC where an under assessment of tax is made by them.

The percentage depends on the reason for the error.

Taxpayer behaviour	Maximum penalty % of tax lost
Mistake	No penalty
Failure to take reasonable care	30%
Deliberate understatement	70%
Deliberate understatement with concealment	100%

The penalties may be reduced at HMRC discretion where the taxpayer discloses information to HMRC. The reduction depends on the circumstances of the penalty and whether the taxpayer discloses the information before HMRC discover the error (unprompted disclosure) or afterwards (prompted disclosure).

Taxpayer behaviour	Minimum penalties	
	Unprompted disclosure % of tax lost	Prompted disclosure % of tax lost
Failure to take reasonable care	Nil	15
Deliberate understatement	20	35
Deliberate understatement with concealment	30	50

 Example

State the maximum and minimum penalties that may be levied on each of the following companies which have submitted incorrect tax returns.

L Ltd   Accidentally provided an incorrect figure even though the return was checked carefully. The company notified HMRC of the error three days after submitting the return.

S Ltd   Was unable to check the return due to staff being on holiday. The return included a number of errors. The return was checked thoroughly the following week and the company provided HMRC with the information necessary to identify the errors.

J Ltd   Deliberately understated its tax liability and attempted to conceal the incorrect information that had been provided. HMRC have identified the understatement and J Ltd is helping them with their enquiries.

Solution

Penalties for incorrect tax returns are a percentage of the under declared tax.

L Ltd   No penalty is charged where a taxpayer has been careful and has made a genuine mistake.

S Ltd   The maximum percentage for failing to take reasonable care is 30%. The minimum percentage for unprompted disclosure is nil.

J Ltd   The maximum percentage for a deliberate understatement with concealment is 100%. The minimum percentage for prompted disclosure of information (where the taxpayer provides information in response to HMRC identifying the error) in respect of deliberate understatement with concealment is 50%.

---

2 HM Revenue and Customs' (HMRC) compliance checks

2.1 Basic rules

HMRC have the right to enquire into a company's tax return under their compliance check powers.

Where a return is submitted on time, notice must normally be given within a year of the actual filing date.

Where a return is submitted late HMRC can give notice of a compliance check (formerly referred to as an enquiry) within a year of the 31 January, 30 April, 31 July or 31 October following the actual date of delivery of the return.

HMRC may also demand that the company produce documents for inspection. If the company fails to do so, a penalty of £300, plus up to £60 a day, may be imposed.

A compliance check (enquiry) ends when HMRC give notice that it has been completed and notify what amendments they believe to be necessary.

 Example

CTS Ltd has produced accounts for the year ended 30 June 2014. The company filed its return on 1 April 2015.

What is the latest date by which HMRC must give notice of a compliance check (enquiry)?

How would your answer differ if CTS Ltd had filed its return on 1 September 2015?

Solution

HMRC must give notice within a year of the actual filing date. The actual filing date is 1 April 2015; therefore notice must be given by 1 April 2016.

If the company had filed its return on 1 September 2015, (i.e. after the due filing date of 30 June 2015) HMRC would need to give notice by 31 October 2016 (i.e. 12 months after 31 October following the actual date of delivery of the return).

2.2 Discovery assessments

A discovery assessment may be issued if HMRC believe that insufficient tax has been collected.

The taxpayer can appeal to the Tribunal against a discovery assessment.

2.3 Appeals procedure

The taxpayer can request an informal review of a disputed decision.

Alternatively, a formal appeal may be made to the Tax Tribunal.

Appeals from the Tax Tribunal on a point of law (but not on a point of fact) may be made to the Court of Appeal and from there to the Supreme Court.

The Tax Tribunal is independent of HMRC.

3 Record keeping requirements

A company and its tax adviser must keep records to assist in dealings with and support evidence given to HMRC.

Companies must keep records until the latest of:

*   six years from the end of the accounting period.

*   the date any enquiries are completed.

*   the date after which enquiries may not be commenced.

Failure to keep records can lead to a penalty of up to £3,000 for each accounting period affected.

4 Payment of corporation tax

4.1 Payment date

All payments of corporation tax must be made electronically.

Companies normally pay corporation tax within 9 months and one day of the end of the chargeable accounting period (CAP).

A company with a year ended 31 January 2015 would pay corporation tax by 1 November 2015.

Note that Edgar Ltd (in an earlier example) which had a long period of account of the 15 months ended 31 March 2015 would have two payment dates.

Edgar Ltd would pay corporation tax for:

- CAP 1 = 12 months ended 31 December 2014, by 1 October 2015.

- CAP 2 = 3 months ended 31 March 2015, by 1 January 2016.

From this we can see that a company with a long period of account can have:

- two separate payment dates;

- but one common filing date.

Note that the payment dates are earlier than the filing date.

This normal payment date rule does not however apply to large companies (see below).

4.2 Payment by instalments

Large companies are required to make quarterly payments on account of their corporation tax liability.

A large company for this purpose is a company which pays corporation tax at the main rate (21% for FY2014).

Note that this is normally where profits exceed £1,500,000. However, remember that the upper limit is divided between associated companies and time apportioned for short accounting periods.

Therefore, a company with two other associates will pay tax at 21% and will be required to pay its corporation tax in instalments if its augmented profits exceed £500,000 (£1,500,000 ÷ 3).

Exceptions to the rule

A company is not required to make quarterly instalment payments in the first period in which it becomes large, unless its profits exceed £10 million.

This £10 million limit is also shared between associated companies and time apportioned for short CAPs.

In addition, a company does not have to make quarterly instalment payments if its CT liability does not exceed £10,000.

Payment amounts and pay days

The quarterly payments should be based on the actual corporation tax liability for the current year.

The first payment is made on the 14th day of the seventh month of the accounting period.

The other quarterly payments are due on the 14th day of months 10, 13 and 16.

Note that the payments begin during the accounting period itself, not afterwards. So you must begin counting months from the start of the accounting period.

 Example

State the instalment payment dates for a company with an accounting period ending on 28 February 2015.

Solution

The payments on account are due on:

* 14 September 2014
* 14 December 2014
* 14 March 2015
* 14 June 2015

Each payment due is a quarter of the corporation tax liability for the year.

Therefore estimates of the corporation tax liability for the year need to be made at each payment date.

At least the first three (and probably all four instalments) usually have to be estimated in practice.

The first instalment payment would be a quarter of the best estimate at that date.

The second payment would require a revised estimate and add or deduct any difference in respect of the first instalment and so on.

HMRC may expect to see some proof that the estimates were made with care.

A penalty may be imposed where a company deliberately makes insufficient quarterly payments.

Activity 1

Russell plc prepares accounts to 31 December each year and its taxable total profits for the year ended 31 December 2014 are £1,600,000.

Russell plc has no subsidiaries, receives no dividend income and its taxable total profits for the year ended 31 December 2013 were £720,000.

Which one of the following statements is correct with respect to Russell plc's corporation tax liability for the year ended 31 December 2014?

A   The liability is payable
     – in 4 equal instalments beginning on 14 July 2014

B   The liability is payable
     – in 4 equal instalments beginning on 14 July 2015

C   The liability is payable on 1 October 2015

D   The liability is payable on 31 December 2015

4.3   Interest

Companies should revise the estimate of their corporation tax liability every quarter. It is a good idea to keep records showing how the estimate has been calculated. This will help to justify the size of a payment if HMRC should dispute the amount paid.

Interest runs from the due date on any underpayments or overpayments.

Interest paid by the company is a deductible expense. Interest received by the company is taxable income. Both are dealt with under the loan relationship rules as non-trade interest.

Penalties may be charged if a company deliberately fails to pay instalments of a sufficient size.

5   Approach to preparing written answers

5.1   Written advice to clients

Task 7 in the AQ2013 assessment will cover a number of syllabus areas including those dealing with filing dates, payments of tax, penalties and interest for companies or individuals (see Chapter 15).

AAT guidance states that this area:

'will be assessed via a free text written response from the learner. The questions will usually be client focussed so learners will be expected to address their answers in a manner appropriate to such an audience'

The chief assessor has written a guidance document to assist learners with written answers in Personal Tax. However, much of the guidance is relevant for Business Tax. Some of the key points from the advice are set out below.

Firstly, it's important you understand that the software in which you are answering the task is not Microsoft Word. So there's no:

- *spell checker*
- *grammar checker*
- *automatic correcting of typos.*

You **must** *proofread what you've written and correct any obvious spelling and grammatical errors.*

There's often a mark for presentation of the answer, and the assessor is looking for whether the way you've presented your work would be acceptable in the workplace. This mark is independent of the technical answer, and what we look for is whether a client would find the answer acceptable from a visual perspective.

Before you start to type:

You must read the question in detail. We've noticed that students often scan read a question, decide what it's about in an instant and then write the answer without giving any thought or consideration to the details. You should:

- *read through once to get the general feel of the question*
- *read through again, slower this time, concentrating on key words or phrases*
- *plan your answer, ensuring all key areas are covered*
- *decide the structure of your answer, considering where you'll use things like an email, a memo or bullet points*
- *type up your answer*
- *proof read your answer, correcting any errors.*

Too many times it would seem that students only follow the fifth of these points. If you do this it **will** *affect your marks.*

Consider exactly who you're writing to. Most likely it will be a client, so this needs to influence your approach.

Remember, if the client is writing to you for advice, they don't know the answer. We often see students give half answers which the assessor will understand, but which a client would not. As a result, they lose marks.

Similarly, be sure to avoid:

- *abbreviations*
- *technical jargon*
- *SMS/text message speak.*

 Activity 2

Space plc, which has taxable total profits of £2 million annually, is preparing its budget for the year ending 31 March 2015. It does not have any dividend income.

Required:

(a) Prepare a plan of projected corporation tax payments based on its results for the year, stating the amounts due and the due dates.

(b) Advise of any other administrative requirements for corporation tax purposes.

Approach to the question

Step 1: Calculate the corporation tax liability.

Step 2: Consider the impact of the instalment system on this large company.

Step 3: Consider the *returns* required, and the impact of late payments.

6 Summary

There are numerous deadlines and penalties under CTSA.

The key points are:

- A company must file a return within
    - 12 months of the end of its period of account or,
    - if later, three months from the date of the notice from HMRC.
- Failure to submit a return on time results in an immediate penalty of £100.
- The company can amend a return within 12 months of the due filing date.
- HMRC can conduct a compliance check (enquiry) into a return provided they give written notice within a year of the actual filing date.
- Companies must keep records for six years from the end of the accounting period. Failure to do so can result in a penalty of up to £3,000.
- The due date for corporation tax is nine months and one day after the end of the accounting period.
- Companies liable at the main rate of CT (21% for FY2014) must pay their liability in quarterly instalments, commencing on the 14th day of the seventh month of the accounting period.

7 Test your knowledge

 Workbook Activity 3

Payment and administration

Read the following statements and state whether they are true or false.

1   Companies must file their corporation tax returns before they pay their corporation tax.

2   The filing date for a company which prepares accounts for the 11 months to 28 February 2015 is 28 February 2016.

3   DEF Ltd filed its corporation tax return for the year ended 31 March 2015 on 19 May 2016. The latest date that it can amend the return is 19 May 2017.

4   The maximum penalty for not filing a corporation tax return on time is £100.

Workbook Activity 4

ABC Ltd

ABC Ltd has four associated companies. In the year to 31 March 2014 its profits were £200,000. In the year to 31 March 2015 it sold its factory and had profits of £3 million.

When is the corporation tax for the year to 31 March 2015 due?

A   The liability is payable in 4 equal instalments beginning on 14 October 2014

B   The liability is payable in 4 equal instalments beginning on 14 October 2015

C   The liability is payable on 1 January 2016

D   The liability is payable on 31 March 2016

Workbook Activity 5

Wendy Windows plc

Wendy Windows plc pays corporation tax at the main rate every year and has taxable total profits in the year ended 31 January 2015 of £2,400,000.

Required:

Calculate the corporation tax liability of Wendy Windows plc for the accounting period to 31 January 2015 and state when this liability is due for payment.

Sole traders and partnerships – principles of taxation

Introduction

In Chapters 2 to 9 we have considered how we tax the profits and gains of one type of business entity – a company.

In the next few chapters we look at how we tax the profits of sole traders and partnerships (unincorporated businesses).

This chapter is an introduction to the main differences in the method of dealing with the tax affairs of these business entities.

KNOWLEDGE	CONTENTS
Identify relevant tax authority legislation and guidance. (1.1 K)	1 Sole trader 2 Partnerships

1 Sole trader

1.1 No separate legal entity

A sole trader is an individual who has set up his/her own business. The business is not a separate legal entity.

1.2 Types of tax payable

The individual who sets up as a sole trader pays:

- income tax, on income including adjusted trading profits; and
- capital gains tax, on chargeable gains.

Example

Which of the following business entities is a sole trader?

(a) Fred Flint, haulage contractors.

(b) Fred Flint Ltd, haulage contractors.

Solution

(a) Fred Flint is a sole trader. Fred pays income tax on his adjusted trading profit and capital gains tax on his gains.

(b) Fred Flint Ltd is a company (a separate legal entity). The company pays corporation tax on income and gains.

2 Partnerships

2.1 No separate legal entity

A partnership is a group of individuals carrying on in business together. The business is not a separate legal entity.

2.2　Types of tax payable

Each partner individually pays:

- income tax, on his share of the partnership's adjusted trading profit in addition to his other personal income.

A partnership is effectively a collection of sole traders working together, each responsible for his own tax liability.

The allocation of partnership profits is considered further in Chapter 12.

3　Summary

Sole traders and partnerships:

- DO NOT pay corporation tax.
- DO pay income tax and capital gains tax.
- ARE NOT separate legal entities.

Taxable trade profits for unincorporated businesses

Introduction

The assessment may include a task that looks at the taxable trading profits of a sole trader or partner (unincorporated businesses).

There are some differences in the computation of adjusted trading profits and capital allowances for unincorporated businesses compared to companies.

KNOWLEDGE
Identify relevant tax authority legislation and guidance. (3.1 K)
Describe the main regulations relating to disallowed expenditure. (4.1 K)
Explain the availability and types of capital allowances. (4.3 K)

SKILLS
Adjust trading profits and losses for tax purposes. (1.1 S)
Prepare computations of capital allowances. (1.4 S)
Make adjustments for private use of assets by owners. (1.5 S)
Complete the self-employed or partnership supplementary pages of the tax return for individuals, and submit them within statutory time limits. (1.10 S)

CONTENTS

1. Adjusted trading profits for individuals
2. Adjustment of trading profits
3. Capital allowances for individuals
4. Income tax return – self employment

1 Adjusted trading profits for individuals

1.1 Badges of trade

We are now concerned with taxing the profits of a trade of an individual.

Statute law defines a 'trade' as including every venture in the nature of trade. This is not particularly helpful in practice and it has been necessary for the Courts to decide in a number of cases whether or not an activity is a trade.

In 1954 a Royal Commission summarised the existing case law relevant to 'trade' by identifying six attributes or 'badges' of trade. The mnemonic 'SOFIRM' as shown below may help you to remember them!

- *Subject matter and the manner of acquisition(S)*

  Assets are generally acquired either for personal use, or as an investment, or as inventory used in a trade (i.e. stock) or as a non-current asset (i.e. fixed asset) used in a trade.

  An investment may be income generating (e.g. shares) or for pleasure (e.g. a painting). If an asset is clearly neither acquired as an investment or for the use of the owner or his family or friends, the inference of trading arises.

  Transactions involving assets acquired via an inheritance or gift are less likely to be regarded as trading.

  A trading activity is more likely to be inferred where a loan is taken out in order to purchase assets, and those assets need to be sold in order for the loan to be repaid.

- *Length of ownership (O)*

  The shorter the period of ownership the more likely this is indicative of a trade.

- *Frequency of transactions and similarity to existing trade (F)*

  The more frequent a transaction the more likely a trade is being conducted.

  Transactions are more likely to be regarded as trading where they are similar to those of an existing trade.

- *Improvements / Supplementary work (I)*

  An asset bought and enhanced in some way before sale is more likely to be a trading asset than a similar asset simply bought and sold without improvement.

- *Circumstances of realisation (R)*

  It can be argued that the forced sale of an asset to relieve a cash flow crisis is less likely to be a disposal in the course of a trade.

- *Motive (M)*

  The presence of a profit motive is indicative of a trade.

In borderline cases it is necessary to look at all the 'badges' together and not give undue weight to any particular test.

In addition to the original 6 badges of trade mentioned above, HMRC guidance adds that the following are also considered to indicate trading:

- *Existence of similar trading transactions*

  Are the transactions are similar to those of an existing trade carried on by the taxpayer?

- *Finance*

  Did the taxpayer take out a loan to buy the asset which they expect to repay from the proceeds of sale?

- *Method of acquisition*

  Has the taxpayer acquired the asset by way of purchase rather than receiving it as a gift or by inheritance?

Remember that no one factor is conclusive. All factors must be considered and an overall view taken.

 Example

James Aslett renovates classic cars as a 'hobby' in his spare time and exhibits them at classic car events. He has accepted the occasional offer to sell and usually makes a profit if the time he has spent is ignored.

Explain whether you think James will be treated as trading in cars by HMRC.

Solution

- The situation has to be measured against the 'badges of trade'.

- A car could be a trading asset or an investment or for personal use so the first test is inconclusive.

- If James owns the cars for only a brief period and is constantly buying, renovating and selling, perhaps even advertising, there comes a point where the hobby becomes a trade.

1.2 Professions and vocations

The profits made by a self employed person from a profession or vocation, such as accountancy, are taxed in the same way as the profits of a trade.

2 Adjustment of trading profits

2.1 Comparison between individuals and companies

The starting point in determining the amount of taxable trading profits is the net profit as shown in the accounts, but this must be adjusted for tax purposes in a similar way to companies.

We have already seen in Chapter 3 in the context of a company how to adjust the accounting profits to find the adjusted trading profits for tax purposes. The first part of this chapter will concentrate on approaching the topic from an individual trader's perspective.

Taxable trading profits for an individual comprise adjusted trading profits (Chapter 3) less capital allowances (Chapter 4) for an accounting period in much the same way as it does for a company.

There are two differences between individuals and companies that are **excluded** from the Business Tax syllabus:

- The use of the cash basis for small businesses.

- The fixed rate deductions available in respect of certain expenses.

This chapter covers the minor adjustments needed to the rules seen earlier in the context of companies.

Outline pro forma for adjustment of profits computation

	Section	£	£
Net profit per accounts			X
Add: Disallowable expenditure	2.2	X	
Income not included in the accounts but taxable as trading income	2.3	X	
		—	X
			X
Less: Income included in the accounts but not taxable as trading income	2.4	X	
Expenditure not in the accounts but allowable as a trading deduction	2.5	X	
		—	(X)
Adjusted trading profit (before deducting capital allowances)			X

The same profit adjustment rules for companies apply for individual (or 'sole') traders but with minor adjustments explained as follows.

2.2 Disallowable expenditure differences

Adjustments for private expenditure

Any private expenditure of the owner of the business deducted in the accounts should be disallowed. This would include any payment of the trader's income tax or national insurance liabilities.

There will sometimes be an estimated proportion of business use, for example with motor expenses or telephone expenses. If this is the case, only the private element should be disallowed and therefore added back.

Under self assessment the trader has to be prepared to justify his estimate of the private element if HMRC enquire into his self assessment return.

Salary to proprietor

The salary or drawings paid to the owner is the equivalent of a dividend paid by a company. It is an appropriation of profit, not a business expense, and must therefore be added back to profit.

> ### ☀️ Example
>
> Gordon has his own business as a motor dealer. His accounts for the year ended 31 December 2014 show the following results:
>
> | | £ | £ |
> |---|---|---|
> | Gross profit | | 80,000 |
> | Less: Expenses | | |
> | Salaries | 30,000 | |
> | Motor expenses | 3,000 | |
> | Allowable expenses | 22,000 | |
> | | ——— | (55,000) |
> | | | ——— |
> | Net profit per accounts | | 25,000 |
> | | | ——— |
>
> Included in motor expenses is £1,000 relating to the cost of running Gordon's car which is used 60% for business purposes and included in salaries is Gordon's 'salary' of £20,000.
>
> Calculate Gordon's adjusted trading profit.
>
> | | £ |
> |---|---|
> | Net profit per accounts | 25,000 |
> | Add: Disallowable expenses | |
> | Gordon's 'salary'/drawings | 20,000 |
> | Private motor expenses (£1,000 × 40%) | 400 |
> | | ——— |
> | Adjusted trading profit | 45,400 |
> | | ——— |
>
> **Note:** Do not add back salaries or private motor expenses of employees. These are allowable expenses for the business (just as they are in a company's computation).

Bad debts / Irrecoverable debts

We saw in Chapter 3 that as companies are required to produce their accounts in accordance with internationally accepted accounting practice, any provisions for irrecoverable debts (bad debts) included within the accounts are specific in nature and therefore allowable for tax purposes.

The accounts of an unincorporated business however are not bound by the Companies Act requirements and therefore may contain *general* provisions which are not allowable for tax purposes.

Movements in general provisions, for example the *general* bad debt provision, are not allowable. An increase in a general provision must be added back, and a decrease in a general provision must be deducted, to arrive at adjusted trading profits.

Movements in *specific* provisions are allowable and do not need adjusting for in calculating the adjusted trading profits.

Note that movements in any other general provisions charged to the statement of profit or loss should also be disallowed (e.g. inventory / stock provisions).

Example

The bad debts account of Greg, an interior designer, for the year ended 30 June 2015 appears as follows:

	£		£
Written off		Balance brought down	
Trade	274	Specific provision	185
Former employee	80	General provision	260
Balance carried down		Recoveries – trade	23
Specific provision	194	Profit and loss account	305
General provision	225		
	773		773

Show the adjustment required in computing the adjusted trading profit.

Solution

The first stage is to establish a breakdown of the statement of profit or loss charge of £305.

Remember that this figure comprises amounts written off and recovered, and movements in provisions.

Statement of profit or loss charge:

	£	Allowable?
Increase in specific provision (£194 – £185)	9	✓
Decrease in general provision (£225 – £260)	(35)	✗
Trade debt written off	274	✓
Former employee loan written off	80	✗
Recoveries – trade	(23)	✓
	305	

The movement in the general provision and the amount owed by the former employee are both disallowed. In this case, the movement in the general provision is a *decrease, so* the adjustment made is to *deduct* it from the profit per the accounts.

The adjustments required to compute the adjusted trading profit are therefore as follows:

		£
Add:	Former employee, debt written off	80
Less:	Decrease in general provision	(35)

Charitable donations

An unincorporated business may make charitable donations. These fall into three categories:

- Small and to a local charity – allowed as trade expenses.

- Donations via the Gift Aid scheme – these are not allowed as a trade expense but the trader will get relief for the payment via their personal income tax computation. This relief is not examinable in Business Tax.

- Other charitable donations – not allowed as a trade expense and no other relief is available.

For a company all charitable donations that are not relieved as trade expenses are given relief as qualifying charitable donations and are deducted from total profits.

2.3 Income not included in the accounts but taxable as trading income

This category does not exist for the adjustment of profits for a company.

The most common example is goods taken by the owner for his own use. The proprietor must be taxed on the profit he would have made if the goods had been sold at market value (i.e. at retail or wholesale price as appropriate).

If the cost of sales in the statement of profit or loss has not been reduced for the goods taken for own use then the amount to be added back to arrive at the adjusted profit will be the *selling price*.

If the cost of sales has been reduced by the cost of the goods taken for own use, then the amount added back will be the *profit.*

Example

Sammy operates a toy store and has taken goods for his own use costing £500 during the year ended 31 December 2014. An adjustment has already been made to reflect the cost of the goods taken.

What is the increase to net profit required if:

(a)   Sammy operates a mark-up basis of pricing of 40%; or alternatively

(b)   Sammy operates on a gross profit margin of 40%?

Read the requirement carefully in the assessment. These will give different results.

Solution

(a)   Mark-up means that the cost of the goods represents 100% and that sales value is therefore 140%.

	%
Sales	140
Less: Cost	(100)
	–––––
Profit	40
	–––––

The profit is therefore (40% of £500) = £200.

(b)   Where a gross profit margin is supplied, sales represent 100% of the value.

If the profit is 40% of sales then the cost of goods is 60%.

	%
Sales	100
Less: Cost	(60)
	–––––
Profit	40
	–––––

Therefore the profit element is (£500 × $\frac{40}{60}$) = £333.

Example

Mr Bean has taken £500 of goods from inventory. An adjustment has been made in the accounts for the cost of the goods taken.

An extract from the statement of profit or loss shows the following:

	£	£
Sales		450,000
Opening inventory	160,000	
Purchases	210,000	
Closing inventory	(120,000)	
Cost of sales		(250,000)
Gross profit		200,000

Explain the adjustments needed if the net profit shown in the accounts is £90,000.

Solution

The increase to net profit for the profit element of goods for own use must be calculated by reference to the correct relationship between cost and gross profit.

If cost of goods used is £500 and £250,000 of costs generates £200,000 of profit then:

Profit element = £500 × $\frac{200}{250}$ = £400

Therefore net profit adjustments are as follows:

	£
Net profit	90,000
Add: Increase in profit for goods for own use	400
Adjusted profit	90,400

2.4 Income included in the accounts but not taxable as trading income

The following are examples of amounts which may be included in the statement of profit or loss, but which are not taxable as trading income. Hence they should be deducted when calculating taxable trading profits.

- Income taxed in another way (e.g. rent, interest receivable).

- Income exempt from income tax (e.g. interest on delayed tax repayments).

- Profits on sales of non-current assets.

These adjustments are essentially the same as those for companies.

2.5 Expenditure not in the accounts but allowable

This category of adjustment does not arise for companies.

Any business expense not charged in the accounts but paid for or borne privately by the proprietor can be deducted as a business expense.

For example, where a home telephone is used for business calls the cost of the business calls can be deducted (although it is more common for the whole amount to be charged to the statement of profit or loss, in which case the private portion should be disallowed).

Activity 1

Capone (1)

Capone is in business as a wine merchant and has prepared accounts to 30 June 2014. His statement of profit or loss was:

	£	£
Sales		183,658
Cost of sales		(119,379)
Gross profit		64,279
Dividend income		300
		64,579
Salaries	9,740	
Rent and business rates	9,860	
Repairs to premises	2,620	
Motor expenses	740	
Depreciation	4,150	
Bad and doubtful debts	6,030	
Sundry expenses	770	
Salary		
– Capone	14,000	
– Wife, as secretary	1,450	
		(49,360)
Net profit		15,219

The following information is given:

Repairs to premises	£
Alterations to flooring in order to install new bottling machine	1,460
Decorations	1,160
	2,620

Bad and doubtful debts account

	£		£
Trade debts written off	1,300	Provision brought forward	
Loan to ex-employee		– General	1,850
written off	400	– Specific	580
Provisions carried forward		Profit and loss account	6,030
– General	5,200		
– Specific	1,560		
	8,460		8,460

Interest on bank overdraft

The overdraft was obtained in order to finance the purchase of inventory

Sundry expenses	£
Fine re breach of Customs bonding regulations	250
Subscription to Wine Retail Trade Association	50
Miscellaneous allowable expenses	470
	770

During the year Capone had withdrawn goods from inventory for his own consumption. The cost of this inventory was £455. The business makes a uniform gross profit of 35% on selling price. No entry had been made in the books in respect of the goods taken.

Most mornings Capone telephoned his importing agent from home; the cost of these calls, extracted from his private British Telecom bills, was £290. No entry has been made in the accounts.

Required:

Compute Capone's adjusted trading profit before capital allowances for the period ended 30 June 2014, giving reasons for the adjustments made.

Note: Reasons for the adjustments are unlikely to be required in the assessment. It is likely that an adjustment of profits question will involve dragging items of expenditure to the appropriate part of the adjustment of profits calculation or choosing the correct adjustment from a few options.

However, understanding why adjustments are made will help you to remember them better.

3 Capital allowances for individuals

3.1 The general rules

The capital allowance rules for plant and machinery (Chapter 4) have already been explained in detail for companies. The modifications needed to apply these rules for sole traders are explained below.

3.2 Private use assets

Any asset used partly *by the proprietor / owner* for private purposes must be given a separate column in the capital allowances working. Such assets cannot be covered by a short life asset election.

The AIA, WDA or FYA on the asset is based on its full cost. However, the allowance actually *claimed* will be reduced for private use. Only the proportion relating to business use can be claimed.

Note that if applicable, the business can choose the expenditure against which the AIA is matched. It will be most beneficial for the AIA to be allocated against the general pool expenditure rather than any private use asset as only the business proportion of any AIA available can be claimed.

However note that in the assessment the assets most commonly used for private purposes are cars, which are not eligible for the AIA.

On disposal, a balancing adjustment will be calculated. However, the balancing adjustment will be similarly reduced for private use. Only the business proportion can be claimed or is taxable.

The following example demonstrates this.

Example

Gerard is a trader preparing accounts for calendar years.

In May 2014 he bought a motor car for £7,200 which has CO_2 emissions of 125 g/km. He sold this car in February 2016 for £5,000 replacing it with a car costing £18,800 which has a CO_2 emission rate of 170 g/km.

Gerard uses his cars for both business and private purposes and estimates an 80% business use proportion.

Show the capital allowances and balancing adjustments on the cars for the years ended 31 December 2014, 2015 and 2016.

Solution

This example involves two private use cars.

Each car will have a separate column, as a private use asset.

The first stage is to calculate the allowances in the normal way. Then multiply these allowances by 80%, the business use proportion, to find the allowances that can be claimed.

On disposal, the balancing allowance or charge will be calculated as usual, and again multiplied by 80% to find the actual amount to be deducted or added back to adjusted trading profits.

The answer is therefore as follows:

Gerard – Capital allowances

	Private use Car 1 £	Private use Car 2 £	Allowances £
Year ended 31 December 2014			
Additions	7,200		
WDA at 18%	(1,296) ×	80%	1,037
TWDV carried forward	5,904		
Year ended 31 December 2015			
WDA at 18%	(1,063) ×	80%	850
TWDV carried forward	4,841		

Year ended 31 December 2016

Additions		18,800
Disposal proceeds	(5,000)	
	————	
	(159)	
Balancing charge	159 × 80%	(127)
	————	
WDA at 8% (note)	(1,504) × 80%	1,203
	————	
TWDV carried forward	17,296	
	————	
Total allowances		1,076
		————

Note: Gerard's new car has emissions of more than 130 g/km and so the WDA is 8%.

 Activity 2

Ernest

Ernest prepares accounts to 31 March annually. On 1 April 2014 he had a qualifying general pool balance of plant and machinery brought forward of £24,000.

The following transactions took place in the year to 31 March 2015.

15 April 2014	Purchased car for £16,000 (wholly business usage)
30 April 2014	Sold plant for £3,200 (original cost £4,800)
16 July 2014	Purchased car for £9,200 (wholly business usage)
17 August 2014	Purchased car for £9,400 (30% private usage by Ernest)

In the following year to 31 March 2016, Ernest sold for £8,100 the car originally purchased on 17 August 2014. The car originally purchased on 15 April 2014 was sold for £9,400 on 9 March 2016. There were no other transactions.

All cars purchased had CO_2 emissions between 96 and 130 g/km.

Assume the rates of allowances for the tax year 2014/15 continue into the future.

Required:

Compute the capital allowances and balancing adjustments for the years ended 31 March 2015 and 31 March 2016.

3.3 The impact of the length of the accounting period (sole traders)

As we have seen, capital allowances are computed for accounting periods and deducted in calculating taxable trading profits.

The writing down allowances calculated so far were all for 12 month accounting periods.

Where the accounting period is more or less than 12 months' long, the AIA and WDA must be scaled up or down accordingly. You must perform this calculation to the nearest month.

Note the important difference between companies and sole traders. A company cannot have a chargeable accounting period greater than 12 months, but a sole trader can. Therefore the WDA is scaled up where there is a long period of account for a sole trader.

Remember however that first year allowances are given in full regardless of the length of the accounting period. They are never scaled up or down according to the length of the accounting period.

Capital allowances for periods which are not twelve months long are very popular in the assessment and you should always watch out for them.

 Example

Ken started to trade on 1 May 2014, and on that day he purchased three cars for the use of his employees at a total cost of £21,900 and plant which cost £22,000. All the cars had CO_2 emissions of 120 g/km.

Calculate the allowances due for his first two accounting periods on the assumption that he prepares his first accounts to:

(i)   30 April 2015

(ii)   28 February 2015

(iii)   31 July 2015

and annually on those dates thereafter.

Assume the rates of allowances for the tax year 2014/15 continue into the future.

Solution

(i) First accounts – 12 months to 30 April 2015

	£	General pool £	Allowances £
12 months to 30.4.15			
Additions:			
No AIA: Cars		21,900	
Qualifying for AIA:			
Plant	22,000		
Less AIA	(22,000)		22,000
	―――――	Nil	
		―――――	
		21,900	
WDA (18%)		(3,942)	3,942
		―――――	
TWDV c/f		17,958	
			―――――
Total allowances			25,942
			―――――
12 months to 30.4.16			
WDA (18%)		(3,232)	3,232
		―――――	―――――
TWDV c/f		14,726	
		―――――	

(ii) First accounts – 10 months to 28 February 2015

	£	General pool £	Allowances £
10 months to 28.2.15			
Additions:			
No AIA: Cars		21,900	
Qualifying for AIA:			
Plant	22,000		
Less AIA	(22,000)		22,000
	―――――	Nil	
		―――――	
		21,900	
WDA (18% × 10/12)		(3,285)	3,285
		―――――	
TWDV c/f		18,615	
			―――――
Total allowances			25,285
			―――――

		General pool	Allowances
12 months to 28.2.16			
WDA (18%)		(3,351)	3,351
TWDV c/f		15,264	

(iii) **First accounts – 15 months to 31 July 2015**

	£	General pool £	Allowances £
15 months to 31.7.15			
Additions:			
No AIA: Cars		21,900	
Qualifying for AIA:			
Plant	22,000		
Less AIA (Note)	(22,000)		22,000
		Nil	
		21,900	
WDA (18% × 15/12)		(4,928)	4,928
TWDV c/f		16,972	
Total allowances			26,928
12 months to 31.7.16			
WDA (18%)		(3,055)	3,055
TWDV c/f		13,917	

Note: Maximum AIA = (£500,000 × 15/12) = £625,000

Activity 3

Anjula runs her own business as a dog groomer. She commenced trading on 1 May 2014 and prepares her first set of accounts to 31 August 2015.

On 2 June 2014 she purchased equipment costing £2,500 and a car costing £6,200 with carbon dioxide emissions of 125 g/km and 100% business use.

What are the capital allowances available for the period ended 31 August 2015?

A   £8,700

B   £3,988

C   £2,088

D   £3,616

 4   Income tax return – self employment

4.1   Self employment supplementary pages

An individual may be required to complete a tax return.

There is a main return (SA100) and several supplementary pages to be completed as appropriate. One of the sets of supplementary pages consists of four pages on self employment (SA103).

In the assessment you will only be asked to complete page SEF 2.

4.2   Page SEF 2

This page records the expenses of the business. The detailed section on expenses need only be completed if the annual turnover of the business is at least £81,000. Otherwise it is only necessary to enter a total expenses figure in Box 31.

- The left hand column includes all expenses shown in the accounts (analysed as appropriate).

- The right hand column shows the disallowable expenditure included within the expenses figures.

It is possible that boxes in both columns could include the same figure; for example, if depreciation in the accounts is £3,000 then:

- Box 29 will show £3,000; and

- Box 44 will show £3,000.

Usually the boxes will show different figures; for example, if wages and salaries of £50,000 included the owner's drawings of £20,000 then:

- Box 19 will show £50,000; and

- Box 34 will show £20,000.

Note that this page **only** records expenses and does not include adjustments for:

- Goods for own use

- Income included in the accounts but not taxable as trading income.

- Capital allowances

The following is important in connection with the completion of forms in the exam.

- When completing the form in the exam, figures must be entered in the correct boxes.

- You will be asked to complete just one page of any form.

- Commas need not be entered for numbers of four digits or more.

- You do not need to fill in every box, only relevant ones.

Business expenses

Please read the *Self-employment (full) notes* before filling in this section.

Total expenses	Disallowable expenses
If your annual turnover was below £79,000 you may just put your total expenses in box 31	Use this column if the figures in boxes 17 to 30 include disallowable amounts

17 Cost of goods bought for resale or goods used

£ _____ · 0 0

32

£ _____ · 0 0

18 Construction industry – *payments to subcontractors*

£ _____ · 0 0

33

£ _____ · 0 0

19 Wages, salaries and other staff costs

£ _____ · 0 0

34

£ _____ · 0 0

20 Car, van and travel expenses

£ _____ · 0 0

35

£ _____ · 0 0

21 Rent, rates, power and insurance costs

£ _____ · 0 0

36

£ _____ · 0 0

22 Repairs and renewals of property and equipment

£ _____ · 0 0

37

£ _____ · 0 0

23 Phone, fax, stationery and other office costs

£ _____ · 0 0

38

£ _____ · 0 0

24 Advertising and business entertainment costs

£ _____ · 0 0

39

£ _____ · 0 0

25 Interest on bank and other loans

£ _____ · 0 0

40

£ _____ · 0 0

26 Bank, credit card and other financial charges

£ _____ · 0 0

41

£ _____ · 0 0

27 Irrecoverable debts written off

£ _____ · 0 0

42

£ _____ · 0 0

28 Accountancy, legal and other professional fees

£ _____ · 0 0

43

£ _____ · 0 0

29 Depreciation and loss/profit on sale of assets

£ _____ · 0 0

44

£ _____ · 0 0

30 Other business expenses

£ _____ · 0 0

45

£ _____ · 0 0

31 Total expenses (total of boxes 17 to 30)

£ _____ · 0 0

46 Total disallowable expenses (total of boxes 32 to 45)

£ _____ · 0 0

SA103F 2014   Page SEF 2

Activity 4

Capone (2)

Complete page 2 of the self employment supplementary pages (see below) for the relevant expenses for Capone in Activity 1.

Business expenses

Please read the *Self-employment (full) notes* before filling in this section.

Total expenses	Disallowable expenses
If your annual turnover was below £79,000 you may just put your total expenses in box 31	Use this column if the figures in boxes 17 to 30 include disallowable amounts

17 Cost of goods bought for resale or goods used
£ · 0 0

32
£ · 0 0

18 Construction industry – *payments to subcontractors*
£ · 0 0

33
£ · 0 0

19 Wages, salaries and other staff costs
£ · 0 0

34
£ · 0 0

20 Car, van and travel expenses
£ · 0 0

35
£ · 0 0

21 Rent, rates, power and insurance costs
£ · 0 0

36
£ · 0 0

22 Repairs and renewals of property and equipment
£ · 0 0

37
£ · 0 0

23 Phone, fax, stationery and other office costs
£ · 0 0

38
£ · 0 0

24 Advertising and business entertainment costs
£ · 0 0

39
£ · 0 0

25 Interest on bank and other loans
£ · 0 0

40
£ · 0 0

26 Bank, credit card and other financial charges
£ · 0 0

41
£ · 0 0

27 Irrecoverable debts written off
£ · 0 0

42
£ · 0 0

28 Accountancy, legal and other professional fees
£ · 0 0

43
£ · 0 0

29 Depreciation and loss/profit on sale of assets
£ · 0 0

44
£ · 0 0

30 Other business expenses
£ · 0 0

45
£ · 0 0

31 Total expenses (total of boxes 17 to 30)
£ · 0 0

46 Total disallowable expenses (total of boxes 32 to 45)
£ · 0 0

SA103F 2014   Page SEF 2

5 Summary

Sole traders must adjust their accounting profits in the same way as companies:

- add back disallowable expenditure
- deduct allowable expenditure which is not shown in the accounts
- deduct income shown in the accounts not taxable as trading income
- add income taxable as trading income which is not shown in the accounts.

The main adjustments applying to individuals but not companies are the disallowance of the proprietor's salary and private expenses, and the adjustment of goods taken for the proprietor's own use.

Capital allowances are then deducted from the adjusted trading profits to give the taxable trading profits. The capital allowances must be restricted for the proprietor's own use of business assets.

6 Test your knowledge

 Workbook Activity 5

Patrick

Patrick is a self-employed businessman. The following expenses are charged in Patrick's statement of profit or loss for the year to 31 December 2014:

	£	✓ or ✗
Patrick's business travelling expenses	5,175	
Christmas presents for staff	250	
Entertaining overseas suppliers	2,750	
Entertaining UK customers	2,300	
Gifts to customers that carry the business name:		
– Boxes of chocolates costing £5.00 each	125	
– Calendars costing £1.50 each	150	
Donation to national charity	50	
Donation to local political party	100	
Subscription to chamber of commerce	25	
A gift to a member of staff upon marriage	45	
Patrick's squash club subscription	250	
Advertising in trade press	280	

Patrick often uses his squash club as a place to take customers since several of them are keen squash players.

Mark each expense with either a ✓ (if the expense is allowable and requires no adjustment) or ✗ (if the expense is disallowable and must be added back).

Workbook Activity 6

Georgina

Georgina runs a business which she started on 1 September 2014 and prepares her first set of accounts to 31 May 2015.

On 1 October 2014, she purchased a car with carbon dioxide emissions of 127 g/km for £10,500 which she uses 30% for business purposes.

What are the capital allowances available to her for the period ended 31 May 2015?

A   £567

B   £1,418

C   £1,890

D   £425

 Workbook Activity 7

Adam

Adam's business accounts for the year to 31 March 2015 include the following items.

For each item state what adjustments, if any, are required?

1   Motor expenses for a car used by an employee, private use estimated at 30%.

2   Motor expenses for a car used by Adam, private use estimated at 30%.

3   Overdraft interest on the business bank account.

4   Bank interest received on the business deposit account.

5   Goods taken by Adam which he paid for at cost.

The choices available are:

A   None

B   Add back full amount

C   Deduct full amount

D   Add back 30%

E   Add back selling price

F   Add back profit

Workbook Activity 8

Manuel Costa (1)

Manuel Costa is a self employed wholesale clothing distributor. His summarised accounts for the year ended 30 June 2014 are as follows:

	£	£
Sales		400,000
Opening inventory	40,000	
Purchases	224,000	
	———	
	264,000	
Closing inventory	(32,000)	
	———	
Cost of sales		(232,000)
		———
Gross profit		168,000
Wages and National Insurance (Note 1)	84,655	
Motor car running expenses		
(Manuel's car) (Note 2)	2,000	
Lighting and heating	4,250	
Rent and business rates	31,060	
Repairs and renewals (all allowable)	3,490	
Legal expenses (Note 3)	1,060	
Depreciation	3,510	
Sundry expenses (all allowable)	5,770	
	———	(135,795)
		———
Net profit		32,205
		———

Notes to the accounts

(1) Wages

Included in wages are Manuel's drawings of £300 per week, his National Insurance contributions of £116 for the year and wages and National Insurance contributions in respect of his wife totalling £11,750. His wife worked full-time in the business as a secretary.

(2) Motor car running expenses

Manuel estimates that one-third of his mileage is private. Included in the charge is £65 for a speeding fine incurred by Manuel whilst delivering goods to a customer.

(3)   Legal expenses

	£
Defending action in respect of alleged faulty goods	330
Defending Manuel in connection with speeding offence	640
Debt collection	90
	1,060

(4)   Capital allowances on plant and machinery for the year to 30 June 2014 are £2,480.

Required:

Calculate the taxable trade profits for the accounting period to 30 June 2014.

Workbook Activity 9

Manuel Costa (2)

Following on from Activity 8, you are required to complete page SEF 2 (disallowable expenses) for Manuel Costa's tax return for 2014/15.

Business expenses

Please read the *Self-employment (full) notes* before filling in this section.

Total expenses	Disallowable expenses
If your annual turnover was below £79,000 you may just put your total expenses in box 31	Use this column if the figures in boxes 17 to 30 include disallowable amounts
17 Cost of goods bought for resale or goods used £ · 0 0	**32** £ · 0 0
18 Construction industry – *payments to subcontractors* £ · 0 0	**33** £ · 0 0
19 Wages, salaries and other staff costs £ · 0 0	**34** £ · 0 0
20 Car, van and travel expenses £ · 0 0	**35** £ · 0 0
21 Rent, rates, power and insurance costs £ · 0 0	**36** £ · 0 0
22 Repairs and renewals of property and equipment £ · 0 0	**37** £ · 0 0
23 Phone, fax, stationery and other office costs £ · 0 0	**38** £ · 0 0
24 Advertising and business entertainment costs £ · 0 0	**39** £ · 0 0
25 Interest on bank and other loans £ · 0 0	**40** £ · 0 0
26 Bank, credit card and other financial charges £ · 0 0	**41** £ · 0 0
27 Irrecoverable debts written off £ · 0 0	**42** £ · 0 0
28 Accountancy, legal and other professional fees £ · 0 0	**43** £ · 0 0
29 Depreciation and loss/profit on sale of assets £ · 0 0	**44** £ · 0 0
30 Other business expenses £ · 0 0	**45** £ · 0 0
31 Total expenses (total of boxes 17 to 30) £ · 0 0	**46** Total disallowable expenses (total of boxes 32 to 45) £ · 0 0

SA103F 2014   Page SEF 2

Workbook Activity 10

Freda Jones

Freda Jones supplies furniture and furnishings. Her summarised accounts for the year ended 31 December 2014 are as follows:

	£	£
Sales of furniture and furnishings (Note 1)		300,000
Cost of sales		(200,000)
		100,000
Design fees		85,000
Gross profit		185,000
Wages and National Insurance (Note 2)	75,000	
Rent and business rates	18,250	
Miscellaneous expenses (all allowable)	12,710	
Taxation (Freda's income tax)	15,590	
Depreciation	2,540	
Lease rental on car (Freda's car) (Note 3)	8,400	
Motor car running expenses (Freda's car) (Note 4)	2,500	
Lighting and heating	1,750	
		(136,740)
Net profit		48,260

Notes to the accounts

(1) Cost of sales has been reduced by £1,000 reimbursed by Freda for furnishings taken from inventory. This reimbursement represented cost price.

(2) Wages include Freda's drawings of £1,000 per month and her National Insurance contributions of £125 for the year.

(3) Lease rental on car. Freda's car was a BMW costing £50,000 with CO_2 emissions of 150 g/km. The lease was entered into on 1 July 2014.

(4) Motor car running expenses. Freda estimates that one-half of her mileage is private.

(5) Capital allowances for the year to 31 December 2014 are £1,200.

Required:

Calculate the taxable trade profits for the accounting period to 31 December 2014.

Workbook Activity 11

Hudson

Hudson has been carrying on a manufacturing business in a South London suburb since 1 April 2010 preparing accounts to 31 March each year.

He decided to retire on 31 October 2015, and drew up his final set of accounts for the 7 month period to 31 October 2015.

The balance on the general capital allowances pool as at 1 April 2014 was £6,500.

The following plant was acquired for cash on the dates shown:

| 1 May 2014 | New plant costing | £10,858 |
| 1 June 2014 | Second-hand plant costing | £1,000 |

On 10 July 2014, Hudson bought a car costing £16,000 through his business. Three-quarters of his usage of the car was for business purposes and one-quarter for private purposes. The car has CO_2 emissions of 125 g/km.

No sale of plant took place during these periods, but at 31 October 2015, when the business closed down, all the plant was sold for £2,450 (no one item realising more than its original cost), and the motor car was disposed of to a dealer, who gave Hudson £14,000 for it.

Required:

Calculate the capital allowances for Hudson for the final two accounting periods to 31 October 2015.

Assume the rates of allowances for the tax year 2014/15 continue into the future.

Workbook Activity 12

Ethan

Ethan prepares accounts to 31 March annually. In the year to 31 March 2015, he bought three cars for use in his business as follows:

11 May 2014	Purchased car for £17,000 (wholly business usage)
21 June 2014	Purchased car for £8,800 (wholly business usage)
16 September 2014	Purchased car for £11,600 (30% private usage by Ethan)

All the cars have CO_2 emissions between 96 and 130 g/km.

He had never previously acquired any plant and machinery for his business.

In the following year to 31 March 2016, Ethan sold for £9,700 the car originally purchased on 16 September 2014. The car originally purchased on 11 May 2014 was sold for £10,000 on 12 June 2015. There were no other transactions.

Required:

Compute the capital allowances and balancing adjustments for the years ended 31 March 2015 and 31 March 2016.

Assume the rates of allowances for the tax year 2014/15 continue into the future.

Workbook Activity 13

Raj

On 1 May 2014, Raj began a small manufacturing business in a rented factory.

He subsequently purchased the following machinery:

		£
2 November 2014	Machinery	20,000
1 February 2015	Car (20% private use with CO_2 emissions 180 g/km)	16,000
1 February 2015	New tool grinder	6,000
2 October 2015	Car for salesman (with CO_2 emissions 120 g/km)	11,600

Accounts are prepared to 31 March in each year.

Required:

Compute the capital allowances for each accounting period up to 31 March 2016.

Assume the rates of allowances for the tax year 2014/15 continue into the future.

Partnership profit allocation

Introduction

Some of the tasks in the assessment will relate to either a sole trader or a partnership (i.e. an unincorporated business).

Both are given the same tax treatment with one extra step for partnerships, which is covered in this chapter.

KNOWLEDGE

Identify relevant tax authority legislation and guidance. (3.1 K)

Explain the basic allocation of trading profits between partners (4.5 K)

SKILLS

Divide profits and losses of partnerships amongst partners. (1.6 S)

Prepare computations to show the changes in partnership structure for new partners and departing partners. (1.7 S)

Complete the self-employed or partnership supplementary pages of the tax return for individuals, and submit them within statutory time limits. (1.10 S)

CONTENTS

1   Allocation of profits
2   Change in profit sharing arrangements
3   Partnership changes
4   Partnership interest income
5   Partnership tax return

1 Allocation of profits

1.1 Computation of taxable trade profits

There is no difference between a sole trader and a partnership when applying the rules for computing the adjustment of the profits of a partnership.

A partnership is merely treated for tax purposes as a collection of sole traders.

Each partner is assessed on his share of partnership profits as if he were a sole trader earning those profits.

1.2 Division of profits between partners

Profits are allocated according to the profit sharing arrangements during the *accounting period* in which profits are earned.

 Example

Andrew and Bernard have been in business for many years, drawing up their accounts to 31 December each year, and sharing profits in the ratio of 2:1.

The partnership's taxable trade profits for the year ended 31 December 2014 were £37,500.

Show how these profits are allocated to partners.

Solution

Year ended 31 December 2014	Total	Andrew	Bernard
Profits split (2:1)	£37,500	£25,000	£12,500

Activity 1

John and Kyle

John and Kyle began in partnership on 6 April 2014 and have taxable trading profits for the year to 5 April 2015 of £24,047.

They have agreed to share profits and losses in the ratio of 3:2.

Calculate each partner's share of the taxable profits for the year ended 5 April 2015.

 ## Example

Vivienne, Caroline and Marie started business on 1 January 2014. They shared profits as follows:

Interest on fixed capital	10%

Salaries	
Vivienne	£3,000 per annum
Caroline	£4,000 per annum
Marie	£3,000 per annum

Share of balance	
Vivienne	60%
Caroline	20%
Marie	20%

Capital account balances were as follows:

Vivienne	£10,000
Caroline	£5,000
Marie	£5,000

The taxable trade profits of the partnership for the year ended 31 December 2014 were £80,000.

Show how these profits are allocated to the partners.

Solution

Profits are allocated as follows:

	Total £	Vivienne £	Caroline £	Marie £
Interest on capital (10% × capital)	2,000	1,000	500	500
Salaries	10,000	3,000	4,000	3,000
Balance (60:20:20)	68,000	40,800	13,600	13,600
Total adjusted trading profits	80,000	44,800	18,100	17,100

It is important to realise that the whole profit of £80,000 is classed as taxable trade profits.

Even though there is reference to salaries and interest, this is merely a means of allocation. For example, Vivienne is now treated as having taxable trade profits of £44,800; she is not regarded as having received interest income or employment income.

2 Change in profit sharing arrangements

2.1 Principle of allocating profits

Where there is a change in the profit sharing arrangements during the accounting period, the period must be split into two or more parts (depending on the number of changes), with a separate division among the partners for each part.

Example

Rosie, Fran and Gilly have been in business for many years.

During the year ended 31 December 2014, their taxable trade profits were £94,000. Profits were shared as follows:

	Rosie £	Fran £	Gilly £
To 30 June 2014			
Salary (per annum)	10,000	6,100	–
Balance	1	1	1
To 31 December 2014			
Salary (per annum)	Nil	Nil	Nil
Balance	2	1	1

Show how the profits would be allocated between the partners.

Solution

Beware, the salaries are quoted per annum; if a change occurs during an accounting period the salary must be pro rated.

Year ended 31 December 2014

	Total £	Rosie £	Fran £	Gilly £
Period 1 January 2014 – 30 June 2014 ($^6/_{12}$)				
Salary	8,050	5,000	3,050	
Balance (1:1:1)	38,950	12,983	12,983	12,984
	————			
(£94,000 × $^6/_{12}$)	47,000			
Period 1 July 2014 – 31 December 2014 ($^6/_{12}$)				
Balance (2:1:1)	47,000	23,500	11,750	11,750
	————	————	————	————
Total	94,000	41,483	27,783	24,734
	————	————	————	————

The profits are deemed to accrue evenly over time.

Each partner now has their own taxable trade profits for the accounting period.

 Activity 2

Read the following statements and state whether they are true or false.

1   A partnership pays tax on the partnership profits.

2   Brian and Mary trade in partnership sharing profits equally and preparing accounts to 31 December. If they want to change their profit shares to 1/3:2/3 on 1 July 2014 they need to prepare accounts to 30 June 2014.

3   Partners' salaries and interest on capital are deductible in computing adjusted trading profit.

3 Partnership changes

3.1 Principle of allocating profits

Where there is a change in the partnership during the accounting period, the period must be split into two or more parts (depending on the number of changes), exactly as for a change in the profit share arrangement.

A change in the partnership may occur when a new partner is admitted.

 Example

Charles and David began to trade in partnership with effect from 1 July 2011, preparing accounts to 30 June each year and sharing profits equally.

On 1 January 2013, Edward joined the partnership. Profits were then split in the ratio 2:2:1.

The tax adjusted trading profits of the partnership were as follows:

	£
Year ended 30 June 2012	70,000
Year ended 30 June 2013	73,200
Year ended 30 June 2014	74,000

Show the profit allocation for each partner for each accounting period.

Solution

Allocate accounting period profits to partners according to profit share, splitting the accounting period where appropriate.

	Total £	C £	D £	E £
Year ended 30 June 2012 (1:1)	70,000	35,000	35,000	–
Year ended 30 June 2013				
1 July 2012 – 31 Dec 2012 (1:1) $^6/_{12}$	36,600	18,300	18,300	–
1 Jan 2013 – 30 June 2013 (2:2:1) $^6/_{12}$	36,600	14,640	14,640	7,320
	73,200	32,940	32,940	7,320
Year ended 30 June 2014 (2:2:1)	74,000	29,600	29,600	14,800

A change in the partnership may also occur when a partner leaves the partnership or dies.

 Example

Fred, George and Harry began to trade in partnership with effect from 1 July 2011, preparing accounts to 30 June each year and sharing profits equally.

On 31 October 2014 George died. Profits and losses were then split in the ratio 3:2.

The tax adjusted trading profits of the partnership were as follows:

	£
Year ended 30 June 2012	60,000
Year ended 30 June 2013	85,200
Year ended 30 June 2014	75,000
Year ended 30 June 2015	75,600

Show the profit allocation for each partner for each accounting period.

Solution

Allocate accounting period profits to partners according to profit share, splitting the accounting period where appropriate.

	Total £	F £	G £	H £
Year ended 30 June 2012 (1:1:1)	60,000	20,000	20,000	20,000
Year ended 30 June 2013 (1:1:1)	85,200	28,400	28,400	28,400
Year ended 30 June 2014 (1:1:1)	75,000	25,000	25,000	25,000
Year ended 30 June 2015				
1 July 2014 – 31 Oct 2014 (1:1:1) $\frac{4}{12}$	25,200	8,400	8,400	8,400
1 Nov 2014 – 30 June 2015 (3:2) $\frac{8}{12}$	50,400	30,240	–	20,160
	75,600	38,640	8,400	28,560

The examiner has confirmed that in the assessment there will be a maximum of three partners in any one scenario.

However, changes to partnerships in terms of changes to the partnership agreement or changes to the actual partners themselves will be assessed.

Activity 3

Michael, Nick and Liz (1)

Michael Peters and Nick Wyatt commenced business as printers on 1 October 2011, preparing accounts to 30 September each year and sharing profits equally.

On 1 January 2013, Liz Stretton was admitted to the partnership and profits continued to be shared equally.

On 30 June 2014, Nick retired. Profits continued to be shared equally.

On 31 December 2015 the partnership was dissolved.

The adjusted profits of the partnership, after deducting capital allowances, were as follows:

	£
Year ended 30 September 2012	30,000
Year ended 30 September 2013	36,000
Year ended 30 September 2014	42,500
Year ended 30 September 2015	40,000
Three months to 31 December 2015	17,500

Required:

Show the allocation of profits to each partner for all accounting periods.

4 Partnership interest income

4.1 Allocation of partnership interest income

Interest received by a partnership must be deducted in the partnership adjustment of profits computation as it is not trading income.

The income must however be assessed on the partners.

The gross interest is therefore apportioned between the partners according to the profit sharing ratio applicable to the balance of trading income, on the date the interest is received.

Each partner then includes his share of the interest in his personal income tax return.

5 Partnership tax return

5.1 Partnership tax return

Although the partnership does not pay its own tax liability, there is still a requirement to file a tax return for the partnership. One partner will be nominated by the other members of the partnership to complete and submit the return.

The return covers details of the partnership income and related information. It also includes a partnership statement, which shows each partner's share of profits, losses and income. Each individual partner will then enter this information on their own personal tax return.

The partnership return consists of 8 pages, broken down as follows:

- Page 1 – There is no information to complete on the first page, which simply sets out the partners' responsibilities.

- The long form return (4 pages) – Pages 2 to 5

- The short form return (2 pages) – Pages 6 and 7

- Page 8 – Other information relevant to the partnership.

In an assessment you will only be required to complete the short form return.

5.2 Partnership tax return: Page 6

This page is the first page of the 'partnership statement (short)', which will be used by the individual partners to make entries on their personal tax returns.

Information is transferred from the remainder of the return and then allocated between the partners.

The tax adjusted trading profit of the partnership is put in Box 11, or the trading loss is inserted in Box 12.

It is possible that the partnership will also have received interest income. If so, the gross amount needs to be entered in Box 22.

The short statement caters for up to 3 partners when page 7 is used but in the assessment you will only have to complete one partner's information on page 6.

You should complete Boxes 6 – 10 for with the information provided in the assessment, if applicable, regarding the name, address, unique taxpayer reference, NI number and date appointed or ceased as a partner.

The trading profit or loss should then be apportioned between the partners according to the profit sharing agreement, and entered in Boxes 11 or 12 on each partner's statement.

The partnership may have received payments under the Construction Industry Scheme (CIS). Any tax deducted from such payments should be entered in Box 24 for the partnership with the appropriate amounts entered in Box 24 for each of the individual partners.

You do not need to give any further information if the split is a simple profit sharing ratio, but if any partner is entitled to a salary or interest on capital, this should be explained in Box 3.116 – 'additional information' on page 5 of the long form return. This explanation on the long form return will not be required in the assessment.

Any gross interest received by the partnership will be apportioned between the partners according to the profit sharing ratio on the date of receipt of the interest, and entered in Box 22 on each partner's statement.

You should ignore the text which says 'Copy this figure to box …' as this is only relevant when completing the partner's individual income tax returns.

5.3   Completing the tax return

The following is important in connection with the completion of forms in the exam.

*   When completing the form in the exam, figures must be entered in the correct boxes.

*   Commas need not be entered for numbers of four digits or more.

*   You do not need to fill in every box, only relevant ones.

Page 6 is shown overleaf.

PARTNERSHIP STATEMENT (SHORT) *for the year ended 5 April 2015*

Please read these instructions before completing the Statement

Use these pages to allocate partnership income if the only income for the relevant return period was trading and professional income or taxed interest and alternative finance receipts from banks and building societies. Otherwise you must download or ask the SA Orderline for the *Partnership Statement (Full)* pages to record details of the allocation of all the partnership income. Go to **hmrc.gov.uk/selfassessmentforms**

Step 1 Fill in boxes 1 to 29 and boxes A and B as appropriate. Get the figures you need from the relevant boxes in the Partnership Tax Return. Complete a separate Statement for each accounting period covered by this Partnership Tax Return and for each trade or profession carried on by the partnership.

Step 2 Then allocate the amounts in boxes 11 to 29 attributable to each partner using the allocation columns on this page and page 7, read the Partnership Tax Return Guide, go to **hmrc.gov.uk/selfassessmentforms** If the partnership has more than three partners, please photocopy page 7.

Step 3 Each partner will need a copy of their allocation of income to fill in their personal tax return.

PARTNERSHIP INFORMATION
If the partnership business includes a trade or profession, enter here the accounting period for which appropriate items in this statement are returned.

Start **1** / /

End **2** / /

Nature of trade **3**

MIXED PARTNERSHIPS

Tick here if this Statement is drawn up using Corporation Tax rules **4**

Tick here if this Statement is drawn up using tax rules for non-residents **5**

Individual partner details

6 Name of partner

Address

Postcode

Date appointed as a partner (if during 2013–14 or 2014–15)
7 / /

Partner's Unique Taxpayer Reference (UTR)
8

Date ceased to be a partner (if during 2013–14 or 2014–15)
9 / /

Partner's National Insurance number
10

Partnership's profits, losses, income, tax credits, etc.

Partner's share of profits, losses, income, tax credits, etc.

*Copy figures in boxes 11 to 29 to boxes in the individual's **Partnership** (short) pages as shown below*

Tick this box if the items entered in the box had foreign tax taken off

● **for an accounting period ended in 2014–15** ▼

		Partnership	Partner's share	
from box 3.83 Profit from a trade or profession **A**	**11** £	Profit **11** £		Copy this figure to box 8
from box 3.82 Adjustment on change of basis	**11A** £	**11A** £		Copy this figure to box 10
from box 3.84 Loss from a trade or profession **B**	**12** £	Loss **12** £		Copy this figure to box 8
from box 10.4 Business Premises Renovation Allowance	**12A** £	**12A** £		Copy this figure to box 15

● **for the period 6 April 2014 to 5 April 2015***

from box 7.9A UK taxed interest and taxed alternative finance receipts	**22** £	**22** £		Copy this figure to box 28
from box 3.97 CIS deductions made by contractors on account of tax	**24** £	**24** £		Copy this figure to box 30
from box 3.98 Other tax taken off trading income	**24A** £	**24A** £		Copy this figure to box 31
from box 7.8A Income Tax taken off	**25** £	**25** £		Copy this figure to box 29
from box 3.117 Partnership charges	**29** £	**29** £		Copy this figure to box 4, 'Other tax reliefs' section on page Ai 2 in your personal tax return

* if you are a 'CT Partnership' see the Partnership Tax Return Guide

Activity 4

Michael, Nick and Liz (2)

Following on from Activity 3, complete page 6 of the partnership return in respect of the year ended 30 September 2014 for Michael.

PARTNERSHIP STATEMENT (SHORT) *for the year ended 5 April 2015*

Please read these instructions before completing the Statement

Use these pages to allocate partnership income if the only income for the relevant return period was trading and professional income or taxed interest and alternative finance receipts from banks and building societies. Otherwise you must download or ask the SA Orderline for the *Partnership Statement (Full)* pages to record details of the allocation of all the partnership income. Go to **hmrc.gov.uk/selfassessmentforms**

Step 1   Fill in boxes 1 to 29 and boxes A and B as appropriate. Get the figures you need from the relevant boxes in the Partnership Tax Return. Complete a separate Statement for each accounting period covered by this Partnership Tax Return and for each trade or profession carried on by the partnership.

Step 2   Then allocate the amounts in boxes 11 to 29 attributable to each partner using the allocation columns on this page and page 7, read the Partnership Tax Return Guide, go to **hmrc.gov.uk/selfassessmentforms** If the partnership has more than three partners, please photocopy page 7.

Step 3   Each partner will need a copy of their allocation of income to fill in their personal tax return.

PARTNERSHIP INFORMATION

If the partnership business includes a trade or profession, enter here the accounting period for which appropriate items in this statement are returned.

Start **1** / /

End **2** / /

Nature of trade **3**

MIXED PARTNERSHIPS

Tick here if this Statement is drawn up using Corporation Tax rules **4**

Tick here if this Statement is drawn up using tax rules for non-residents **5**

Individual partner details

6 Name of partner

Address

Postcode

Date appointed as a partner (if during 2013–14 or 2014–15) **7** / /

Date ceased to be a partner (if during 2013–14 or 2014–15) **9** / /

Partner's Unique Taxpayer Reference (UTR) **8**

Partner's National Insurance number **10**

Partnership's profits, losses, income, tax credits, etc.

Tick this box if the items entered in the box had foreign tax taken off

Partner's share of profits, losses, income, tax credits, etc.

*Copy figures in boxes 11 to 29 to boxes in the individual's **Partnership** (short) pages as shown below*

● **for an accounting period ended in 2014–15** ▼

from box 3.83 Profit from a trade or profession	**A**	**11** £	Profit **11** £	Copy this figure to box 8
from box 3.82 Adjustment on change of basis		**11A** £	**11A** £	Copy this figure to box 10
from box 3.84 Loss from a trade or profession	**B**	**12** £	Loss **12** £	Copy this figure to box 8
from box 10.4 Business Premises Renovation Allowance		**12A** £	**12A** £	Copy this figure to box 15

● **for the period 6 April 2014 to 5 April 2015***

from box 7.9A UK taxed interest and taxed alternative finance receipts	**22** £	**22** £	Copy this figure to box 28
from box 3.97 CIS deductions made by contractors on account of tax	**24** £	**24** £	Copy this figure to box 30
from box 3.98 Other tax taken off trading income	**24A** £	**24A** £	Copy this figure to box 31
from box 7.8A Income Tax taken off	**25** £	**25** £	Copy this figure to box 29
from box 3.117 Partnership charges	**29** £	**29** £	Copy this figure to box 4, 'Other tax reliefs' section on page Ai 2 in your personal tax return

* if you are a 'CT Partnership' see the Partnership Tax Return Guide

SA800 2014   PARTNERSHIP TAX RETURN: PAGE 6

6 Summary

The taxable trade profits of a partnership are apportioned amongst the partners in accordance with the profit sharing arrangements during the accounting period.

Where there are salaries and interest on capital these should be dealt with first, and then any balance shared out using the profit sharing ratio.

Interest income is apportioned according to the profit sharing ratio on the date the interest is received.

7 Test your knowledge

 Workbook Activity 5

Lindsay, Tricia and Kate (1)

Lindsay and Tricia have been in partnership for many years, running a dry cleaning business. They prepare their accounts to 31 March each year. Their profit sharing ratio has always been 3:2.

On 1 August 2014, Kate joined the partnership and the profit sharing ratio was changed to 4:3:2 for Lindsay, Tricia and Kate.

For the year ended 31 March 2015, the trading profit was £150,000.

The division of profit would be calculated as:

	Total	Lindsay	Tricia	Kate
	£	£	£	£
Period to	1	2	3	
Period to	4	5	6	7

Options

1	A	£150,000
	B	£75,000
	C	£50,000
	D	£100,000
2	A	£30,000
	B	£20,000
	C	£45,000
	D	£90,000
3	A	£30,000
	B	£20,000
	C	£60,000
	D	£40,000

4	A	£150,000
	B	£75,000
	C	£50,000
	D	£100,000
5	A	£33,333
	B	£22,222
	C	£66,667
	D	£44,445
6	A	£22,222
	B	£25,000
	C	£33,333
	D	£44,445
7	A	£16,667
	B	£22,222
	C	£33,333
	D	£44,445

 Workbook Activity 6

Anne, Betty, Chloe and Diana

Anne and Betty have been in partnership since 1 January 2002 sharing profits equally.

On 30 June 2013, Betty resigned as a partner and was replaced on 1 July 2013 by Chloe. Diana was admitted as a partner on 1 April 2014. Profits were shared equally throughout.

The partnership's taxable trade profits are as follows:

		£
Year ended	31 December 2013	60,000
Year ended	31 December 2014	72,000

Required:

Show the allocation of the taxable trade profits between the partners for each of the years to 31 December 2013 and 2014.

Workbook Activity 7

Bert and Harold

Bert and Harold have traded in partnership for several years. Their accounts for the year ended 30 September 2014 show taxable trade profits of £16,500.

Bert and Harold changed their profit-sharing ratio on 1 July 2014. The old profit-sharing ratio applies until 30 June 2014, and the new ratio applies from 1 July 2014.

	Bert	*Harold*
Old ratio:		
Salaries p.a.	£3,000	£2,000
Share of balance	3/5	2/5
New ratio:		
Salaries p.a.	£6,000	£4,000
Share of balance	2/3	1/3

Required:

Show the allocation of the taxable trade profits between the partners for the year to 30 September 2014.

 Workbook Activity 8

Peter and Nathan Flannery

Brothers Peter and Nathan Flannery have traded in partnership as Superhero Supplies for many years, trading in books and comics.

Their tax adjusted trading profits for the year ended 31 March 2015 are £130,400, and the partnership received gross interest of £16,210.

Peter and Nathan have always shared the profits of their business in the ratio 4:3.

Required:

Complete page 6 of the partnership tax return in respect of the year ended 31 March 2015 for the partnership as a whole and for Peter.

PARTNERSHIP STATEMENT (SHORT) *for the year ended 5 April 2015*

Please read these instructions before completing the Statement

Use these pages to allocate partnership income if the only income for the relevant return period was trading and professional income or taxed interest and alternative finance receipts from banks and building societies. Otherwise you must download or ask the SA Orderline for the *Partnership Statement (Full)* pages to record details of the allocation of all the partnership income. Go to **hmrc.gov.uk/selfassessmentforms**

Step 1 Fill in boxes 1 to 29 and boxes A and B as appropriate. Get the figures you need from the relevant boxes in the Partnership Tax Return. Complete a separate Statement for each accounting period covered by this Partnership Tax Return and for each trade or profession carried on by the partnership.

Step 2 Then allocate the amounts in boxes 11 to 29 attributable to each partner using the allocation columns on this page and page 7, read the Partnership Tax Return Guide, go to **hmrc.gov.uk/selfassessmentforms** If the partnership has more than three partners, please photocopy page 7.

Step 3 Each partner will need a copy of their allocation of income to fill in their personal tax return.

PARTNERSHIP INFORMATION
If the partnership business includes a trade or profession, enter here the accounting period for which appropriate items in this statement are returned.

Start **1** / /

End **2** / /

Nature of trade **3**

MIXED PARTNERSHIPS

Tick here if this Statement is drawn up using Corporation Tax rules **4**

Tick here if this Statement is drawn up using tax rules for non-residents **5**

Individual partner details

6 Name of partner

Address

Postcode

Date appointed as a partner (if during 2013–14 or 2014–15) **7** / /

Partner's Unique Taxpayer Reference (UTR) **8**

Date ceased to be a partner (if during 2013–14 or 2014–15) **9** / /

Partner's National Insurance number **10**

Partnership's profits, losses, income, tax credits, etc.

Tick this box if the items entered in the box had foreign tax taken off

Partner's share of profits, losses, income, tax credits, etc.

Copy figures in boxes 11 to 29 to boxes in the individual's Partnership (short) pages as shown below

● **for an accounting period ended in 2014-15** ▼

from box 3.83 Profit from a trade or profession **A**	**11** £	Profit **11** £	*Copy this figure to box 8*
from box 3.82 Adjustment on change of basis	**11A** £	**11A** £	*Copy this figure to box 10*
from box 3.84 Loss from a trade or profession **B**	**12** £	Loss **12** £	*Copy this figure to box 8*
from box 10.4 Business Premises Renovation Allowance	**12A** £	**12A** £	*Copy this figure to box 15*

● **for the period 6 April 2014 to 5 April 2015***

from box 7.9A UK taxed interest and taxed alternative finance receipts	**22** £	**22** £	*Copy this figure to box 28*
from box 3.97 CIS deductions made by contractors on account of tax	**24** £	**24** £	*Copy this figure to box 30*
from box 3.98 Other tax taken off trading income	**24A** £	**24A** £	*Copy this figure to box 31*
from box 7.8A Income Tax taken off	**25** £	**25** £	*Copy this figure to box 29*
from box 3.117 Partnership charges	**29** £	**29** £	*Copy this figure to box 4, 'Other tax reliefs' section on page Ai 2 in your personal tax return*

* if you are a 'CT Partnership' see the Partnership Tax Return Guide

SA800 2014 PARTNERSHIP TAX RETURN: PAGE 6

Workbook Activity 9

Lindsay, Tricia and Kate (2)

For Lindsay in Workbook Activity 5, complete page 6 in the partnership return in respect of the year ended 31 March 2015.

PARTNERSHIP STATEMENT (SHORT) *for the year ended 5 April 2015*

Please read these instructions before completing the Statement

Use these pages to allocate partnership income if the only income for the relevant return period was trading and professional income or taxed interest and alternative finance receipts from banks and building societies. Otherwise you must download or ask the SA Orderline for the *Partnership Statement (Full)* pages to record details of the allocation of all the partnership income. Go to **hmrc.gov.uk/selfassessmentforms**

Step 1 Fill in boxes 1 to 29 and boxes A and B as appropriate. Get the figures you need from the relevant boxes in the Partnership Tax Return. Complete a separate Statement for each accounting period covered by this Partnership Tax Return and for each trade or profession carried on by the partnership.

Step 2 Then allocate the amounts in boxes 11 to 29 attributable to each partner using the allocation columns on this page and page 7, read the Partnership Tax Return Guide, go to **hmrc.gov.uk/selfassessmentforms** If the partnership has more than three partners, please photocopy page 7.

Step 3 Each partner will need a copy of their allocation of income to fill in their personal tax return.

PARTNERSHIP INFORMATION
If the partnership business includes a trade or profession, enter here the accounting period for which appropriate items in this statement are returned.

Start **1** / /

End **2** / /

Nature of trade **3**

MIXED PARTNERSHIPS

Tick here if this Statement is drawn up using Corporation Tax rules **4**

Tick here if this Statement is drawn up using tax rules for non-residents **5**

Individual partner details

6 Name of partner

Address

Postcode

Date appointed as a partner (if during 2013–14 or 2014–15)

7 / /

Partner's Unique Taxpayer Reference (UTR)

8

Date ceased to be a partner (if during 2013–14 or 2014–15)

9 / /

Partner's National Insurance number

10

Partnership's profits, losses, income, tax credits, etc.

Partner's share of profits, losses, income, tax credits, etc.

Tick this box if the items entered in the box had foreign tax taken off ▼

Copy figures in boxes 11 to 29 to boxes in the individual's Partnership (short) pages as shown below

• **for an accounting period ended in 2014–15**

from box 3.83 Profit from a trade or profession **A**	**11** £	Profit **11** £	Copy this figure to box 8
from box 3.82 Adjustment on change of basis	**11A** £	**11A** £	Copy this figure to box 10
from box 3.84 Loss from a trade or profession **B**	**12** £	Loss **12** £	Copy this figure to box 8
from box 10.4 Business Premises Renovation Allowance	**12A** £	**12A** £	Copy this figure to box 15

• **for the period 6 April 2014 to 5 April 2015***

from box 7.9A UK taxed interest and taxed alternative finance receipts	**22** £	**22** £	Copy this figure to box 28
from box 3.97 CIS deductions made by contractors on account of tax	**24** £	**24** £	Copy this figure to box 30
from box 3.98 Other tax taken off trading income	**24A** £	**24A** £	Copy this figure to box 31
from box 7.8A Income Tax taken off	**25** £	**25** £	Copy this figure to box 29
from box 3.117 Partnership charges	**29** £	**29** £	Copy this figure to box 4, 'Other tax reliefs' section on page Ai 2 in your personal tax return

* if you are a 'CT Partnership' see the Partnership Tax Return Guide

SA800 2014   PARTNERSHIP TAX RETURN: PAGE 6

Basis periods

13

Introduction

Sole traders and partners must complete a tax return each year.

There are rules to determine which profits go into each tax return, with special rules for the opening and closing years of a business.

KNOWLEDGE
Identify relevant tax authority legislation and guidance. (3.1 K)
Explain the basis of assessment for unincorporated businesses. (4.2 K)

SKILLS
Apply the basis of assessment for unincorporated businesses, including opening and closing years and overlap profits. (1.2 S)

CONTENTS

1   Tax years
2   Current year basis
3   Opening year rules
4   Closing year rules
5   Partnerships

1 Tax years

1.1 Tax year

An individual in business will need to complete a tax return for a tax year. A tax year runs from 6 April to the following 5 April.

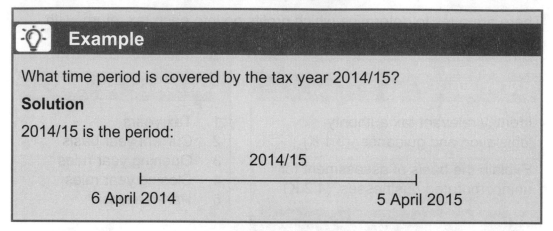

> ### Example
>
> What time period is covered by the tax year 2014/15?
>
> **Solution**
>
> 2014/15 is the period:
>
> 2014/15
>
> 6 April 2014   5 April 2015

We need to determine which taxable trade profits are to be assessed in each tax year.

2 Current year basis

2.1 Ongoing business

The basic rule is that the taxable trade profits assessed in any tax year will be based on the profit for the 12 month period of account ending in that tax year. This is known as the current year basis.

>
>
> ### Example
>
> Vivienne prepares accounts to 30 April each year.
>
> Her taxable trade profits after making all necessary adjustments, including capital allowances, were as follows:
>
> | | £ |
> | ------------------------ | ------ |
> | Year ended 30 April 2013 | 20,000 |
> | Year ended 30 April 2014 | 25,000 |
>
> State in which tax years these profits will be taxed.

Solution

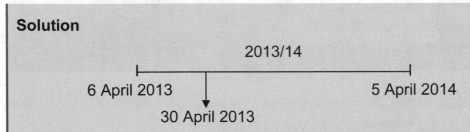

2013/14

6 April 2013   5 April 2014

30 April 2013

The year ended 30 April 2013 ends in 2013/14 and therefore all of the profits of that year will be taxed in the tax year 2013/14.

The year ended 30 April 2014 ends in 2014/15 and therefore all of the profits of that year will be taxed in the tax year 2014/15.

An individual can choose whichever accounting period end date he wants for his business, but care must be taken to tax the profits in the correct tax year.

Example

In which tax years will the following profits be taxed?

Profits for year ending: 30 April 2015
                                    31 March 2015
                                    30 June 2015
                                    31 January 2015
                                    31 December 2014

Solution

Profits for year ending:	Tax year of assessment
30 April 2015	2015/16
31 March 2015	2014/15
30 June 2015	2015/16
31 January 2015	2014/15
31 December 2014	2014/15

It often helps to draw a diagram showing the beginning and end of the tax year and mark on the accounting period end date to ensure you select the correct tax year.

3 Opening year rules

3.1 Special rules

Over the life of a business, it is important that:

• the total taxable trading profits of the business should be taxed, and

• there should be an assessment for each tax year of trading.

Suppose a business starts trading on 1 July 2014 and prepares accounts up to 30 June 2015.

Although the business starts in 2014/15 there is no accounting period ending in 2014/15, so if the normal 'current year basis' is applied, there would be no tax assessment in 2014/15.

To make sure that there is an assessment in every year the business trades, there are special opening year rules.

These are explained below.

(a) **First tax year**

The first tax year is the tax year in which the business started to trade.

The basis of assessment for the first tax year is *always* the period:

– from the date of commencement

– to the following 5 April.

This is known as the *actual basis of assessment*.

(b) **Second tax year**

In the second tax year, you need to ask the question:

Is there a set of accounts that ends in the second tax year?

If no accounts are prepared to a date ending in the second tax year, the basis of assessment is:

• the actual profits of the second tax year (6 April to 5 April).

If accounts are prepared to a date ending in the second tax year, you need to ask another question:

How long are the accounts that end in the second tax year?

If the accounts are:

- 12 months or more after the business started:
  - the basis of assessment is the profits of the 12 months to the end of that period.
- less than 12 months after the business started:
  - the basis of assessment is the profits of the first 12 months trading.

(c) **Third year**

In the third tax year, the basis of assessment is:

- the profits of the 12 months to the accounting date ending in the third year.

This is usually the *current year basis*.

For the purposes of your assessment, any apportionments of profit are made on a monthly basis (not daily).

The following examples will illustrate the three possibilities for the second tax year.

Example

Lara started in business on 1 November 2012, preparing accounts to 31 October each year.

Her adjusted profits were as follows:

	£
Year ended 31 October 2013	18,000
Year ended 31 October 2014	37,500
Year ended 31 October 2015	44,000

State the taxable trade profits for the first four tax years of trading.

Solution

Her taxable trade profits are therefore as follows:

Year of Assessment	Basis period	Assessment £
2012/13	1 November 2012 – 5 April 2013 (£18,000 × $\frac{5}{12}$)	7,500
2013/14	1 November 2012 – 31 October 2013	18,000
2014/15	1 November 2013 – 31 October 2014	37,500
2015/16	1 November 2014 – 31 October 2015	44,000

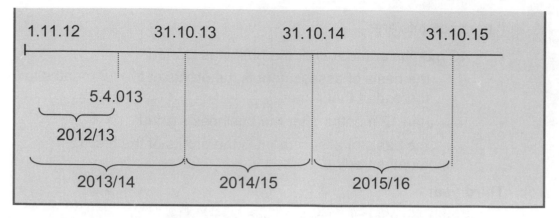

3.2   Overlap profits

When an individual starts to trade, some profits may be taxed twice. Profits assessed in more than one year are called overlap profits.

In the previous example, the following profits are assessed in both 2012/13 and 2013/14:

1 November 2012 to 5 April 2013 = (£18,000 × $^5/_{12}$) = £7,500

However, as stated before, it is very important that over the life of the business, the trader will be taxed on the total taxable profits of the business – and only once.

Therefore, relief for overlap profits is given by deducting them from the final assessment when an individual ceases to trade.

Note that there will be no overlap profits if the trader has a 5 April year end. Since we work to the nearest month for exams, this means that starting business and choosing a 31 March year end will also have no overlap profits.

 Example

Edrich started in business on 1 July 2012. He prepared his first set of accounts for the six months ended 31 December 2012 and then for calendar years thereafter.

His adjusted profits were as follows:

	£
Six months ended 31 December 2012	3,100
Year ended 31 December 2013	7,600
Year ended 31 December 2014	8,200
Year ended 31 December 2015	6,400

Show the taxable trade profits for the tax years 2012/13 to 2015/16 inclusive, and calculate the amount of any overlap profits.

Solution

His taxable trade profits are therefore as follows:

Year of assessment	Basis period	Assessment £
2012/13	1 July 2012 – 5 April 2013	
	£3,100 + (£7,600 × ³⁄₁₂)	5,000
2013/14	1 January 2013 – 31 December 2013	7,600
2014/15	1 January 2014 – 31 December 2014	8,200
2015/16	1 January 2015 – 31 December 2015	6,400

There are overlap profits of £1,900 (£7,600 × ³⁄₁₂) for the period from 1 January 2013 to 5 April 2013.

 Example

Hammond started in business on 1 January 2013. He prepared his first set of accounts for the seven months ended 31 July 2013 and annually to 31 July thereafter.

His adjusted profits were as follows:

	£
Seven months ended 31 July 2013	10,500
Year ended 31 July 2014	33,600
Year ended 31 July 2015	19,800

Show the taxable trade profits for the tax years 2012/13 to 2015/16 inclusive, and calculate the amount of any overlap profits.

Solution

The business commenced on 1 January 2013, which is in 2012/13.

The second tax year is 2013/14 and the accounts ending in that period are those for the seven months to 31 July 2013. This date is less than 12 months after the business started. Therefore the second year assesses the first 12 months trading.

Remember we must tax 12 months of profits in the second year.

Hammond's taxable trade profits are therefore as follows:

Year of Assessment	Basis period	Assessment £
2012/13	1 January 2013 – 5 April 2013 £10,500 × 3/7	4,500
2013/14	1 January 2013 – 31 December 2013 £10,500 + (£33,600 × 5/12)	24,500
2014/15	1 August 2013 – 31 July 2014	33,600
2015/16	1 August 2014 – 31 July 2015	19,800

The overlap profits are:

	£
1 Jan 2013 – 5 April 2013 (£10,500 × 3/7)	4,500
1 Aug 2013 – 31 Dec 2013 (£33,600 × 5/12)	14,000
	18,500

Example

Yallop started in business on 1 February 2013. He prepared his first set of accounts for the 18 months to 31 July 2014 and annually to 31 July thereafter.

His adjusted profits were as follows:

	£
18 months ended 31 July 2014	9,000
Year ended 31 July 2015	2,680

Show the taxable trade profits for the tax years 2012/13 to 2015/16 inclusive, and calculate the amount of any overlap profits.

Solution

The taxable trade profits are as follows:

Year of Assessment	Basis period	Assessment £
2012/13	1 February 2013 – 5 April 2013 £9,000 × $^{2}/_{18}$	1,000
2013/14	6 April 2013 – 5 April 2014 £9,000 × $^{12}/_{18}$	6,000
2014/15	1 August 2013 – 31 July 2014 £9,000 × $^{12}/_{18}$	6,000
2015/16	1 August 2014 – 31 July 2015	2,680

The overlap profits are:

1 Aug 2013 – 5 April 2014 (£9,000 × 8/18)	£4,000

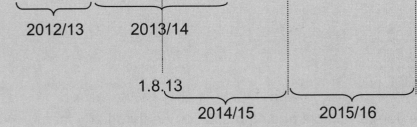

Note: In this example there is an 18 month period of account ending in the third tax year 2014/15.

In the second tax year where there are no accounts ending in that year, the actual profits from 6 April to 5 April are assessed.

In the third tax year, because we must only assess 12 months of profits, we take the last 12 months ending on the accounting date (i.e. 12 m/e 31 July 2014).

Activity 1

Jane

Jane started trading on 1 November 2011. She prepares her accounts to 30 April each year. The adjusted profits were as follows:

	£
Period ended 30 April 2012	12,000
Year ended 30 April 2013	27,000
Year ended 30 April 2014	30,000

1   In which tax year did Jane start trading?

    A   2010/11
    B   2011/12
    C   2012/13
    D   2013/14

2   What are Jane's taxable trading profits for the first tax year of trading?

    A   £25,500
    B   £12,000
    C   £10,000
    D   £9,600

3   What are Jane's taxable trading profits for the second tax year of trading?

    A   £12,000
    B   £25,500
    C   £26,750
    D   £27,000

4   What are Jane's taxable trading profits for the third tax year of trading?

    A   £30,000
    B   £29,750
    C   £27,000
    D   £26,750

5   What are Jane's overlap profits?   £ _____

6   Her overlap profits are relieved as follows:

    A   There is no relief for overlap profits
    B   From the taxable profits of her choice
    C   From her taxable profits in the first year of trade
    D   From her taxable profits in the final year of trade

Activity 2

Robert and Jack

(a)   Robert started in business on 1 May 2012.

His first set of accounts was prepared to 30 September 2012 and he then retained 30 September as his year end.

tax adjusted results in the early years were as follows:

	£
1 May 2012 – 30 September 2012	20,250
Year ended 30 September 2013	29,700
Year ended 30 September 2014	36,450
Year ended 30 September 2015	28,350

(b)   Jack started in business on 1 January 2012 and prepared his first set of accounts to 30 April 2013.

He then continued to prepare his accounts to 30 April and the tax adjusted results in the early years were as follows:

	£
1 January 2012 – 30 April 2013	37,800
Year ended 30 April 2014	26,325
Year ended 30 April 2015	28,350

Required:

Show the amounts assessable for all tax years affected by these results and compute any overlap profits.

4 Closing year rules

4.1   Method of assessment

When an individual trader ceases to trade, any profits not yet assessed will be taxed in the tax year in which trading ceases.

The penultimate year (and the years prior to the penultimate year) is assessed on a current year basis. The final tax year assesses those profits that have not yet been assessed.

Note that this could result in the profits of more than one accounting period being assessed in the final tax year, as shown in the next example.

Example

Hutton has been in business for many years, preparing his accounts to 30 June each year. Owing to ill-health, he stopped trading on 31 January 2015.

His adjusted profits were as follows:

	£
Year ended 30 June 2013	12,000
Year ended 30 June 2014	10,000
Seven months ended 31 January 2015	3,640

Show the taxable trade profits for the last two tax years of assessment.

Solution

Step 1: **Identify in which tax year the last few accounting periods end.**

Accounting period	Ends in
Year ended 30 June 2013	2013/14
Year ended 30 June 2014	2014/15
Seven months ended 31 January 2015	2014/15

Step 2: **Assess the profits in the tax years shown on the right hand side in step 1.**

His taxable trade profits are therefore as follows:

Year of assessment	Basis period	Assessment £
2013/14	1 July 2012 – 30 June 2013	12,000
2014/15	1 July 2013 – 31 January 2015 (£10,000 + £3,640)	13,640

4.2 Overlap profits

As previously stated, over the life of the business, a trader will be taxed on his total taxable profits – and only once.

Therefore relief for overlap profits in the opening years is given by deducting them from the assessment of the final tax year.

Example

Barrington started in business on 1 August 2011, preparing accounts to 31 July each year. He ceased to trade on 31 July 2015, on which date his business was acquired by another firm.

His adjusted profits were as follows:

	£
Year ended 31 July 2012	15,000
Year ended 31 July 2013	23,000
Year ended 31 July 2014	27,000
Year ended 31 July 2015	35,600
Total adjusted profits	100,600

Show the taxable trade profits for the tax years 2011/12 to 2015/16 inclusive and calculate the amount of any overlap profits.

Solution

Step 1: Identify the tax year in which trade commences

In this year profits from the date of commencement to 5 April will be assessed (1 August 2011 is in 2011/12).

Step 2: Deal with the second tax year

The second tax year has a 12 month period ending in it therefore those 12 months profits are assessed.

After this you should be able to identify the amount of the overlap profits.

Step 3: Work out assessments for all years up to year of cessation

All other years will be taxed on the current year basis until the year of cessation.

Step 4: Work out the final year assessment

In the tax year of cessation (2015/16) all profits not yet assessed are taxed.

In this example it is straightforward as all periods are 12 months long.

Step 5: Deduct overlap profits

Finally, deduct from the final assessment the overlap profits.

The taxable trade profits are as follows.

Year of assessment	Basis period	Assessment £
2011/12	1 August 2011 – 5 April 2012	
	£15,000 × $^8/_{12}$	10,000
2012/13	1 August 2011 – 31 July 2012	15,000
2013/14	1 August 2012 – 31 July 2013	23,000
2014/15	1 August 2013 – 31 July 2014	27,000
2015/16	1 August 2014 – 31 July 2015	
	(£35,600 – £10,000)	25,600
Total assessments		100,600

The overlap profits amount to £10,000. This sum is deducted from the assessment for the final tax year (2015/16).

Barrington's aggregate profits over his four years of trading total £100,600 and his aggregate taxable trade profits for the five tax years involved come to exactly the same figure.

5 Partnerships

5.1 Separate traders

A partnership is treated as a collection of individual traders.

Therefore, if some individuals have been trading in partnership for many years, each will be assessed on his own share of the profits on a current year basis.

5.2 Partners joining

Where an individual joins the partnership, he alone will be assessed using the opening year rules on his share of the partnership profits.

The remaining partners will use the current year basis.

5.3 Partners leaving

Where an individual leaves the partnership, he alone will be assessed using the closing year rules on his share of the partnership profits.

The remaining partners will use the current year basis.

5.4 Procedure for partnerships

The correct procedure to follow for partnerships is:

Step 1: Adjust profits of the accounting period (including calculating capital allowances) for the partnership as a whole.

Step 2: Allocate the profits of the accounting period to the partners using the profit share arrangement.

Step 3: Consider each partner in turn, as if they were sole traders, to determine whether to apply current year basis, opening year rules or closing year rules.

 Example

Using the results of the Fred, George and Harry example in Chapter 12 as set out below, calculate the taxable trade profits for each partner for the tax years 2011/12 to 2014/15.

	Total £	F £	G £	H £
Year ended 30 June 2012 (1:1:1)	60,000	20,000	20,000	20,000
Year ended 30 June 2013 (1:1:1)	85,200	28,400	28,400	28,400
Year ended 30 June 2014 (1:1:1)	75,000	25,000	25,000	25,000
Year ended 30 June 2015				
1 July 2014 – 31 Oct 2014 (1:1:1) ($\frac{4}{12}$)	25,200	8,400	8,400	8,400
1 Nov 2014 – 30 June 2015 (3:2) ($\frac{8}{12}$)	50,400	30,240	–	20,160
	75,600	38,640	8,400	28,560

Solution

Steps 1 and 2 of the procedure have already been completed above.

Step 3: Determine the basis of assessment for each partner.

- Fred and Harry both commenced in partnership on 1 July 2011, hence apply the opening year rules. The following figures relate to Fred.

Year of assessment	Basis period	Assessment £
2011/12	1 July 2011 – 5 April 2012 (£20,000 × $^9/_{12}$)	15,000
2012/13	Year ended 30 June 2012	20,000
2013/14	Year ended 30 June 2013	28,400
2014/15	Year ended 30 June 2014	25,000
2015/16	Year ended 30 June 2015	38,640

Overlap profits = £15,000

- Harry would be the same as Fred until 2015/16 when his assessment would be £28,560

- George commenced in partnership on 1 July 2011, and ceased on 31 October 2014, hence apply both opening and closing year rules:

Year of assessment	Basis period	Assessment £
2011/12	1 July 2011 – 5 April 2012 (£20,000 × $^9/_{12}$)	15,000
2012/13	Year ended 30 June 2012	20,000
2013/14	Year ended 30 June 2013	28,400
2014/15	1 July 2013 – 31 October 2014 (£25,000 + £8,400 – £15,000)	18,400

Overlap profits = £15,000

In the assessment you will probably only need to perform Step 3 for one of the partners.

Activity 3

Adam, Ben and Catrina

Adam, Ben and Catrina have been in partnership since 1 April 2009. The partnership prepares accounts to 31 December each year. On 1 November 2014, Adam retired from the partnership and the profit sharing arrangements were changed from that date onwards.

Which one of the following statements is correct?

A   The partnership is deemed to cease on Adam's retirement and the partners will apply the closing year rules to calculate their trading income assessments for the final years.

B   The final year of trading for Adam, Ben and Catrina will be 2014/15.

C   Ben and Catrina will have to apply the opening year rules to calculate their trading income assessments for 2014/15.

D   Adam will apply the closing year rules in order to calculate his trading income assessment for 2014/15.

6 Summary

As the final step in assessing profits of an individual, we must consider whether to apply the:

- current year basis

- opening year rules (and calculate overlap profits)

- closing year rules (and deduct overlap profits).

7 Test your knowledge

 Workbook Activity 4

Xavier

Xavier commenced trading on 1 January 2014 and prepares his first set of accounts to 31 May 2015.

The period of profits which will be taxed in the second tax year is:

A   1 January 2014 to 5 April 2014

B   1 January 2014 to 31 December 2014

C   6 April 2014 to 5 April 2015

D   12 months ended 31 May 2015

 Workbook Activity 5

Mario

Mario commenced trading on 1 February 2014 and intends to prepare his accounts to 31 May each year. His first set of accounts is prepared to 31 May 2015.

For 2014/15, he will be assessed on trading profits for the 12 month period to 31 May 2015.

A   True

B   False

Workbook Activity 6

Rupert

Rupert commenced in business as a fashion designer on 1 July 2013, and prepared his first set of accounts to 30 April 2015.

His profit for the period, adjusted for taxation, was £33,000.

What is the amount of overlap profit that arises on the commencement of Rupert's trade?

A   £18,000

B   £16,500

C   £4,500

D   £Nil

 Workbook Activity 7

Katrina

Katrina ceased trading on 28 February 2015. Her tax adjusted trading profits for the final periods of trading are as follows:

	£
Year ended 30 June 2013	30,000
Year ended 30 June 2014	27,000
Period ended 28 February 2015	20,000

She has unrelieved overlap profits of £12,000.

What is Katrina's trading income assessment for 2014/15?

A   £8,000

B   £47,000

C   £35,000

D   £65,000

Workbook Activity 8

James

James started in business on 1 January 2011 and prepared his first set of accounts to 30 April 2012.

He then continued to prepare his accounts to 30 April and his taxable trade profits in the early years were as follows:

	£
1 January 2011 – 30 April 2012	75,600
Year ended 30 April 2013	52,650
Year ended 30 April 2014	56,900

Required:

Show the amounts assessable for all tax years affected by these results and calculate the overlap profits arising.

 Workbook Activity 9

Avril

Avril commenced trading on 1 January 2012. She prepared accounts to 30 June each year.

Her taxable trade profits for the first few years of trading were:

Period		£
6 months to	30 June 2012	80,000
Year ended	30 June 2013	100,000
Year ended	30 June 2014	110,000

Required:

Calculate the amounts assessable for 2011/12 to 2014/15, and show the overlap profit arising to be carried forward.

Workbook Activity 10

Benny

Benny, a fashion designer, decided to commence his own business on 1 July 2012. He prepared accounts on a calendar year basis and his taxable trade profits for the first few periods of trading are as follows:

Period		£
6 months to	31 December 2012	14,000
Year ended	31 December 2013	36,000
Year ended	31 December 2014	28,000

Required:

Show the amounts assessable for 2012/13 to 2014/15, and state the overlap profit to be carried forward.

 Workbook Activity 11

Elle

Elle prepares accounts to 31 May annually.

Recent taxable trade profits have been as follows:

	£
Year ended 31 May 2013	22,000
Year ended 31 May 2014	26,000

Elle had overlap profits on commencement of the business totalling £5,000.

Required:

Show the assessments for all relevant tax years for the following alternative dates for cessation of trading.

(a)   31 May 2015 with taxable trade profits of £27,000.

(b)   31 January 2015 with taxable trade profits of £22,500.

Workbook Activity 12

Bernadette

Bernadette opened a riding school on 1 October 2011.

Accounts were prepared regularly to 30 September and her taxable trade profits are as follows:

		£
Year ended	30 September 2012	21,280
Year ended	30 September 2013	24,688
Year ended	30 September 2014	28,816
Year ended	30 September 2015	30,304

She intends to cease trading on 28 February 2016. The forecast taxable trade profits for the period from 1 October 2015 to 28 February 2016 have been estimated at £16,792.

Required:

Show the assessable amounts for all tax years of the business.

 Workbook Activity 13

Bay

Bay, who has been carrying on a manufacturing business in a South London suburb since 1 January 2011, decided to retire on 31 October 2014, having reached 65 years of age.

His adjusted profits (before capital allowances) and capital allowances (CAs) over the life of the business are:

		Profits £	CAs £
Year ending	31 December 2011	19,487	4,343
Year ending	31 December 2012	17,840	3,879
Year ending	31 December 2013	16,928	3,310
Period ending	31 October 2014	18,040	1,326

Required:

Compute all the assessable amounts for Bay for the years 2010/11 to 2014/15 inclusive.

Approach to the question

Note that you must proceed in the following order:

- Deduct the capital allowances from the adjusted profits.

- Apply the basis period rules to the profits after the deduction of capital allowances.

 Workbook Activity 14

Ranjit

On 1 November 2012, Ranjit commenced a manufacturing business preparing accounts to 30 September in each year.

The adjusted profits for income tax purposes but before deducting capital allowances and the capital allowances are as follows:

		Profits £	CAs £
Period ended	30 September 2013	6,106	3,800
Year ended	30 September 2014	8,845	5,000
Year ended	30 September 2015	19,087	9,950

Required:

Compute the assessable amounts for each of the years affected by the results and calculate the amount of overlap profits.

 Workbook Activity 15

Period of assessment

Read the following statements and state whether they are true or false.

1 The basis of assessment is always the 12 months to the accounting date ending in the tax year.

2 If Paul started trading on 1 August 2013 and prepares account to 5 April each year, he will have no overlap profits.

3 When a new partner joins a partnership, he is immediately taxed on his share of the profits of the accounting period ending in the tax year.

Workbook Activity 16

John and Edward

John and Edward started trading on 1 April 2014 and made a tax adjusted trading profit for the year ended 31 March 2015 of £60,000. They agreed to split the profits equally.

Joe joined the partnership on 1 January 2015, at which point the profit sharing arrangement was changed and John, Edward and Joe agreed to share profits in the ratio 3:2:1.

What is Joe's trading income assessment for 2014/15?

A   £2,500

B   £5,000

C   £10,000

D   £7,500

 Workbook Activity 17

Richard and Brenda

Richard and Brenda commenced in business on 1 October 2011 as hotel proprietors, sharing profits equally.

On 1 October 2013 their son Michael joined the partnership and from that date each of the partners was entitled to one third of the profits.

Recent profits of the partnership adjusted for income tax are:

	£
Year ended 30 June 2014	50,000
Year ended 30 June 2015	60,000

What amount of profit is assessable on Michael for 2014/15?

A   £12,500

B   £17,500

C   £8,333

D   £18,750

Trading losses for individuals

Introduction

As for companies, individuals can also make trading losses. This chapter discusses how a loss is calculated and how it can be relieved.

KNOWLEDGE

Identify relevant tax authority legislation and guidance. (3.1 K)

Identify alternative loss reliefs, demonstrating how best to utilise that relief. (4.4 K)

SKILLS

Divide profits and losses of partnership amongst partners. (1.6 S)

CONTENTS

1   Identification of a trading loss
2   Ongoing businesses
3   New businesses and closing years
4   Trading losses set against capital gains
5   Partnership losses

1 Identification of a trading loss

A trading loss is identified in exactly the same way as a trading profit.

In other words, the accounting profit (or loss) is adjusted for tax purposes, and capital allowances are taken into account.

The adjusted loss is then identified with the tax year in which it arose. This is shown in the examples below.

 Example

A trader has a net accounting profit of £9,000 for the year ended 31 December 2014 which includes £3,000 of disallowable expenses. Capital allowances of £14,000 are available.

Calculate the taxable trade profits assessed in 2014/15 and the trading loss available for relief.

Solution

Year ended 31 December 2014	£
Net profit	9,000
Add: Disallowable expenses	3,000
	12,000
Less: Capital allowances	(14,000)
Adjusted loss	(2,000)

In this situation when a loss has arisen, the 2014/15 trading profits assessment is determined as £Nil and there is a (£2,000) trading loss available for relief.

Example

A trader has a net accounting loss of £9,000 for the year ended 31 December 2014 which includes £3,000 of disallowable expenses. Capital allowances of £14,000 are available.

Calculate the taxable trade profits assessed in 2014/15 and the trading loss available for relief.

Solution

	£
Accounting loss	(9,000)
Add: Disallowable expenses	3,000
	─────
	(6,000)
Less: Capital allowances	(14,000)
	─────
Adjusted loss	(20,000)
	─────

The assessment for 2014/15 is £Nil.

The trading loss available is £20,000.

It is easy to identify the wrong amount of loss available by not paying sufficient attention to the arithmetic.

Capital allowances, which normally reduce a profit, will increase a loss.

2 Ongoing businesses

2.1 Options available

There are two main ways of relieving a trading loss in an ongoing business.

- relief against total income of the current and/or the preceding tax year.

- relief against future trading profits only.

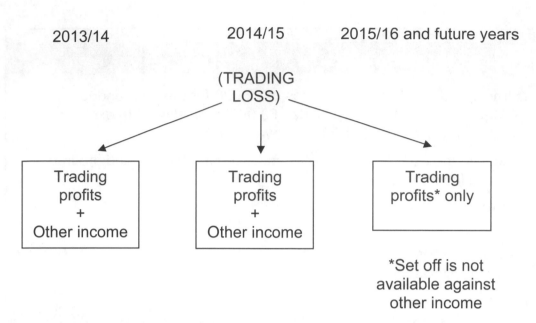

2013/14   2014/15   2015/16 and future years

(TRADING LOSS)

| Trading profits + Other income | Trading profits + Other income | Trading profits* only |

*Set off is not available against other income

2.2   Set off of trading loss against total income

This relief allows the trading loss to be set **against total income** of:

(i)   the **tax year of the loss**, and / or

(ii)   the **preceding tax year**.

A claim can be made to obtain relief in either year in isolation, or in both years, in any order.

When applying the loss relief it cannot be restricted to preserve the personal allowance. The personal allowance is deducted from income after loss relief has been deducted.

The personal allowance for 2014/15 is £10,000. This means that if a trader has total income of £10,000 or less, it is not worth claiming loss relief against total income for that year as the income is covered by the personal allowance.

Any excess loss over and above total income is available for relief by carrying forward.

Example

Beryl has a trading loss in her accounting year ended 30 September 2014 of £18,000.

Her other income is as follows:

	2013/14	2014/15
	£	£
Taxable trade profits	14,000	Nil
Other income	2,000	6,000

State the alternative claims Beryl could make to obtain loss relief against her total income.

Solution

The loss for the year ended 30 September 2014 is identified with the tax year 2014/15 as the trading year ends in the tax year 2014/15.

As a result the taxable trade profits for 2014/15 are £Nil.

The loss could be offset against her total income in that year (2014/15) and/or the previous tax year (2013/14) as follows:

- Set off £6,000 in 2014/15 and relieve the balance of £12,000 in 2013/14, or

- Set off £6,000 in 2014/15 and make no claim for 2013/14, or

- Set off £16,000 in 2013/14 and relieve the balance of £2,000 in 2014/15, or

- Set off £16,000 in 2013/14 and make no claim for 2014/15.

It is important to identify all of the available options before deciding the course of action you will take.

2.3 Future relief for trading losses

The individual taxpayer does not *have* to claim relief for the loss against total income as described in section 2.2. If no such claim is made, all of the loss will be carried forward for relief in the future.

Alternatively a claim may have been made for loss relief against total income, but as it can only be used in the same tax year as the loss and/or the previous year, there may be an amount of trading loss still unrelieved after this relief. This remaining amount will be available to carry forward.

Whatever the reason, any trading loss *not* relieved in the same or previous tax year is automatically carried forward.

The trading loss carried forward must be relieved against the **first available** taxable **trading profits** from the **same trade**.

The set off cannot be restricted. If there are sufficient losses, future taxable trade profits will be reduced to £Nil.

Trading losses carried forward cannot be set against other sources of income.

 Example

Derek has been trading for some time preparing accounts to 31 July.

His recent adjusted trading results are as follows:

		£
Year ended 31 July 2012	Profit	18,000
Year ended 31 July 2013	Loss	43,200
Year ended 31 July 2014	Profit	13,000
Year ended 31 July 2015	Profit	15,000

Derek's other income in each year is £12,000 (gross).

Show Derek's net income after loss relief for all tax years affected by the above results assuming:

(a) no claim is to be made against total income for the trading loss.

(b) full claims are to be made to obtain relief against total income as early as possible.

Solution

(a) **If no claim is made against total income**

The trading loss of 2013/14 is carried forward against future trading profits.

	2012/13 £	2013/14 £	2014/15 £	2015/16 £
Taxable trade profits	18,000	Nil	13,000	15,000
Less: Loss relief b/f			(13,000)	(15,000)
	18,000	Nil	Nil	Nil
Other income	12,000	12,000	12,000	12,000
Net income after reliefs	30,000	12,000	12,000	12,000

Loss memorandum

	£
Year ended 31 July 2013 – Loss	43,200
Less: Utilised – 2014/15	(13,000)
– 2015/16	(15,000)
Loss left to carry forward to 2016/17	15,200

(b) **Full claims made against total income**

Claims against total income can only be made for 2012/13 and / or 2013/14, and any balance is carried forward for relief against future trading profits.

	2012/13 £	2013/14 £	2014/15 £	2015/16 £
Taxable trade profits	18,000	Nil	13,000	15,000
Less: Loss relief b/f			(1,200)	–
			11,800	15,000
Other income	12,000	12,000	12,000	12,000
	30,000	12,000	23,800	27,000
Less: Loss relief				
– current year		(12,000)		
– preceding year	(30,000)			
Net income after reliefs	Nil	Nil	23,800	27,000

Loss memorandum

	£
Year ended 31 July 2013 – Loss	43,200
Less: Relief against total income – 2012/13	(30,000)
– 2013/14	(12,000)
	1,200
Less: Utilised in 2014/15	(1,200)
Loss left to carry forward	Nil

Activity 1

Caroline

Caroline has been in business as a gourmet caterer since 1 July 2011.

She prepares accounts for calendar years and her adjusted trading results were as follows:

	£
Six months ended 31 December 2011	4,900
Year ended 31 December 2012	10,500
Year ended 31 December 2013	(25,000)
Year ended 31 December 2014	350

Caroline also receives a salary of £2,000 per annum from part-time secretarial work.

She has also received gross interest as follows:

2012/13	£220
2013/14	£8,715
2014/15	£8,700

Required:

Calculate Caroline's net income after reliefs (but before the personal allowance) for the years 2012/13 to 2014/15 inclusive, assuming reliefs for losses are claimed as early as possible.

3 New businesses and closing years

When an individual sets up a business or ceases to trade, the rules for trading loss relief are different.

However, only ongoing trading loss relief will be examined in your assessment.

4 Trading losses set against capital gains

If a trader still has loss remaining after offset against their total income for the year, they may treat the loss like a capital loss and set it off against capital gains of the tax year. The claim can also be made for the previous tax year. Capital gains are dealt with in Chapter 20.

5 Partnership losses

5.1 Reliefs available to partners

Partners are allocated losses in the same way as profits. Each partner is then entitled to decide independently on how to use their individual share of the loss.

An ongoing partner could use their loss against total income in the current and/or preceding year or carry the loss forward against trading profits.

A new partner joining a partnership or an existing partner ceasing to be involved in the partnership has other loss relief opportunities available, however these are not examinable.

 Activity 2

Read the following statements and state whether they are true or false.

1   A sole trader can restrict the amount of loss relief claimed against total income in the current year so that the personal allowance is not lost.

2   Kate has been trading for many years. A trading loss for the year to 31 December 2014 can be relieved by set off against total income of 2013/14 and/or 2014/15 (in any order). Any balance unrelieved can be carried forward and set against future trading profits of the same trade.

3   If a partnership makes a loss, all partners must claim loss relief in the same way.

---

6 Summary

The loss reliefs available to an ongoing business are summarised below.

- Relief against total income – current and/or preceding year

- Carry forward against future profits of the same trade

- Relief against gains – current and preceding year provided a claim is made against income first.

7 Test your knowledge

 Workbook Activity 3

Sole trader losses

Which one of the following statements is correct with regard to sole trader's losses?

A   A loss can only be relieved against trading profits made in the same tax year

B   A loss can be relieved in the preceding tax year, but only after a claim for relief has been made in the current tax year

C   A carried forward loss must be relieved against profits from the same trade in future years

D   A loss can be relieved against total income arising in future years

 Workbook Activity 4

Belinda

Belinda has been trading for many years and incurred a tax adjusted trading loss for the period ended 31 December 2014.

Which one of the following statements is correct with regard to the use of the trading loss?

A   The trading loss may be carried forward and set against trading income for 2014/15 arising from the same trade

B   The trading loss can be set against total income for 2014/15, but only after the loss is set against total income for 2013/14

C   The trading loss can be set against total income for 2013/14, irrespective of whether the loss has been set against total income for 2014/15

D   The trading loss can be set against total income for 2013/14, but only after the loss is set against total income for 2014/15

Workbook Activity 5

Bourbon

Bourbon has been trading as a self employed biscuit maker for many years. His taxable trade profits or losses are given below.

		£
Year to 31 March 2014	Profit	12,200
Year to 31 March 2015	Loss	(24,050)
Year to 31 March 2016	Profit	12,750

Details of other income for Bourbon is as follows:

	2013/14 £	2014/15 £	2015/16 £
Building society received (gross)	7,250	15,250	5,250

Required:

Set out the options available to an established continuing trade for relief of the loss and, together with calculations, advise Bourbon as to the best method of obtaining loss relief.

Payment and administration – individuals

Introduction

This chapter covers tax returns and amendments, the payment of tax and enquiries for individuals.

KNOWLEDGE

Identify relevant tax authority legislation and guidance. (3.1 K)

Explain the system of penalties and interest as it applies to income tax, corporation tax and capital gains tax. (3.2 K)

Explain the self-assessment process including payment of tax and filing of returns for unincorporated businesses. (4.6 K)

Identify due dates of payments, including payments on account. (4.7 K)

SKILLS

Complete the self-employed or partnership supplementary pages of the tax return for individuals, and submit them within statutory time limits. (1.10 S)

CONTENTS

1 Introduction to the self assessment return
2 Payment of income tax and capital gains tax
3 Interest and penalties on payments of tax
4 HM Revenue and Customs' compliance checks
5 Penalties for incorrect returns

1 Introduction to the self assessment return

1.1 The self assessment return

Certain individuals are required to complete a return for every tax year.

Amongst other things this covers trading income and capital gains and, in some cases, a calculation of the tax payable.

The key details to grasp concerning the return are the filing dates.

The taxpayer has the choice of filing a paper return or filing electronically online. The date by which a return must be filed depends on the method used.

All completed and signed paper returns must be filed by:

* 31 October following the end of the tax year

All online electronic returns must be filed by:

* 31 January following the end of the tax year.

The relevant dates for a 2014/15 return are therefore 31 October 2015 and 31 January 2016.

HMRC normally issue an individual with a tax return in April / May following the end of the tax year.

However, where HMRC issue a tax return late, the taxpayer has until the later of the filing dates mentioned above and 3 months after the date the return is issued in which to file their return.

An individual who receives a 2014/15 tax return from HMRC on 15 August 2015 therefore has until 15 November 2015 to file a paper return or until 31 January 2016 to file the return electronically.

31 January following the end of the tax year is known as the 'filing date', regardless of whether the return is filed on paper or electronically. This must be distinguished from the date on which the return is filed / submitted to HMRC (known as the 'actual' filing date).

The return consists of an eight page summary form with six supplementary pages for self employed individuals.

In the assessment you will only be required to complete page 2 of the self employment supplementary pages and/or page 6 of the partnership return.

Where a tax return is not issued, an individual is required to notify HMRC by *5 October* following the tax year where there is chargeable income (i.e. new sources of income) or gains arising.

Notification is not required where there are no assessable gains or where the income is either covered by allowances or the full tax liability has been deducted at source.

Failure to notify may result in a penalty. The penalty is calculated in broadly the same way as penalties for incorrect returns (see below) and is a maximum of 100% of the tax outstanding.

The taxpayer is permitted to correct or 'repair' his self assessment return within 12 months of the filing date (i.e.by 31 January 2017 for a 2014/15 return). HMRC can correct 'obvious errors' and anything else which they believe to be incorrect by reference to the information they hold in the period of nine months from actual filing.

1.2 Records

An individual must retain certain records to support the completed tax return, to assist with providing evidence to support information given to HMRC.

Self employed people (i.e. sole traders and partners in a partnership) must keep records for five years after the filing date (i.e. until 31 January 2021 for 2014/15 information).

Examples of records to be kept include the following:

- Accounts.

- Documentation, receipts, invoices.

- Dividend vouchers.

Failure to keep records can lead to a penalty of up to £3,000.

1.3 Penalties for late filing

Failure to submit a return by 31 January following a tax year will result in a flat rate penalty. The penalties are the same as for Corporation Tax (see Chapter 9).

 Activity 1

Bob

Bob understands that he has responsibilities under the self assessment system and is required to meet a number of deadlines. In particular he needs confirmation of the deadlines for the following actions.

1   Notifying HMRC that he started receiving rent for the first time on 1 January 2015.

2   Filing a paper return for 2014/15.

3   Filing his 2014/15 return electronically.

4   Amending his 2014/15 tax return.

Match each of Bob's responsibilities with the correct deadline:

A   5 October 2015

B   31 January 2016

C   31 October 2015

D   31 January 2017

2 Payment of income tax and capital gains tax

2.1 The instalment system

The submission of information, and the penalties relating thereto, should not be confused with the fact that certain individuals will also need to make payments of tax.

Self employed individuals are subject to an instalment system based upon total liability.

The instalment system operates as follows:

- 31 January in the tax year: first payment on account (POA).

- 31 July *following* the tax year: second payment on account (POA).

- 31 January *following* the tax year: final payment

For example, for 2014/15 the following dates are relevant:

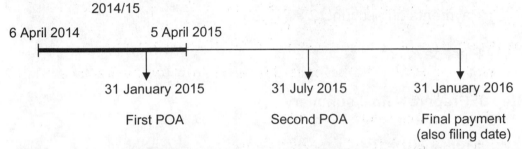

2014/15

6 April 2014   5 April 2015

31 January 2015   31 July 2015   31 January 2016

First POA   Second POA   Final payment
(also filing date)

The payments on account are estimated, in that they are based on the previous year's tax and Class 4 NIC payable.

The taxpayer can claim to make reduced payments on account where this year's income tax payable is expected to be less than that of last year. The taxpayer will be charged a penalty if the claim to make reduced payments on account was made either fraudulently or negligently.

The examiner has stated that a detailed understanding of the payments on account system is expected, including when payments are due and how to pay them.

 Example

Roderic is self employed. His only source of income is from his trade. The income tax payable for 2013/14 was £5,100.

His tax payable for 2014/15 based on his taxable trade profits for the year ended 31 July 2014 is £7,032.

Ignoring NICs, state Roderic's payments in respect of his 2014/15 income tax liability.

Solution

Step 1: Determine the relevant dates

31 January 2015   –   first payment on account

31 July 2015   –   second payment on account

31 January 2016   –   final payment

Step 2: Determine the amounts due

- The amounts due for the 'payments on account' are based on an equal division of the previous year's tax payable, hence £2,550 (£5,100 ÷ 2).

- The final payment on account will be based on the final liability for 2014/15 less the payments on account already made.

	£
2014/15 IT liability	7,032
Payments on account (2 × £2,550)	(5,100)
	————
Final payment	1,932
	————

Step 3: Prepare a final summary

	£
31 January 2015	2,550
31 July 2015	2,550
31 January 2016	1,932

The amount due on 31 January following the end of the tax year consists of the final payment on account for the year just ended and the first payment on account for the new tax year.

In Roderic's case this means that on 31 January 2016 he will start the instalment option all over again, by making the first payment on account of his 2015/16 liability based on 2014/15 tax payable.

Hence his 31 January 2016 payment is £5,448 ((£7,032 × ½) + £1,932).

The Class 4 National Insurance contributions payable by a self employed person are also paid by the instalment system (see Chapter 16).

2.2 No requirement for payments on account

Payments on account are not required in the following circumstances:

- The income tax and Class 4 NIC payable for the previous tax year by self assessment is less than £1,000, or

- More than 80% of the income tax liability for the previous year was met through tax deducted at source.

2.3 Capital gains tax

The capital gains tax due for a tax year (see Chapter 20) is payable on 31 January following the end of the tax year, together with the final payment of income tax.

CGT is therefore paid in one instalment on 31 January following the tax year regardless of whether there was a CGT liability for the previous year.

The CGT liability is not taken into account when determining the payments on account for income tax.

Payments on account of capital gains tax are never required.

 Activity 2

Required:

(a)   State the latest date by which the taxpayer should submit the 2014/15 tax return if:

    (i)   he wishes to file his return online; or

    (ii)   he wishes to file a paper return.

(b)   State:

    (i)   the normal dates of payment of income tax and Class 4 NIC for a sole trader in respect of the tax year 2014/15; and

    (ii)   how the amounts of these payments are calculated.

(c)   State:

    (i)   the penalties that will be charged where a tax return is submitted within six months after the due date;

    (ii)   the penalties that will be charged where a tax return is submitted more than six months late.

2.4 How to pay

There are a number of ways to pay your tax liability.

HMRC recommends that you make your payments electronically using one of the methods described below.

Electronic payments are generally more efficient and secure, provided you give HMRC an accurate reference number.

Electronic payment methods

- Internet or telephone banking

- Direct debit

- Payment by debit or credit card over the Internet: (BillPay)
- Bank Giro
- By cheque at the Post Office (this is regarded by HMRC as an electronic payment)

Payment by post

HMRC highly recommends using one of the other electronic methods set out above, however, it is also possible to pay by post with a cheque and an HMRC payslip.

If the tax payer does not have a payslip they must provide their name, address, telephone number, self assessment reference and confirm the amount of tax they are paying.

2.5 Recovery of overpaid tax

A taxpayer who believes that they have paid too much income tax or capital gains tax can submit a claim in order to have the excess tax repaid. The claim must be submitted within 4 years of the end of the relevant tax year.

3 Interest and penalties on payments of tax

3.1 Interest

Failure to make payments, whether payments on account (POA) or final payments, by the due date will attract interest.

Interest is not perceived as being a penalty but merely as commercial compensation for late payment. It is not a deductible expense when computing taxable income.

Interest is charged from the day the tax is due until the day before it is paid. The calculation of interest on tax paid late is not within the syllabus.

In addition to the interest charge there is also a penalty where tax is paid late.

An individual who receives a tax repayment may receive interest in respect of the amount repaid. This interest income is not taxable.

The tax treatment of interest on underpayments/overpayments of corporation tax paid by or to companies is different from that for individuals and is covered in Chapter 9.

Example

Rodney was due to make the following payments of tax for 2014/15.

		Actual date of payment
31 January 2015	£2,100	28 February 2015
31 July 2015	£2,100	31 August 2015
31 January 2016	£1,000	31 March 2016

For what periods will interest be charged?

Solution

On first POA	31 January 2015 – 27 February 2015	1 month
On second POA	31 July 2015 – 30 August 2015	1 month
On final payment	31 January 2016 – 30 March 2016	2 months

3.2 Penalty for late payment of tax

A penalty will be charged where there is income tax or capital gains tax outstanding after the day on which the final payment of tax is due (31 January after the end of the tax year). This penalty is in addition to any interest that is charged.

- More than 30 days late   5% of tax overdue

- More than six months late   further 5% of tax overdue

- More than 12 months late   further 5% of tax overdue

A late payment penalty may be mitigated (i.e. reduced) where the taxpayer can provide a reasonable excuse, for example a serious illness.

Insufficiency of funds or lack of knowledge of self assessment are not reasonable excuses.

Example

Star submitted the final payment in respect of his 2013/14 self assessment return on 30 April 2015.

What penalties will be charged in respect of the late payment of the tax?

Solution

The final payment in respect of the 2013/14 self assessment return was due on 31 January 2015. The payment is more than 30 days but less than 6 months late.

Because the return is more than 30 days late there will be a penalty of 5% of the tax outstanding.

(Note that Star will also be charged interest on the late paid tax from 31 January 2015 to 29 April 2015. However, the question only asked for the penalties.)

 HM Revenue and Customs' compliance checks

4.1 Introduction

HMRC have the right to enquire into an individual's tax return (similar to the system on corporation tax returns) under their compliance check powers.

They must make their compliance check (enquiry) within 12 months of the date the return was filed.

4.2 Compliance check (enquiry) procedure

Once the compliance check notice is given, an Officer can request relevant documents and written particulars.

At the end of the compliance check a completion notice is issued stating the outcome of the enquiry, for example, no amendment made or business profits increased by £10,000!.

The taxpayer has 30 days from completion to ask for their case to be reviewed.

4.3 Discovery assessments

Although HMRC usually only have 12 months from the date a return is filed to open an enquiry, they can replace a self assessment at a later date by making a discovery assessment.

A discovery assessment can be made where tax has been lost perhaps because of insufficient information in the tax return.

The taxpayer can appeal to the Tax Tribunal against a discovery assessment.

4.4 Appeals procedure

The taxpayer can request an informal review of a disputed decision.

Alternatively, a formal appeal may be made to the Tax Tribunal.

Appeals from the Tax Tribunal on a point of law (but not on a point of fact) may be made to the Court of Appeal and from there to the Supreme Court.

The Tax Tribunal is independent of HMRC.

5 Penalties for incorrect returns

The common penalty regime described in Chapter 9 applies to income tax returns as well as corporation tax returns.

The penalties are the same for individuals in that a penalty will be charged where an inaccurate return is submitted to HMRC or where the individual fails to notify HMRC where an under assessment of tax is made by them.

 Example

State the maximum and minimum penalties that may be levied on each of the following individuals who have submitted incorrect tax returns.

Lars   Deliberately understated his tax liability and attempted to conceal the incorrect information that he had provided. HMRC have identified the understatement and Lars is helping them with their enquiries.

Sven   Accidentally provided an incorrect figure even though he checked his tax return carefully. He realised his mistake a few days later and notified HMRC.

Jo   Completed his tax return too quickly and made a number of errors. The day after he had submitted the tax return he decided to check it thoroughly and immediately provided HMRC with the information necessary to identify the errors.

Solution

Penalties for incorrect tax returns are a percentage of the under declared tax.

Lars   The maximum percentage for a deliberate understatement with concealment is 100%. The minimum percentage for prompted disclosure of information (where the taxpayer provides information in response to HMRC identifying the error) in respect of deliberate understatement with concealment is 50%.

Sven   No penalty is charged where a taxpayer has been careful and has made a genuine mistake.

Jo   The maximum percentage for failing to take reasonable care is 30%. The minimum percentage for unprompted disclosure is nil.

Activity 3

1   James commenced his own business in February 2015.

     If he does not receive a tax return to complete for 2014/15, by what date should he notify HMRC that he is chargeable to tax for 2014/15?

2   Isabel made her second payment on account of tax for 2014/15 on 15 September 2015.

     What are the consequences?

3   Mike filed his 2014/15 tax return on 18 January 2016.

     What is the latest date for HMRC to open a compliance check (enquiry)?

6 Summary

This chapter covers a core topic – self assessment.

Traders have to self assess because they receive trading income gross.

Payment dates

31 January 2015

- Balance of income tax and Class 4 NIC payable for 2013/14.

- CGT liability for 2013/14.

- First POA for 2014/15 (based on previous year's liability).

31 July 2015

- Second POA for 2014/15.

Filing returns (2014/15 return)

Paper return   –   31 October 2015

Electronic return   –   31 January 2016 (the 'filing date')

Main surcharges/penalties

Late filing – same as Corporation tax (see Chapter 9)

Incorrect returns – same as Corporation tax (see Chapter 9)

Tax unpaid 30 days after 31 January – 5% penalty with further 5% penalties if the tax remains outstanding after 6 and 12 months.

If no compliance check (enquiry) notice issued by the anniversary of the date the return is filed, the taxpayer can assume it is 'final'.

However, if HMRC are able to show they had insufficient information supplied in the tax return, they can make a 'discovery' assessment.

7 Test your knowledge

 ## Workbook Activity 4

Payments on account

State the appropriate dates in respect of the following payments.

1   First instalment for tax year – 2014/15

2   Second instalment for tax year – 2014/15

3   Final instalment for tax year – 2014/15

4   Payment date for capital gains tax for tax year – 2014/15

 ## Workbook Activity 5

Income tax self assessment

Read the following statements and state whether they are true or false.

1   An individual must retain their tax records for 2014/15 until 5 April 2020.

2   If an individual is two months late in submitting their tax return for 2014/15, they will receive a penalty of £100.

3   Penalties for errors made by individuals in their tax return vary from 30% to 100%.

4   Late payment penalties can be imposed on balancing payments made late.

Workbook Activity 6

Kazuo

Kazuo is required to pay tax in instalments.

For 2013/14, his income tax liability was £18,700, of which £2,000 was collected at source. He estimates that his income tax payable for 2014/15 will be £22,000.

What is the amount of the first payment on account that Kazuo should make on 31 January 2015 in respect of his income tax liability for 2014/15?

Ignore National Insurance.

A   £8,350

B   £9,350

C   £10,000

D   £11,000

 Workbook Activity 7

Income tax self assessment

Clark is a new client who has come to you for information about the self assessment system.

Explain to Clark:

(a)   The latest date by which income tax returns for the year 2014/15 should be submitted to HM Revenue and Customs (HMRC).

(b)   The date by which Clark should notify HMRC that he has received income in the year 2014/15 which is liable to income tax where no income tax return has been issued.

(c)   The penalties for the late submission of income tax returns and when they apply.

(d)   The penalty for the submission of an incorrect income tax return.

(e)   The penalty for failing to maintain or retain adequate records to back up an income tax return.

National Insurance contributions payable by self employed individuals

Introduction

A self employed individual has his/her own National Insurance contributions to pay, but may also have to pay contributions as an employer.

KNOWLEDGE
Identify relevant tax authority legislation and guidance. (3.1 K)
Explain the self assessment process including payment of tax and filing of returns for unincorporated businesses. (4.6 K)
Identify due dates of payments, including payments on account. (4.7 K)

SKILLS
Calculate the national insurance contributions payable by self employed persons. (1.8 S)

CONTENTS
1 Contributions as an employer
2 Contributions as a sole trader
3 Effect of partnerships

1 Contributions as an employer

1.1 Class 1 secondary and Class 1A contributions

A sole trader or partnership may employ staff.

As an employer, they may be liable to Class 1 secondary and Class 1A contributions in relation to the remuneration paid to their employees.

However, calculations of these contributions are outside the syllabus for business tax.

2 Contributions as a sole trader

2.1 Class 4 NICs

A self employed person, whether operating as a sole trader or as a partner, pays two types of National Insurance contributions:

- Class 2 and
- Class 4.

Class 4 NICs are calculated by applying a fixed percentage (currently 9%) to the amount by which the taxpayer's 'profits' (or share of 'profits', where the taxpayer is a member of a partnership) exceed a lower limit (£7,956 for 2014/15).

> ### 💡 Example
>
> If Nicholas has 'profits' of £12,670 for 2014/15, he will be liable to pay Class 4 NICs calculated as follows:
>
> | | £ |
> |---|---|
> | 'Profits' | 12,670 |
> | Less Lower limit | (7,956) |
> | Excess | 4,714 |
> | Class 4 NICs (9% × £4,714) | 424.26 |

The 9% rate only applies up to an upper limit of profits (£41,865 for 2014/15).

Where a taxpayer's 'profits' exceed the upper limit, the excess profit is liable to Class 4 NICs at 2%.

For example, if a taxpayer has taxable trading profits of £50,000 for 2014/15 he is liable to Class 4 NICs of £3,203.55 calculated as follows:

	£ p
(£41,865 – £7,956) × 9%	3,051.81
(£50,000 – £41,865) × 2%	162.70
	3,214.51

Note that where a taxpayer's 'profits' do not exceed the lower limit (i.e. £7,956 for 2014/15); there is no liability to Class 4 NICs.

2.2 Profits

The 'profits' to be used in the calculation of the taxpayer's liability to Class 4 NICs are:

	£
Taxable trade profits	X
Less: Trading losses brought forward	(X)
Profits for Class 4 NICs	X

2.3 Payments of Class 4 NICs

Class 4 NICs are payable under self assessment at the same time as the related income tax liability (i.e. two payments on account and a balancing payment).

Interest will be charged on late payments.

A taxpayer does not have to pay Class 4 NICs if they are:

- of retirement age or over at the beginning of the tax year.

- aged under 16 at the beginning of the tax year.

Retirement age is currently 65 for men and is gradually being increased for women from 60 to 65. You would be told in an assessment if a woman had reached retirement age.

2.4 Class 2 NICs

In addition to Class 4 NICs, a trader is also liable for Class 2 NICs which are payable at a fixed rate of £2.75 per week. The liability relates to the individual trader, such that it does not increase where an individual has more than one trade.

There is no liability if the 'profits' are below the small earnings limit of £5,885.

'Profits' for Class 2 NICs purposes are the accounts profits (i.e. not tax adjusted) falling in the tax year, excluding any charges for the owner's drawings.

Class 2 is payable in two instalments on 31 January and 31 July but is not part of the payment on accounts calculations described in Chapter 15. Alternatively, taxpayers can opt to pay monthly.

A taxpayer does not have to pay Class 2 NICs in respect of any week in which they are:

- aged under 16; or
- of retirement age or over.

Retirement age is currently 65 for men and is gradually being increased for women from 60 to 65. You would be told in an assessment if a woman had reached retirement age.

3 Effect of partnerships

3.1 Each partner is treated as a separate sole trader

Each partner must pay:

- their own Class 2 contributions; and
- their own Class 4 contributions.

The Class 4 contributions are based on his share of profits, as assessed to income tax for the tax year.

Activity 1

1   A taxpayer has self employed income of £80,000 for the tax year 2014/15. The amount of his income which will be chargeable to Class 4 NICs at 2% is £ [   ]

2   A taxpayer has self employed income of £30,000. The amount of Class 4 NIC payable would be £ [   ]

3   Anne has tax adjusted trading profits for 2014/15 of £5,600.

    Her accounts show a net profit of £5,900 for the year to 31 March 2015.

    •   What Class 4 NICs are due?   £ [   ]

    •   What Class 2 NICs are due?   £ [   ]

4   Which one of the following statements is correct?

    A   Self employed taxpayers pay either Class 2 or Class 4 NICs, but not both

    B   Every self employed taxpayer must pay Class 2 NICs, regardless of the level of their profits

    C   Class 4 NICs are based on the amount of income a taxpayer withdraws from the business

    D   In a partnership, each partner is responsible for their own NICs

4   Summary

Sole traders and partners may have to pay the following contributions:

•   Class 2, and

•   Class 4.

5 Test your knowledge

 Workbook Activity 2

Naomi

Naomi, aged 45, has been self employed for many years.

Her accounting profits always exceed her taxable trade profits.

Required:

State the National Insurance contributions payable by Naomi for 2014/15, assuming her taxable trade profits are:

(a) £5,900

(b) £24,500

(c) £44,500

 Workbook Activity 3

Adrian

Adrian's tax liability for 2013/14 was as follows:

	£
Income tax	9,400
Less: Tax deducted at source	(2,100)
	7,300
Class 4 NIC	700
CGT	5,000
	13,000

What will each of the payments on account be for 2014/15?

A   £6,500

B   £4,700

C   £4,000

D   £3,650

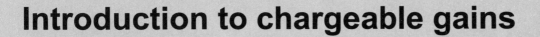

Introduction to chargeable gains

Introduction

Both individuals and companies pay tax on chargeable gains.

This chapter helps identify when chargeable gains arise.

KNOWLEDGE

Identify relevant tax authority legislation and guidance. (3.1 K)

Identify capital gains exemptions and reliefs on assets. (6.1 K)

Identify methods by which chargeable assets can be disposed of. (6.2 K)

SKILLS

Identify and value any chargeable assets that have been disposed of and calculate the chargeable gain/or allowable loss and relevant reliefs as applicable under current tax law. (2.8 S)

CONTENTS

1   Principle of a chargeable gain
2   Chargeable disposal
3   Chargeable person
4   Chargeable asset

1 Principle of a chargeable gain

1.1 The three essential elements

In order for a chargeable gain to be calculated there are three essential requirements.

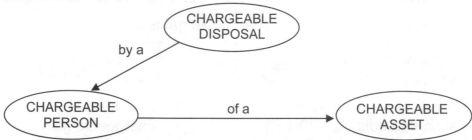

2 Chargeable disposal

2.1 Main types of disposal

A chargeable disposal includes:

- a sale of an asset (whole or part of an asset),
- a gift of an asset,
- an exchange of an asset,
- the loss or destruction of an asset.

Where a gift is made the sale proceeds are deemed to be its market value.

Where an asset is lost or destroyed the sale proceeds are likely to be nil or insurance proceeds.

2.2 Exempt disposals

The following occasions are exempt disposals and so no CGT computation is required:

- the sale is a trading disposal (badges of trade – Chapter 11).
- on the death of an individual
- on a gift to a charity.

In the assessment it will be obvious whether the disposal is of:

- stock/inventory, therefore dealt with as trading income; or

- a capital item (for example land), therefore calculate a gain.

3 Chargeable person

3.1 Types of person

Chargeable gains will be calculated on disposals by:

- Individuals
- Partners in partnership } – pay capital gains tax

- Companies – pay corporation tax on chargeable gains (see Chapter 5 pro forma)

4 Chargeable asset

4.1 Exempt assets

All assets are chargeable unless they are on the specific list of exempt assets. The main types of exempt asset are listed below.

Exempt assets in the list below need to be learned so that you can identify them in a question.

- Motor vehicles, including vintage and veteran cars.

- Cash (i.e. legal tender in the UK)

- Any form of loan stock (i.e. qualifying corporate bonds, loan notes, debentures, gilt edged securities, Treasury stock, Exchequer stock).

- Wasting chattels:

    - a chattel is property that is tangible and moveable.

    - 'wasting' means that it has a life of less than or equal to 50 years.

The most common examples of wasting chattels that you will encounter in an assessment are:

    - all animals (racehorses, greyhounds etc.), boats and caravans.

- Non-wasting chattels, which have both sale proceeds and cost of £6,000 or less.

  The most common examples of non-wasting chattels are works of art, jewellery and antiques.

 Activity 1

Chargeable disposals

For each of the following transactions, state whether it is a chargeable disposal or exempt from capital gains.

1   Bill gave his trading premises to his daughter Beatrice.

2   ABC Ltd is a building company. It built a small development of 5 houses and sold them.

3   DEF Ltd, a manufacturing company, sold a racehorse for £10,000.

4   DEF Ltd also sold a portrait for £10,000 which had been hanging in the boardroom.

---

5 Summary

The requirements for a chargeable gain to be calculated are:

- a chargeable disposal; by
- a chargeable person; of
- a chargeable asset.

6 Test your knowledge

 Workbook Activity 2

Chargeable disposals

For each of the following transactions, state whether it is a chargeable or an exempt disposal for the purpose of capital gains.

1   Sale of a motor car that was purchased for £12,000 and sold for £13,000 and used for business purposes throughout the period of ownership

2   Sale of a half share in a racehorse that was purchased for £12,000 and sold for £17,000.

3   Gift of a painting which was purchased for £5,000 and sold for £8,500.

4   Sale of land that was purchased for £2,900 and sold for £5,800.

Gains and losses for companies

Introduction

A company pays corporation tax on its chargeable gains.

A calculation of gains is likely to be required in Section 2 of your assessment.

This chapter sets out the pro forma for calculating the chargeable gain, and explains the separate entries required in the computation.

KNOWLEDGE	CONTENTS
Identify relevant tax authority legislation and guidance. (3.1 K) Identify methods by which chargeable assets can be disposed of. (6.2 K)	1 Pro forma computation 2 The chargeable gain computation 3 Special rules
SKILLS	
Identify and value any chargeable assets that have been disposed of and calculate the chargeable gain/or allowable loss and relevant reliefs as applicable under current tax law. (2.8 S)	

1   Pro forma computation

1.1   The pro forma computation (for corporation tax)

Gains and losses are calculated for chargeable accounting periods.

Once you have calculated all the individual chargeable gains and allowable capital losses for an accounting period, summarise them as follows:

	£
Chargeable gain (1)	X
Chargeable gain (2)	X
Allowable loss (3)	(X)
	——
Net chargeable gains/(losses) for the current year	X
Less: Capital losses brought forward	(X)
	——
Net chargeable gains	X
	——

The net chargeable gains are then put into the computation of taxable total profits and the corporation tax liability is calculated in the normal way.

If there is an overall capital loss, it is carried forward and set against future chargeable gains. It cannot be relieved against other income.

Example

Alpha Ltd made three disposals in its year ended 31 March 2015, giving the following results:

Asset	Gain/(loss)
	£
1	20,000
2	5,000
3	(8,000)

Calculate the net chargeable gains shown on the corporation tax computation.

Solution

Included within taxable total profits will be net chargeable gains of £17,000 (£20,000 + £5,000 − £8,000).

If the loss on asset 3 had been £28,000, the corporation tax computation would show net chargeable gains of nil.

A net loss of £3,000 (£20,000 + £5,000 − £28,000) would then be carried forward to offset against the next available net chargeable gains.

 Activity 1

Bubbles Ltd

Bubbles Ltd disposed of two assets during its accounting period to 31 March 2015, realising a chargeable gain of £13,000 and an allowable loss of £4,000.

It had allowable losses brought forward of £2,000.

How much will be included in taxable total profits for the year to 31 March 2015?

The remainder of this chapter considers how to calculate the gains and losses on each chargeable disposal made by a company.

2 The chargeable gain computation

2.1 The standard pro forma

The following pro forma should be used:

	Notes	£
Gross sale proceeds	1	X
Less: Selling costs	2	(X)
Net sale proceeds (NSP)		X
Less: Allowable cost	3	(X)
Unindexed gain	4	X
Less: Indexation allowance (IA) = Cost × 0.XXX	5	(X)
Chargeable gain		X

Notes to the pro forma

1   The sale proceeds are usually given in the question.

     However, where a disposal is not a sale at arm's length (e.g. a gift) then *market value* will be substituted for sale proceeds in the computation.

2   The selling costs incurred on the disposal of an asset are an allowable deduction.

     Examples of such allowable costs include valuation fees, advertising costs, legal fees, auctioneer's fees.

3   The purchase price of an asset is the main allowable cost, but this will also include any incidental purchase expenses, including legal fees, stamp duty, etc.

4   The gain after deducting the costs above is known as an unindexed gain.

5   An indexation allowance (IA) may then be available to reduce that gain.

     The indexation allowance is intended to give relief for inflation and is based upon the movement in the Retail Prices Index (RPI).

2.2   The indexation allowance (IA)

The IA is relief for inflation covering the period since the asset was purchased up to the date of disposal.

The indexation allowance runs:

*   from the month of the purchase (i.e. when the cost was incurred)

*   to the month of disposal.

It is computed by multiplying the acquisition cost by an indexation factor.

The formula for calculating the indexation factor is:

$$\frac{\text{RPI for month of disposal} - \text{RPI for month of acquisition}}{\text{RPI for month of acquisition}}$$

This produces a decimal figure which must be rounded to three decimal places.

In the assessment you will be given the indexation factor or the amount of the indexation allowance.

Example

Eli Ltd sells a chargeable asset on 31 March 2015 for £24,600 after deducting auctioneer's fees of £400. The asset was acquired on 1 May 2002 for £10,000.

Calculate the chargeable gain. Assume that the indexation factor for May 2002 to March 2015 is 0.473.

Solution

	£
Gross sales proceeds (March 2015)	25,000
Less: Incidental costs	(400)
Net sale proceeds	24,600
Less: Allowable cost (May 2002)	(10,000)
Unindexed gain	14,600
Less: Indexation allowance (£10,000 × 0.473)	(4,730)
Chargeable gain	9,870

Be careful to ensure that you index the allowable expenditure and not the unindexed gain – a very easy mistake to make!

Note also that the indexation allowance:

- cannot be used to turn a gain into a loss
- is not available where there is an unindexed loss.

 Example

JNN Ltd is considering selling a field at auction in August 2014. It acquired the field in August 1990 for £10,000 and the sale proceeds are likely to be one of three results.

(a)   £25,000

(b)   £12,000

(c)   £8,000

Calculate the chargeable gain or loss under each of these alternatives.

Assume the indexation factor from August 1990 to August 2014 is 1.005.

Solution

	(a) £	(b) £	(c) £
Sale proceeds	25,000	12,000	8,000
Less: Cost	(10,000)	(10,000)	(10,000)
Unindexed gain or (loss)	15,000	2,000	(2,000)
Less: Indexation allowance			
(1.005 × £10,000) = £10,050	(10,050)	(2,000)*	Nil**
Chargeable gain/(allowable loss)	4,950	Nil	(2,000)

Notes:

* Restricted, because indexation cannot create a loss.

** No indexation because indexation cannot increase a loss.

 Activity 2

JHN Ltd

JHN Ltd made the following disposals in the year ended 31 March 2015.

1   On 9 June 2014 it sold some plant for £15,000. The plant was bought in October 1996 for £8,000.

2   On 5 September 2014 it sold a building which had been purchased for £27,500 in November 1997. Sale proceeds were £26,500.

3   On 1 March 2015 it sold a car, a Trabant, which was bought in February 1991 for £3,000. By the time of the sale, it had become a collector's item and JHN Ltd managed to obtain proceeds of £9,000, out of which it paid £450 in auctioneer's fees.

4   On 3 March 2015 it sold a collection of military memorabilia for £19,000. The collection had cost £7,000 in March 1991.

5   Also on 3 March 2015, it sold some land which was purchased in April 1990 for £15,000. The land was sold for £25,000.

Required:

Calculate the chargeable gain on each of the above transactions in the year ended 31 March 2015.

You should use the following indexation factors.

April 1990 – March 2015	1.075
Feb 1991 – March 2015	0.983
March 1991 – March 2015	0.976
Oct 1996 – June 2014	0.664
Nov 1997 – Sept 2014	0.612

Approach to the question

It is important that the chargeable gain or allowable loss on each transaction is *separately* computed.

Finally, prepare a summary adding gains and losses together to arrive at one overall figure.

3 Special rules

3.1 Changes to the calculation of the gain

There are a number of special situations that will give rise to slight changes in the calculation of the gains. They are:

- Enhancement expenditure (see section 3.2 below)
- Part disposals (see section 3.3 below)
- Non-wasting chattels (see section 3.4 below).

3.2 Enhancement expenditure

The main allowable cost in computing an unindexed gain is the purchase cost (including incidental costs).

Any additional capital expenditure incurred at a later date on the asset is also an allowable cost. This normally takes the form of improvement (i.e. enhancement) expenditure.

As the additional expenditure is incurred later than the original expenditure, there will be an impact on the calculation of indexation allowance.

Indexation allowance can only be calculated from the actual date of expenditure; therefore, where there is cost plus enhancement expenditure, *two* indexation allowance calculations will be required.

 Example

RMY Ltd bought a shop in November 1994 for £13,200. The company spent £3,800 on improvements in May 1997. The shop was sold for £49,000 in October 2014.

The indexed rise from November 1994 to October 2014 is 0.773 and from May 1997 to October 2014 is 0.642.

Calculate the chargeable gain on the sale of the shop.

Solution

	£
Sale proceeds (October 2014)	49,000
Less: Cost (November 1994)	(13,200)
Enhancement (May 1997)	(3,800)

Unindexed gain	32,000
Less: Indexation allowance	
Cost £13,200 × 0.773	(10,204)
Enhancement £3,800 × 0.642	(2,440)

Chargeable gain	19,356

 Activity 3

Linda Ltd

On 15 February 2015, Linda Ltd sold a factory building for £420,000.

The factory had been purchased on 14 October 2001 for £194,000, and was extended at a cost of £58,000 during March 2003.

During May 2005, the roof of the factory was repaired at a cost of £12,000 following damage in a fire.

Linda Ltd had incurred legal fees of £3,600 in connection with the original purchase of the factory, and £6,200 in connection with the disposal.

What is the chargeable gain on the disposal?

A   £20,191

B   £36,391

C   £61,969

D   £158,200

You should use the following indexation factors, where relevant.

October 2001 – February 2015	0.487
March 2003 – February 2015	0.441
May 2005 – February 2015	0.350

3.3   Part disposal

A disposal can be of all or part of an asset. It could for example apply to a disposal of part of a plot of land.

When only part of an asset is sold, we know how much the proceeds are, but we cannot immediately determine what the cost was of that part of the asset.

The allowable cost of the part disposed of is calculated using the following formula:

Allowable cost of the part disposed of = Cost of whole asset $\times \dfrac{A}{A+B}$

Where   A =   gross sale proceeds of part disposed of
(i.e. before deducting selling costs).

          B =   market value of the remaining part
(will be given in assessment).

 Example

John Ltd bought a piece of land in January 1998 for £5,000.

In March 2015 the company sold part of the land for £4,500. At the same time the remaining part was valued at £20,500.

The indexation factor from January 1998 to March 2015 is 0.628.

Calculate the chargeable gain arising on the part disposal of land.

Solution

	£
Sale proceeds	4,500
Less: Allowable cost (£5,000 × $\frac{£4,500}{£4,500 + £20,500}$)	(900)
Unindexed gain	3,600
Less: Indexation allowance (0.628 × £900)	(565)
Chargeable gain	3,035

Activity 4

Smith Ltd

Smith Ltd sold three acres out of a 12 acre plot of land on 14 December 2014 for £15,000. The whole plot had been purchased for £4,500 on 15 June 2010. On 14 December 2014 the unsold acres had an agreed market value of £25,000.

What is the chargeable gain?

You should use an indexation factor of 0.153.

3.4 Non-wasting chattels

In the previous chapter we noted that wasting chattels (i.e. expected life of no more than 50 years) are exempt (e.g. animals, boats, caravans).

Special rules apply to non-wasting chattels (e.g. furniture, works of art, jewellery, antiques).

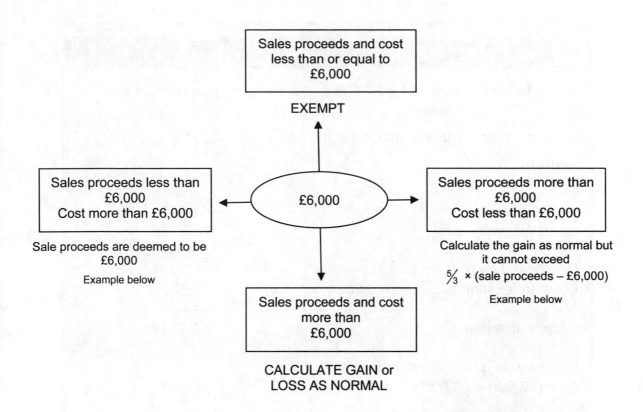

Sales proceeds and cost
less than or equal to
£6,000

EXEMPT

£6,000

Sales proceeds less than
£6,000
Cost more than £6,000

Sale proceeds are deemed to be
£6,000

Example below

Sales proceeds more than
£6,000
Cost less than £6,000

Calculate the gain as normal but
it cannot exceed

$\frac{5}{3}$ × (sale proceeds – £6,000)

Example below

Sales proceeds and cost
more than
£6,000

CALCULATE GAIN or
LOSS AS NORMAL

Example

Harry Ltd sold an antique table for £5,000 in January 2014. It had originally purchased the table in August 2003 for £8,000.

Calculate the chargeable gain or allowable loss on disposal.

Solution

	£
Sale proceeds (deemed)	6,000
Less: Allowable cost	(8,000)
Unindexed loss	(2,000)
Less: Indexation allowance	Nil
(restricted as it cannot increase a loss)	
Allowable loss	(2,000)

Example

Kevin Ltd sold a painting for £6,600 that it originally purchased for £2,000. The indexation factor is 0.800.

Calculate the chargeable gain on disposal.

Solution

	£
Sale proceeds	6,600
Less: Allowable cost	(2,000)
Unindexed gain	4,600
Less: Indexation allowance (0.800 × £2,000)	(1,600)
Chargeable gain	3,000
Chargeable gain cannot exceed: $\frac{5}{3}$ × (£6,600 – £6,000)	1,000

 Activity 5

Chattel disposals

1 ABC Ltd sold a non-wasting chattel for £6,500 realising a gain of £2,000.

What is the chargeable gain?

2 DEF Ltd sold a non-wasting chattel for £4,000. It had originally cost £7,500.

How much of the loss is allowable?

3 GHI Ltd sold a painting for £14,000 in March 2015. The painting had been acquired for £5,000 in November 2006. The indexation factor from November 2006 to March 2015 was 0.291.

Complete the following computation.

£

Proceeds	☐
Less: Cost	☐
	──
	☐
Less: Indexation allowance	☐
	──
Gain	☐
Chargeable gain cannot exceed:	☐
	──
Chargeable gain	☐
	──

4   Summary

There is a pro forma computation for calculation of individual gains and losses.

The gains and losses of the accounting period are netted off to give the net chargeable gains to include in the company's corporation tax computation.

Special rules exist for the treatment of improvement costs, part disposals (using the formula A/A+B), and for chattels.

5 Test your knowledge

 Workbook Activity 6

RBQ Ltd

RBQ Ltd made the following disposals in the year ended 31 March 2015.

(1) On 11 August 2014, it sold a shop for £15,000. The shop was bought in May 2001 for £8,000.

(2) On 16 October 2014, it sold a painting which had been purchased for £30,000 in November 1998. Sale proceeds were £25,000.

(3) On 1 February 2015, it sold a car, a VW Beetle, which was bought in February 1995 for £2,000.

By the time of the sale, it had become a collector's item and RBQ Ltd managed to obtain proceeds of £10,000.

(4) On 3 January 2015, it sold a piece of land for £29,000. It had cost £6,000 in May 1999.

Required:

Calculate the total chargeable gains on the above transactions in the year ended 31 March 2015.

You should use the following indexation factors, where relevant:

February 1995 – February 2015	0.764
November 1998 – October 2014	0.567
May 1999 – January 2015	0.563
May 2001 – August 2014	0.474

Workbook Activity 7

Jackson Ltd

During the year to 30 September 2014, Jackson Ltd had the following capital transactions:

(a) In October 2013 it sold land for £27,000. It bought the land in February 1996 for £14,000.

(b) It also sold a factory unit in December 2013 for £100,000. Out of that the company had to pay legal fees of £1,200. It had originally bought the factory unit in March 1995 for £10,500, extended it in April 1999 for £3,000 and extended it again in June 2002 for £4,600.

(c) In March 2014, Jackson Ltd sold a racehorse for £22,000. It had purchased the horse for £4,000 on 1 December 2007.

Required:

Calculate the chargeable gain on each of the above transactions in the year ended 30 September 2014.

Use the following indexation factors, where relevant:

March 1995 – December 2013	0.718
February 1996 – October 2013	0.669
April 1999 – December 2013	0.534
June 2002 – December 2013	0.438
December 2007 – March 2014	0.208

Workbook Activity 8

Alphabet Ltd

1 Alphabet Ltd sold an antique table for £7,500 realising an indexed gain of £3,000. What will be the chargeable gain?

2 Delta Ltd sold a painting for £3,000. It had originally cost £8,500.

How much of the loss is allowable?

3 Golf Ltd sold an antique desk for £17,000 in January 2015. The desk had been acquired for £4,000 in September 2007. The indexation factor from September 2007 to January 2015 was 0.244.

Complete the following computation.

	£
Proceeds	
Less: Cost	
Less: Indexation allowance	
Gain	
Chargeable gain cannot exceed	
Chargeable gain	

Shares and securities – disposals by companies

Introduction

A company may hold another company's shares as an investment. Special rules apply to the calculation of chargeable gains on the disposal of shares.

KNOWLEDGE

Identify relevant tax authority legislation and guidance. (3.1 K)

Identify methods by which chargeable assets can be disposed of. (6.2 K)

SKILLS

Identify and value any chargeable assets that have been disposed of and calculate the chargeable gain/or allowable loss and relevant reliefs as applicable under current tax law. (2.8 S)

CONTENTS

1 The matching rules
2 Bonus issues and rights issues
3 Approach to assessment questions

1 The matching rules

1.1 Disposal of shares and securities

What distinguishes a share disposal from other asset disposals is the need for matching rules.

Before considering what these matching rules are, it helps to understand why we need them.

1.2 Principle of matching rules

Suppose that a company makes the following purchases of shares in another company, A plc:

1 September 1993	800 shares for	£2,000
3 February 1996	300 shares for	£1,000
1 July 2002	500 shares for	£1,000

On 1 November 2014, 400 of these shares are sold – but which 400?

- It could be the 300 acquired in 1996 and 100 acquired in 1993.

- It could be 400 out of the 500 acquired in 2002.

- It could be based on 400 out of the total 1,600 with costs being averaged.

We need matching rules so that we can establish *which* shares have been sold, and consequently what allowable costs and indexation allowances can be deducted from the sale proceeds.

The matching rules dictate the order in which the shares disposed of are matched with purchases.

1.3 The matching rules for companies

Shares of the same type in the same company (for example Lionel Ltd ordinary shares) are matched as follows:

(1) first, with shares bought on the same day; then

(2) second, with shares bought in the previous nine days (on a first in first out basis);

(3) third, with shares in the 'share pool' (sometimes referred to as the s104 pool or the FA1985 pool).

The 'share pool' is considered in detail below. For companies, shares are pooled together from 10 days after purchase.

It is possible that the matching rules could form part of a task. However, the majority of the time we will just be dealing with the share pool.

Note that the matching rules for individuals are different and are covered in Chapter 21.

 Example

Minnie Ltd has sold 3,000 shares in Mickey plc for £15,000 on 2 February 2015. The shares in Mickey plc were purchased as follows:

Date	Number	Cost
		£
1 July 1995	1,000	2,000
1 September 2005	1,000	2,500
27 January 2015	500	1,200
2 February 2015	1,500	6,000

Explain which shares Minnie Ltd is deemed to have sold.

Solution

Using the matching rules, the 3,000 shares sold are as follows:

	Number
2 February 2015 (same day purchase)	1,500
27 January 2015 (in previous 9 days)	500
	–––––
	2,000

Share pool:
All other shares were purchased more than 9 days ago, therefore must be in the pool.

1 July 1995	1,000	
1 September 2005	1,000	
	–––––	
Total number of shares in pool	2,000	
	–––––	
Out of the pool (1,000 out of 2,000)		1,000
		–––––
Shares disposed of		3,000
		–––––

Note: When dealing with the pool we do not identify which 1,000 shares are sold.

1.4 Calculation of gains on same day and previous 9 day purchases

If a disposal is matched with the first two rules (i.e. matching against a same day purchase or purchases in the previous 9 days), there will be no indexation allowance available.

Hence, the gain is calculated as:

	£
Sale proceeds	X
Less: Allowable cost	(X)
Chargeable gain	X

Example

For Minnie Ltd in the previous example, calculate the gains on the shares purchased:

(1) on the same day; and

(2) in the previous 9 days.

Solution

Step 1: Calculate the gain on the same day purchase (1,500 shares)

3,000 shares are sold for £15,000.

	£
Sale proceeds (1,500/3,000 × £15,000)	7,500
Less: Allowable cost	(6,000)
Chargeable gain	1,500

Step 2: Calculate the gain on the previous 9 days purchase (500 shares)

	£
Sale proceeds (500/3,000 × £15,000)	2,500
Less: Allowable cost	(1,200)
Chargeable gain	1,300

KAPLAN PUBLISHING

1.5 The operation of a share pool

Any purchases from 1 April 1982 are 'pooled' in the 'share pool'.

Purchases before 1 April 1982 are not in the syllabus.

Indexation will apply to the pool from the date of acquisition to the date of disposal.

To enable the correct indexation to be calculated, a separate working is needed to identify the amount available. The working is also used to find the average cost of a partial disposal.

The pool is initially set up with three columns as follows:

	Number	Cost £	Indexed cost £
Purchases (say) June 1989	1,000	2,000	2,000

Then every time there is an 'operative event' (an event involving cash – i.e. a sale or a purchase), two steps must be performed.

Step 1: An indexation update.

In the indexed cost column, add in indexation from the last operative event until this one.

This is calculated by multiplying the balance in the indexed cost column by the increase in the RPI since the last operative event.

Step 2: Deal with the operative event.

– for a purchase add in the new shares. The cost must be added in to both the cost and indexed cost columns.

– for a sale eliminate some shares. The amounts to be deducted from the cost and indexed cost columns are calculated in proportion to the number of shares being removed from the pool.

The following working should be produced:

Pro forma for the share pool

	Number	Cost	Indexed cost
		£	£
Purchase	X	X	X
Index to next event			X
Record next event (e.g. purchase)	X	X	X
	X	X	X
Index to next event			X
	X	X	X
Record next event (e.g. sale)	(X)	(X) (W1)	(X) (W2)
Pool carried forward	X	X	X

Note: For the 'indexed rises' the indexation factor is **not** rounded in practice. This is the only situation where a non-rounded factor is ever used.

However, in the assessment you will always to be given a rounded indexation factor, therefore use the factor given.

Workings:

(W1) Total cost × (number of shares sold / number of shares in pool)

(W2) Total indexed cost × (number of shares sold / number of shares in pool)

The purpose of the share pool working is to find:

- the average pool cost of shares disposed of = working 1 (W1).

- the *indexation* of shares disposed of = (working 2 – working 1).

The gain on the shares is then calculated as normal:

	£
Sale proceeds	X
Less: Cost (W1)	(X)
Unindexed gain	X
Less: Indexation allowance (W2 – W1)	(X)
Chargeable gain	X

The indexation factor is **always** applied to the total on the indexed cost column (**not** cost).

A partial disposal from a share pool uses straight line apportionment of cost and indexation.

In your CBT you will be provided with a grid to enter your calculations (Section 3).

 Example

For Minnie Ltd in the previous example, calculate the gain on the disposal from the share pool.

The indexation factors to use are as follows:

July 1995 – September 2005	0.295
September 2005 – February 2015	0.342

Solution

Step 1: Calculate cost and indexed cost from the share pool.

	Number	Cost	Indexed cost
		£	£
July 1995 purchase	1,000	2,000	2,000
Index to next event			
(July 1995 to September 2005)			
Indexed cost × 0.295			
(£2,000 × 0.295)			590
September 2005 purchase	1,000	2,500	2,500
	2,000	4,500	5,090
Index to next event			
(September 2005 to February 2015)			
(£5,090 × 0.342)			1,741
	2,000	4,500	6,831
February 2015 sale (half)	(1,000)	(2,250)	(3,416)
Pool carried forward	1,000	2,250	3,415

Step 2:   Calculate the gain on share pool shares.

	£
Sale proceeds (1,000/3,000 × £15,000)	5,000
Less: Allowable cost	(2,250)
Unindexed gain	2,750
Less: Indexation allowance	
(£3,416 – £2,250)	(1,166)
Chargeable gain	1,584

Step 3:   Calculate total chargeable gains on the disposal of all 3,000 shares in Minnie Ltd

The total chargeable gains
= (£1,500 + £1,300 + £1,584) = £4,384

 Activity 1

FDC Ltd

FDC Ltd has purchased shares in DCC Ltd. The share pool information of the shares in DCC Ltd is given below.

		Cost £
1 June 1991	4,000 shares for	8,000
30 July 2000	1,800 shares for	9,750

FDC Ltd disposed of 2,000 of its shares in DCC Ltd for £20,571 in March 2015.

The indexation factors to use are as follows:

June 1991 – July 2000	0.269
July 2000 – March 2015	0.523

Required:

Calculate the chargeable gain on the share pool shares.

KAPLAN PUBLISHING

2 Bonus issues and rights issues

2.1 Principle of bonus issues and rights issues

A bonus issue is the distribution of free shares to shareholders based on existing shareholdings.

A rights issue involves shareholders paying for new shares, usually at a rate below market price and in proportions based on existing shareholdings.

Matching

In both cases, therefore, the shareholder is making a new acquisition of shares. However, for *matching* purposes, such acquisitions arise out of the original holdings.

Bonus and rights issues therefore attach to the original shareholdings for the purposes of the identification rules.

 Example

Alma Ltd acquired shares in S plc, a quoted company, as follows:

- 2,000 shares acquired June 1992 for £11,500.

- In October 1993 there was a 1 for 2 bonus issue.

- In December 1999 there was a 1 for 4 rights issue at £3 per share.

Alma Ltd sold 2,600 shares in December 2014 for £30,000.

Calculate the number of shares in the share pool.

Solution

	Number
June 1992 purchase	2,000
October 1993 bonus issue (1 for 2)	
½ × 2,000	1,000
	3,000
December 1999 rights issue (1 for 4)	
¼ × 3,000	750
	3,750
December 2014 sale	(2,600)
Balance in pool c/f	1,150

2.2 Bonus issue

A bonus issue is the issue of free shares (i.e. no cost is involved). As there is no expenditure involved it is not an operative event and therefore no indexation is calculated before recording the event.

Simply add the number of bonus issue shares received to the pool.

When the next event occurs (a sale, purchase or rights issue) index from the operative event prior to the bonus issue.

 Example

For Alma Ltd in the previous example, set up the share pool and deal with events up to and including the bonus issue.

Solution

Share pool	Number	Cost	Indexed cost
		£	£
Purchase June 1992	2,000	11,500	11,500
Bonus issue October 1993			
(1 for 2) ½ × 2,000	1,000	Nil	Nil
	3,000	11,500	11,500

Note: We have NOT indexed the pool before recording the bonus issue (as no cost is involved).

Therefore, next time there is an operative event we will index from June 1992 (the last operative event involving cost).

2.3 Rights issue

A rights issue involves a payment for new shares. Accordingly, it is treated simply as a purchase of shares (usually at a price below the market rate).

Hence, it should be treated in the same way as a purchase in the share pool:

- index up to the rights issue; then
- add in the new shares and cost.

Example

For Alma Ltd in the previous example, you are required to calculate the gain on disposal.

Assume that the indexed rise from June 1992 to December 1999 is 0.201 and from December 1999 to December 2014 is 0.545.

Solution

Share pool	Number	Cost	Indexed cost
		£	£
Purchase June 1992	2,000	11,500	11,500
Bonus issue October 1993 (1 for 2)	1,000	Nil	Nil
	3,000	11,500	11,500
Indexed rise to December 1999 (£11,500 × 0.201)			2,312
	3,000	11,500	13,812
Rights issue (1 for 4) at £3	750	2,250	2,250
	3,750	13,750	16,062
Indexed rise to December 2014 (£16,062 × 0.545)			8,754
	3,750	13,750	24,816
Disposal December 2014	(2,600)		
Allocate costs (2,600 / 3,750) × £13,750 / £24,816		(9,533)	(17,206)
Balance c/f	1,150	4,217	7,610

Computation of gain – share pool

	£
Proceeds	30,000
Less: Cost	(9,533)
Unindexed gain	20,467
Less: Indexation (£17,206 – £9,533)	(7,673)
Chargeable gain	12,794

Note that the indexed cost is updated prior to the rights issue, because there is a purchase which involves additional cost.

Following the disposal there are 1,150 shares in the pool with a cost of £4,217 and an indexed cost of £7,610. This will be used as the starting point when dealing with the next operative event.

In the assessment you may be given details of brought forward amounts, rather than the complete history of the share pool.

 Activity 2

Scarlet Ltd

On 20 September 2014, Scarlet Ltd sold 1,500 ordinary shares in Red plc for £4,725. The company's previous transactions were as follows.

Balance on the share pool at 5 May 2002 is 2,500 shares with a qualifying cost of £3,900 and an indexed cost of £4,385.

Transactions from 5 May 2002 were as follows:

4 April 2003	Took up 1 for 2 bonus issue
19 January 2004	Took up 1 for 3 rights issue at 140p per share

The indexed rise from May 2002 to January 2004 is 0.039 and from January 2004 to September 2014 is 0.405.

Required:

Calculate Scarlet Ltd's chargeable gain on the disposal on 20 September 2014.

---

3 Approach to assessment questions

In the assessment you will normally be asked to calculate a gain on shares. If so, this question will be manually marked. Hence it is important that you enter your answer into the table supplied correctly and show your workings.

In the specimen assessment a four column table is supplied. The first column is for description and narrative whilst the three other columns are for numerical entry.

This should allow you to enter your answer in the same layout as used throughout this chapter although with a little less detail. For example, you do not need to include lines marking totals and subtotals.

 Example

JTD Ltd bought 1,000 shares in VPZ plc for £4.40 each in December 2004.

In July 2013 it received a 1 for 5 rights issue at £4.80 each.

In May 2014 it sold 400 shares for £35,000.

The indexed rise from December 2004 to July 2013 is 0.315 and from July 2013 to May 2014 is 0.024.

What is the chargeable gain? Your answer should clearly show the balance of shares carried forward. Show all workings.

Solution

Pool	Number	Cost (£)	Indexed cost (£)
12.04 Purchase	1,000	4,400	4,400
Index to 7.13			
(£4,400 × 0.315)			1,386
			5,786
7.13 Rights issue			
1,000/5 × £4.80	200	960	960
			6,746
Index to 5.14			
(£6,746 × 0.024)			162
	1,200	5,360	6,908
5.14 Sale			
(400/1,200) ×	(400)		
£5,360 / £6,908		(1,787)	(2,303)
Balance c/f	800	3,573	4,605
		£	
Proceeds		35,000	
Less cost (pool)		(1,787)	
		33,213	
Indexation			
(£2,303 − £1,787)		(516)	
Gain		32,697	

4 Summary

When disposing of shares we apply matching rules to identify which shares have been disposed of.

These rules are needed so that we can deduct the appropriate acquisition costs from the disposal proceeds.

The matching rules for companies generally match disposals with shares held in the share pool.

Bonus and rights issues attach themselves to the original shareholdings.

5 Test your knowledge

 Workbook Activity 3

Share disposals for companies

Read the following statements and state whether they are true or false.

1   The matching rules for a company are as follows:

  – first with same day acquisitions;

  – then with acquisitions within the previous nine days;

  – and finally with the share pool.

2   You must apply an indexed rise when there is a bonus issue.

3   For identification purposes rights issues are treated as separate acquisitions.

4   You must apply an indexed rise when there is a rights issue.

 Workbook Activity 4

Jerry Ltd

Jerry Ltd sold ordinary 25p shares in Blue plc as follows:

	Number of shares	Proceeds
September 1997	2,000	£9,000
March 2015	2,000	£14,500

At 1 July 1993, Jerry Ltd had 4,100 shares in the share pool, with an indexed cost of £10,744 and a cost of £8,200.

Purchases were made as follows:

	Number of shares	Cost
January 1999	200	£450

Required:

Compute the gains arising on all of the above transactions in quoted securities.

Use the following indexation factors as appropriate:

July 1993 – September 1997	0.132
September 1997 – January 1999	0.026
January 1999 – March 2015	0.589

 Workbook Activity 5

Purple Ltd

On 8 August 2014, Purple Ltd sold 5,000 ordinary shares in Indigo plc for £15,000. The company's previous transactions were as follows.

Balance on share pool at 9 June 1996, 3,000 shares with a qualifying cost of £4,000 and an indexed cost of £5,010.

Transactions from 9 June 1996 were as follows:

12 August 2001	Took up 1 for 3 bonus issue
7 May 2006	Took up 1 for 2 rights issue at 150p per share
4 August 2014	500 shares purchased for £1,410

The indexed rise from June 1996 to May 2006 is 0.292 and from May 2006 to August 2014 is 0.299.

Required:

Calculate Purple Ltd's chargeable gain on the disposal on 8 August 2014.

Workbook Activity 6

Chrome Ltd

Chrome Ltd sold all of its ordinary shares in Copper plc for £17,760 on 1 October 2014.

Chrome Ltd acquired its shares in Copper plc as follows:

10 May 2005	Purchased 3,200 shares for £9,600
9 June 2009	Took up 1 for 4 rights issue at 260p per share
20 January 2011	Purchased 2,100 shares for £4,400

Indexation factors were:

May 2005 to June 2009	0.111
June 2009 to January 2011	0.073
January 2011 to October 2014	0.125

Required:

Calculate Chrome Ltd's chargeable gain on the disposal on 1 October 2014.

Gains and losses for individuals

Introduction

An individual (including a sole trader or a partner) pays capital gains tax on his chargeable gains.

This chapter compares and contrasts the rules for capital gains for individuals with those for companies.

KNOWLEDGE

Identify relevant tax authority legislation and guidance. (3.1 K)

Identify capital gains exemptions and reliefs on assets. (6.1 K)

Identify the rate of tax payable on gains on capital assets disposed of by individuals and entitlement to relevant reliefs. (6.3 K)

SKILLS

Identify and value any chargeable assets that have been disposed of, calculate the chargeable gain/or allowable loss and relevant reliefs as applicable under current tax law; and calculate any tax liability. (1.9 S)

CONTENTS

1 Individual v company
   – similarities
2 Individual v company
   – differences

1 Individual v company – similarities

1.1 Calculation of individual gains and losses

The standard pro forma used to calculate a gain or loss on disposal of an asset is essentially the same as for companies except that individuals are not entitled to an indexation allowance.

	£
Gross sale proceeds	X
Less: Selling costs	(X)
	____
Net sale proceeds (NSP)	X
Less: Allowable cost	(X)
	____
Capital gain	X
	____

1.2 Special rules

The special rules discussed in Chapter 18 also apply for individuals, namely:

- Enhancement expenditure
- Part disposals
- Non-wasting chattels.

2 Individual v company – differences

2.1 Capital gains tax

Individuals pay capital gains tax on their taxable gains for the tax year (e.g. 2014/15).

Individuals are entitled to an annual exempt amount for each tax year (£11,000 in 2014/15).

The annual exempt amount is deducted from the total net chargeable gains of the year to give the taxable gains.

	£
Capital gains	X
Less: Capital losses	(X)
Net chargeable gains	X
Less: Annual exempt amount	(11,000)
Taxable gains	X

If an individual has trading losses for the tax year they can claim to set them against their income, but if any loss remains then a claim can be made to treat the trade loss like a capital loss of the year.

Note that this does not work the other way round. Capital losses cannot be offset against income.

Capital gains tax is then calculated on the taxable gains.

2.2 The annual exempt amount and brought forward losses

Brought forward capital losses are not allocated against gains where this would lead to wastage of the annual exempt amount.

The loss relief is restricted to preserve the annual exempt amount.

This rule does not apply to current tax year capital losses, which must be set off against current year gains and cannot be restricted to preserve the annual exempt amount.

The offset of current year losses may therefore result in wastage of the annual exempt amount.

Example

Mica has the following capital gains and losses for the two years ended 5 April 2015.

	2013/14	2014/15
	£	£
Gains	12,500	13,300
Losses	(14,000)	(2,000)

What gains (if any) are chargeable after considering all reliefs and exemptions?

Solution

	2013/14 £	2014/15 £
Current gains	12,500	13,300
Current losses	(12,500)	(2,000)
Brought forward losses*		(300)
	Nil	11,000
Less: Annual exempt amount	Wasted	(11,000)
Taxable gain	Nil	Nil
Loss carried forward		
(£14,000 – £12,500)	1,500	
(£1,500 – £300)		1,200

*Utilised to reduce gains to annual exempt amount.

 Activity 1

Manuel made chargeable gains and allowable losses for 2014/15 as set out below:

> Gain of £60,000
>
> Gain of £12,000
>
> Capital loss of £4,000

Calculate Manuel's taxable gains for 2014/15.

A £57,000

B £61,000

C £68,000

D £72,000

2.3 Calculating the tax payable

Taxable gains are treated as an additional amount of income in order to determine the rates of CGT. However, the gains must not be included in the income tax computation.

Where the taxable gains fall within any remaining basic rate band (after income has been taxed) they are taxed at 18%. For 2014/15 the basic rate band is £31,865.

The balance of the taxable gains is taxed at 28%.

Example

Carl sold three assets in 2014/15 and made two chargeable gains of £9,400 and £21,700 and a capital loss of £2,500.

Carl has capital losses brought forward as at 6 April 2014 of £3,300.

Carl's taxable income for the year, after deducting the personal allowance, is £30,000.

What is Carl's CGT liability for 2014/15?

Solution

	£
Chargeable gains for the year (£9,400 + £21,700)	31,100
Less: Current year capital losses	(2,500)
Net chargeable gains for the year	28,600
Less: Capital losses brought forward	(3,300)
Net chargeable gains	25,300
Less: Annual exempt amount	(11,000)
Taxable gains	14,300
CGT	
£1,865 (£31,865 – £30,000) × 18%	335.70
£12,435 (£14,300 – £1,865) × 28%	3,481.80
Capital gains tax liability	3,817.50

2.4 Connected persons

Where a disposal is between connected persons:

(i)   sale proceeds are deemed to be market value (any real sale proceeds are ignored); and

(ii)   if a loss arises on a disposal to a connected person it can only be offset against a gain made on a disposal to the **same** connected person.

Connected persons are mainly relatives and their spouses/civil partners or relatives of your spouse/civil partner.

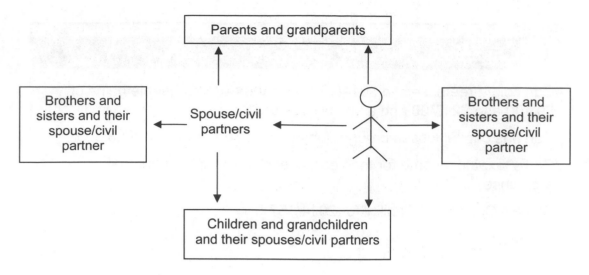

An individual is also connected with a company they control and a partner is connected with their other business partners.

Whilst an individual is connected to their spouse, transactions between spouses are not made at market value but on the basis that no gain or loss arises.

Transfers between civil partners also take place on a no gain/no loss basis.

 Activity 2

Fred sold a painting to his wife on 1 March 2015 for £10,000. The market value of the property at that date was £20,000.

Fred had purchased the painting in June 2005 for £22,000.

A loss arises on the disposal which can only be offset against gains arising on future disposals to his wife.

True or False?

3 Summary

The main differences between calculating gains for individuals and those for companies are:

- Individuals are not entitled to the indexation allowance.

- Individuals are entitled to an annual exempt amount which is deducted from chargeable gains in arriving at taxable gains.

- Individuals pay capital gains tax on the taxable gains arising in a tax year at 18% and 28% depending on the level of their taxable income and gains.

4 Test your knowledge

 Workbook Activity 3

Which of the following transactions carried out by an individual may give rise to a chargeable gain?

Select yes or no for each disposal.

1	Sale of shares	yes / no
2	Sale of a motor car	yes / no
3	Gift of a holiday home	yes / no
4	Sale of an antique (which cost £4,000) for £5,000	yes / no
5	Gift of an antique (which cost £4,000) when it was valued at £15,000.	yes / no

 Workbook Activity 4

Read the following statements and state whether they are true or false.

1 Capital losses are deducted before the annual exempt amount.

2 Excess capital losses can be offset against taxable income.

3 Excess trading losses can be offset against capital gains.

4 Any available capital losses must always be relieved in full.

5 Capital gains are taxed at 40% for higher rate taxpayers.

Workbook Activity 5

1   Mary made a capital loss of £4,000 in 2013/14. In 2014/15 she
     made a chargeable gain of £12,400 and a capital loss of £3,000.

     How much capital loss is carried forward at the end of 2014/15?

     A   £Nil

     B   £4,000

     C   £5,600

     D   £7,000

2   What would your answer be if Mary had only made the chargeable
     gain of £12,400 in 2014/15 and not the capital loss?

     A   £Nil

     B   £1,400

     C   £2,600

     D   £4,000

 Workbook Activity 6

Bert made capital gains of £13,300 and capital losses of £5,000 in
2014/15. He had losses brought forward of £3,000.

What losses will be carried forward to 2015/16?

 Workbook Activity 7

Misha has sold two assets in 2014/15 and made two chargeable gains
of £17,000 and £11,300. Her taxable income for the year, after
deducting the personal allowance, is £20,765.

What is Misha's capital gains tax liability for 2014/15?

Workbook Activity 8

John

John made the following disposals in the tax year 2014/15. John is a higher rate taxpayer for the purposes of income tax.

(1) On 20 June 2014 he sold a holiday cottage for £73,600. The cottage was bought in October 2001 for £29,000.

(2) On 12 August 2014 he sold an investment property. It had been purchased for £30,000 in November 1998. Sale proceeds were £26,000.

(3) On 31 March 2015 he sold 2 acres out of a 10 acre plot of land that he had acquired in June 2007 for £50,000. He sold the 2 acres for £60,000.

In March 2015 the remaining 8 acres were worth £250,000.

Required:

Calculate John's capital gains tax liability for 2014/15.

Shares and securities – disposals by individuals

Introduction

As part of the assessment you may be required to calculate the gain on a disposal of shares by an individual.

As for companies, there are special rules applying to share disposals as it is necessary to determine which particular shares have been sold.

KNOWLEDGE

Identify relevant tax authority legislation and guidance. (3.1 K)

Identify methods by which chargeable assets can be disposed of. (6.2 K)

SKILLS

Identify and value any chargeable assets that have been disposed of; calculate the chargeable gain/or allowable loss and relevant reliefs as applicable under current tax law; and calculate any tax liability. (1.9 S)

CONTENTS

1   The matching rules
2   Same day and next 30 days
3   Share pool
4   Bonus issues and rights issues
5   Approach to assessment questions

1 The matching rules

As for companies, matching rules are required so that, if only some of the shares are sold we know which they are in order to identify their cost.

However, the matching rules for individuals are different to those for companies.

In relation to *individuals,* we match shares disposed of in the following order:

- first, with shares acquired on the same day as the disposal

- second, with shares acquired within the *following* 30 days (using the earliest acquisition first, i.e. on a FIFO basis)

- third, with the share pool (sometimes referred to as the s104 pool or the FA1985 pool).

  This pool of shares brings together the shares bought by the individual since 6 April 1982 to the date before the day of disposal.

Example

Frederic had the following transactions in the shares of DEF plc, a quoted company.

1 June 1992	Bought	4,000 shares for	£8,000
30 July 1999	Bought	1,800 shares for	£9,750
20 May 2007	Bought	1,000 shares for	£8,500
15 March 2015	Sold	3,500 shares for	£36,000
20 March 2015	Bought	400 shares for	£3,900

You are required to match the shares sold with the relevant acquisitions.

Solution

	Number	Number
Shares sold		3,500
(1) Shares acquired on same day		Nil
(2) Shares acquired in following 30 days		(400)
		3,100
(3) Share pool		
1 June 1992	4,000	
30 July 1999	1,800	
20 May 2007	1,000	
	6,800	
The disposal from the pool is therefore 3,100 out of 6,800		(3,100)
		Nil

 Activity 1

Petra sold 200 shares in Red plc on 13 December 2014. She had acquired her shares in the company as follows:

	Number of shares
1 January 2005	650
14 February 2006	250
5 January 2015	50

In accordance with the share matching / identification rules the 200 shares sold by Petra are correctly identified as follows:

A   The 50 shares acquired on 5 January 2015 and then 150 of the remaining 900 shares in the pool.

B   The 50 shares acquired on 5 January 2015 and then 150 of the shares acquired on 14 February 2006

C   200 of the shares acquired on 1 January 2005

D   200 shares in the share pool which includes all 950 shares acquired

Once the correct acquisition is identified, then the computation of the gains can be carried out. This is looked at in detail over the next few sections.

2 Same day and next 30 days

2.1 Calculation of the gain

The calculation of the gain on disposal is straightforward.

	£
Sale proceeds or market value	X
Less: Allowable cost	(X)
Chargeable gain	X

Example

Using the example details above (Frederic) calculate the gain on the sale of the shares acquired in the 30 days following the sale.

Solution

This consists of the sale of 400 shares.

Sale proceeds of £36,000 relates to 3,500 shares so must be apportioned. The proceeds relating to 400 shares will be:

$$\frac{400}{3,500} \times £36,000 = £4,114$$

	£
Sale proceeds	4,114
Less: Cost	(3,900)
Chargeable gain	214

The balance of the proceeds (£36,000 – £4,114) = £31,886 will be applied to shares sold from the share pool.

KAPLAN PUBLISHING

3 Share pool

3.1 Calculation of the pooled cost

The share pool consists of all shares of the same type in the same company purchased since 6 April 1982 (we do not need to consider those purchased before 6 April 1982).

The pool is used to calculate the cost of shares sold by reference to the average cost of all shares purchased.

The pool is set up with two columns; number (of shares) and cost.

Shares purchased are added to the pool and shares sold are deducted.

- For a purchase, add the number of shares acquired to the number column and the cost to the cost column.

- For a sale, deduct the number of shares sold from the number column and an appropriate proportion of the cost from the cost column.

Note that there is no indexed cost column for individuals, as individuals are not entitled to indexation.

Example

Using the example details above (Frederic), calculate the cost to be eliminated from the pool.

Solution

Share pool

		Number	Cost £
1 June 1992	purchase	4,000	8,000
30 July 1999	purchase	1,800	9,750
20 May 2007	purchase	1,000	8,500
		6,800	26,250
15 March 2015	disposal		
£26,250 × (3,100 / 6,800)		(3,100)	(11,967)
Pool balance c/f		3,700	14,283

3.2 Calculation of the gain on the share pool

The gain is calculated as normal:

	£
Sale proceeds	X
Less: Allowable cost	(X)
	___
Chargeable gain	X
	___

☀ Example

Using the details from the example Frederic, what is the gain on the share pool disposals?

Solution

Sale proceeds are £31,886 (from Frederic example above).

	£
Sale proceeds	31,886
Less: Allowable cost (above)	(11,967)
	___
Chargeable gain on share pool shares	19,919
	___

Hence, the total chargeable gain on disposal of the 3,500 shares = (£214 + £19,919) = £20,133

Activity 2

Ken has carried out the following transactions in shares in CYZ plc.

	Number	Cost £
Purchase (8 February 1998)	1,800	3,100
Purchase (12 September 2007)	1,200	4,400
Purchase (10 October 2014)	400	6,000
	Number	Proceeds
Sale (10 October 2014)	2,000	33,000

What is the chargeable gain?

---

4 Bonus issues and rights issues

4.1 Principles of bonus issues and rights issues

A bonus issue is the distribution of free shares to existing shareholders based on existing shareholdings.

The number of shares acquired is added to the number column but there is no cost to add to the cost column.

A rights issue involves shareholders acquiring new shares in proportion to their existing shareholdings. The shares are not free but are usually priced at a rate below the market price.

The number of shares acquired is added to the number column and the cost to the cost column. Accordingly, a rights issue is no different from any other purchase of shares.

 Example

Alma acquired shares in S plc, a quoted company, as follows.

2,000 shares acquired in June 1993 for £11,500.

In October 2003 there was a 1 for 2 bonus issue.

In December 2005 there was a 1 for 4 rights issue at £3 per share.

Alma sold 1,350 shares in November 2014 for £30,000.

What is the chargeable gain?

Solution

	£
Sale proceeds	30,000
Less: Cost (W)	(4,950)
Chargeable gain	25,050

Working: Share pool

	Number	Cost £
June 1993 purchase	2,000	11,500
October 2003 bonus issue (1 for 2) No cost so simply add in new shares	1,000	–
	3,000	11,500
December 2005 rights issue (1 for 4) (£3 × 750)	750	2,250
	3,750	13,750
November 2014 disposal $\dfrac{1,350}{3,750} \times £13,750$	(1,350)	(4,950)
Pool carried forward	2,400	8,800

 Activity 3

Mr Jones

In October 2014 Mr Jones sold 3,000 shares in Smith plc for £36,000.

He had purchased 4,200 shares in June 1991 for £11,600. In August 2005 there was a 1 for 3 rights issue at £5.60 per share.

Required:

Calculate the chargeable gain on disposal.

5 Approach to assessment questions

In the assessment you will normally be asked to calculate a gain on shares. If so, this question will be manually marked. Hence it is important that you enter your answer correctly into the table supplied and show your workings.

In the specimen assessment a four column table is supplied. The first column is for description and narrative whilst the three other columns are for numerical entry.

This should allow you to enter your answer in the same layout as used throughout this chapter although with a little less detail. You will not be able to type in lines to indicate totals and subtotals.

 Example

Jason bought 1,000 shares in VZ plc for £4.20 each in December 2004.

In July 2013 he received a 1 for 5 rights issue at £6.52 each.

On 4 May 2014 he sold 400 shares for £45,000.

On 12 May 2014 he bought 100 shares for £10,000.

What is the chargeable gain? Your answer should clearly show the balance of shares carried forward. Show all workings.

Solution

100 shares (following 30 days)		£	
Proceeds	100/400 × £45,000	11,250	
Cost		(10,000)	
Gain		1,250	
300 shares – pool			
Proceeds	£45,000 – £11,250	33,750	
Less cost (pool)		(1,376)	
Gain		32,374	
Total gain		33,624	

Pool		Number	Cost (£)
12.04 Purchase		1,000	4,200
7.13 Rights issue	1,000/5 × £6.52	200	1,304
		1,200	5,504
5.14 Sale	300/1,200 ×	(300)	
	£5,504		(1,376)
Balance c/f		900	4,128

6 Summary

Share disposals require special matching rules.

Shares sold by individuals are matched with:

- purchases on the same day
- purchases within the following 30 days
- share pool.

Bonus issues increase the number of shares held in the pool.

Rights issues affect both the number of shares held in the pool and the pool cost.

7 Test your knowledge

Workbook Activity 4

Ben bought 1,000 shares in XYZ plc on 1 May 2005 and a further 500 shares on 5 September 2014. He sold 750 shares on 25 August 2014.

Which shares are the shares sold identified with?

A   750 of the shares acquired on 1 May 2005

B   500 of the shares acquired on 1 May 2005 and 250 of the shares acquired on 5 September 2014

C   The 500 shares acquired on 5 September 2014 and 250 of the remaining 1,000 shares in the pool

D   750 of the shares in the share pool which includes 1,500 shares acquired

Workbook Activity 5

Tony bought 15,000 shares in Last Chance Ltd for £6 per share in August 2003. He received a bonus issue of 1 for 15 shares in January 2006.

In November 2014 Tony sold 9,000 shares for £14 per share.

Required:

Calculate the gain made on the sale of the shares and show the balance of shares and their value to carry forward.

All workings must be shown in your calculations.

Workbook Activity 6

Conrad sold all of his 2,145 ordinary shares in Turnip plc on 19 November 2014 for net sale proceeds of £8,580.

His previous dealings in these shares were as follows:

July 2010 purchased 1,750 shares for £2,625

May 2011 purchased 200 shares for £640

June 2012 took up 1 for 10 rights issue at £3.40 per share

Required:

Calculate the gain made on the sale of the shares.

All workings must be shown in your calculations.

 Workbook Activity 7

David bought 2,000 shares in PQR plc for £4,000 on 6 October 2001 and a further 1,000 shares for £3,000 in March 2007.

PQR plc made a rights issue of 1 new share for every 5 held at £4 per share in February 2009. David sold 400 shares in September 2014 for £4,150.

What is the cost of the shares sold?

A   £3,106

B   £1,600

C   £933

D   £1,044

Workbook Activity 8

Irving sold 1,500 ordinary shares in Corniche plc on 9 September 2014 for net sale proceeds of £5,550.

His previous dealings in these shares were as follows:

3 June 2009	purchased 4,800 shares for £15,360
11 April 2013	received a 1 for 4 bonus issue
4 October 2014	purchased 700 shares for £2,450

Required:

Calculate the gain on the sale of the shares on 9 September 2014.

All workings must be shown in your calculations.

Chargeable gains – reliefs

Introduction

The sale of a substantial asset within a business, or the sale of a business, could give rise to a large gain. If all of the gain was subject to tax it would make it difficult for business assets to be sold if the owner could not afford the tax due.

Reliefs exist to reduce the gain in specific circumstances, including when a replacement asset is acquired or when an asset is given away.

KNOWLEDGE

Identify relevant tax authority legislation and guidance. (3.1 K)

Identify capital gains exemptions and reliefs on assets (6.1 K)

Identify the rate of tax payable on gains on capital assets disposed of by individuals and entitlement to relevant reliefs. (6.3 K)

SKILLS

Identify and value any chargeable assets that have been disposed of, calculate the chargeable gain/or allowable loss and relevant reliefs as applicable under current tax law; and calculate any tax liability. (1.9 S)

Identify and value any chargeable assets that have been disposed of and calculate the chargeable gain/or allowable loss and relevant reliefs as applicable under current tax law. (2.8 S)

CONTENTS

1   Entrepreneurs' relief
2   Rollover relief
3   Gift relief

1 Entrepreneurs' relief

Entrepreneurs' relief reduces the capital gains tax payable by an individual on qualifying business disposals; for example where an individual sells all or part of their unincorporated business.

1.1 The relief

The relief operates as follows:

* Gains on 'qualifying business disposals' of up to £10 million are taxed at 10% only.

* Any qualifying gains above the limit are taxed at the normal rates of 18% and 28%.

* The limit is a lifetime limit that is diminished each time a claim for the relief is made.

* In order to maximise tax savings, allowable losses and the annual exempt amount should be deducted from gains on disposals of assets that do not qualify for entrepreneurs' relief wherever possible.

* The amount of qualifying gains that is taxed at 10% must be deducted from the remaining basic rate band when determining the rate of tax to be paid on non-qualifying gains (which will usually be 28%).

The relief must be claimed within 12 months of the 31 January following the end of the tax year in which the disposal is made.

For 2014/15 disposals, the relief must be claimed by 31 January 2017.

The relief is not available to companies.

1.2 Qualifying business disposals

The relief applies to the disposal of:

* the whole or part of a business carried on by the individual either alone or in partnership

* assets of the individual's or partnership's trading business that has **now ceased**

- shares, provided:

  - the shares are in the individual's 'personal trading company', and

  - the individual is an employee of the company (part time or full time).

An individual's 'personal trading company' is one in which the individual:

- owns at least 5% of the ordinary shares

- which carry at least 5% of the voting rights.

Note in particular that:

- the disposal of an individual business asset used for the purposes of a continuing trade does not qualify. There must be a disposal of the whole or part of the trading business; the sale of an asset in isolation does not qualify.

1.3   Qualifying ownership period

The asset(s) being disposed of must have been owned by the individual making the disposal in the 12 months prior to the disposal.

Where the disposal is of an asset of the individual's or partnership's trading business that has now ceased the disposal must also take place within three years of the cessation of trade.

1.4   Applying the relief

When a qualifying disposal is made:

- Calculate the qualifying gains arising on the disposal of the individual assets as normal.

- Add the individual qualifying gains arising on the disposal together.

- Deduct any capital losses and the annual exempt amount from gains that do **not** qualify for the relief.

- Deduct any remaining capital losses and/or annual exempt amount from the gains qualifying for the relief.

- The taxable qualifying gains are taxed at 10%.

- The non-qualifying gains are taxed at 18%/28% depending on the amount of basic rate band (currently £31,865) available.

Example

In July 2014, Katie sold her unincorporated trading business which she set up in 1994. The following gains arose on the disposal of the business:

	£
Factory	275,000
Goodwill	330,000
Warehouse	100,000

In August 2014 Katie also realised a gain of £20,000 on the sale of a painting.

Calculate the capital gains tax payable by Katie in respect of 2014/15

Solution

	Qualifying gains £	Non-qualifying gains £
Business:		
Factory	275,000	
Goodwill	330,000	
Warehouse	100,000	
Painting		20,000
Less: Annual exempt amount		(11,000)
Taxable gains	705,000	9,000
£705,000 × 10%		70,500.00
£9,000 × 28%		2,520.00
Capital gains tax payable		73,020.00

Note: The gain on the painting is taxed at 28% because the gains qualifying for Entrepreneurs' relief are deemed to use up any basic rate band available.

Activity 1

Oliver

In 2014/15 Oliver made a total gain on the disposal of his business assets of £600,000. He also made a gain of £9,300 on the sale of an antique table. Oliver has capital losses brought forward as at 6 April 2014 of £22,000.

How much of the gain on the sale of the business is taxed at 10%?

A £576,300

B £600,000

C £567,000

D £578,000

2 Rollover relief

2.1 Principle of rollover relief

Rollover relief allows a company to defer a chargeable gain, provided certain conditions are met.

This relief is also available for unincorporated businesses (sole traders and partnerships).

This is the only relief in this chapter which is available to both companies and unincorporated businesses.

In order to qualify for relief, the company, sole trader or partnership must reinvest the proceeds from the sale of a qualifying business asset into another qualifying business asset.

Any gain on the disposal of the first asset is then 'rolled over' (i.e. deferred) against the capital gains cost of the new asset.

Unlike Entrepreneurs' relief, which *reduces* the tax paid, rollover relief simply *defers* the gain on the sale of the asset until the later disposal of the replacement asset.

A typical situation can be depicted as follows.

A company sells a building and then buys a new bigger building.

		£
Building (1)	Sale proceeds	100,000
	Less: Cost and indexation allowance	(40,000)
	Indexed gain	60,000
	Less: Rollover relief	(60,000)
	Chargeable gain	Nil
Building (2)	Purchase price	150,000
	Less: 'Rolled over gain'	(60,000)
	Base cost	90,000

The gain on building (1) has been deferred against the base cost of building (2).

Provided that *at least* an amount equal to the proceeds received is reinvested, then *full* deferral applies.

On the sale of the second building, a higher gain will result, as this represents both the gain on the second asset and the deferred gain from the first.

	If no rollover relief claimed on building (1) £		If rollover relief is claimed on building (1) £
Sale of building (2)			
Sale proceeds, say	200,000	Sale proceeds	200,000
Less: Original cost	(150,000)	Less: Base cost	(90,000)
Unindexed gain	50,000	Unindexed gain	110,000

The benefit of rollover relief is that tax which would otherwise be payable now is deferred, possibly for many years.

There is a drawback however in that, for companies, the indexation allowance on the second gain is calculated on a lower base cost if rollover relief is claimed.

2.2 Conditions for relief

Now that we have considered the mechanics, it is necessary to look at the other conditions which apply.

There must be a disposal of and reinvestment in:

- a qualifying business asset,
- within a qualifying time period.

Qualifying business assets

The assets must be used in a *trade.* Where they are only partly used in a trade then only the gain on the trade portion is eligible.

The main qualifying assets are:

- Land and buildings (freehold and leasehold).
- Fixed plant and machinery.
- Goodwill (for unincorporated business only, see below).

The following assets are **not** qualifying assets:

- Shares in a company
- Buildings rented out to tenants.

Note that the replacement asset does not have to be the same type as the asset sold. A company could sell a factory and reinvest in fixed plant and still claim the relief.

Qualifying time period.

The qualifying period for reinvestment in the replacement asset is up to 12 months before the sale to within 36 months after the sale.

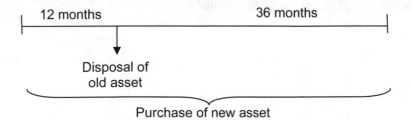

Goodwill

For a company, goodwill acquired on or after 1 April 2002 is not a chargeable asset so cannot be used as a qualifying replacement asset for rollover relief purposes.

However, goodwill is a qualifying asset for unincorporated businesses (sole traders and partnerships).

Claims

A claim for rollover relief must be made within four years from the end of the later of the year of assessment (individuals) or accounting period (companies) in which:

*   the disposal takes place or
*   the replacement asset is purchased.

Therefore, for a sole trader disposal and replacement in 2014/15, the election must be made by 5 April 2019.

For a company disposal and replacement in the year ended 31 December 2014, the election must be made by 31 December 2018.

Note that it is not possible to make a partial claim for rollover relief. If a claim is made then the whole of the eligible gain must be rolled over.

2.3   Partial reinvestment

Rollover relief may still be available even where only part of the proceeds is reinvested. However, it will be restricted, as there is some cash retained which is available to settle tax liabilities. This is logical as the main purpose of the relief is not to charge tax where cash has been reinvested in the business.

The amount which is chargeable now is the lower of:

*   the proceeds not reinvested.
*   the chargeable gain.

This amount cannot be rolled over (i.e. cannot be deferred).

The following example will demonstrate where full relief is available, partial relief is available and no relief is available.

Example

AB Ltd sold an office block for £500,000 in December 2014. The office block had been acquired for £200,000 and was used throughout AB Ltd's ownership for trade purposes. The indexation allowance on the disposal was £213,100. A replacement office block was acquired in February 2015.

Assuming rollover relief is claimed where possible, calculate the gain assessable on AB Ltd and the base cost of the replacement office block if it cost:

(a)   £610,000

(b)   £448,000

(c)   £345,000

Solution

Gain on sale of old office block.

	£
Proceeds	500,000
Less: Cost	(200,000)
Unindexed gain	300,000
Less: Indexation allowance	(213,100)
Chargeable gain before reliefs	86,900

(a)   **New asset cost £610,000**

As all the proceeds have been reinvested, the full gain is rolled over and no gain is immediately chargeable.

	£
Chargeable gain before reliefs	86,900
Less: Rollover relief	(86,900)
Chargeable gain	Nil
Base cost of new asset	
Cost	610,000
Less: Gain rolled over	(86,900)
Base cost	523,100

Note that it is not possible to elect to rollover less than £86,900 i.e. a partial claim cannot be made.

(b) **New asset cost £448,000**

As not all of the proceeds have been reinvested, a gain arises when the old office block is sold as follows:

Gain chargeable now = lower of

(i)	Proceeds not reinvested (£500,000 – £448,000)	£52,000
(ii)	The whole of the chargeable gain	£86,900

	£
Chargeable gain before reliefs	86,900
Less: Rollover relief (£86,900 – £52,000)	(34,900)
Chargeable gain now	52,000

Base cost of new asset	
Cost	448,000
Less: Gain rolled over	(34,900)
Base cost	413,100

(c) **New asset cost £345,00**

As not all of the proceeds have been reinvested, a gain arises immediately

Gain chargeable now = lower of

(i)	Proceeds not reinvested (£500,000 – £345,000)	£155,000
(ii)	The whole of the chargeable gain	£86,900

	£
Chargeable gain before reliefs	86,900
Less: Rollover relief (balance)	(Nil)
Chargeable gain now	86,900

As the proceeds not reinvested exceed the gain, the full gain of £86,900 is chargeable and no rollover relief is available.

Base cost of new asset	£345,000

Activity 2

Karim

Karim purchased a freehold building in September 1993 and sold it for £450,000 in May 2014, generating a chargeable gain before reliefs of £190,000.

The asset qualifies as a business asset. Karim purchased a new building in February 2015 for £415,000.

Assuming a claim for rollover relief is made, what is the chargeable gain on the sale of the building?

A   £190,000

B   £155,000

C   £35,000

D   £14,778

3   Gift relief

3.1   Principle of gift relief

When a gift is made by an individual, the capital gains tax rules require any gain to be calculated as if the disposal had been a sale at full market value.

The legislation allows a claim to defer the gain where the asset is a qualifying 'business asset' as defined for 'gift relief' purposes.

The broad purpose of gift relief is to enable sole traders and shareholders of family companies to pass on their business or shares to the next generation. Note that this relief is not available for gifts by companies.

Gift relief works by 'deducting' the gain (often described as 'holding over' the gain) from the base cost to the donee (i.e. the person receiving the asset).

	Donor		Donee
	£		£
Market value	50,000	Deemed cost	50,000
Less: Cost	(10,000)		
	————		
	40,000		
Less: Gift relief	(40,000)	Less: Held over gain	(40,000)
	————		————
Chargeable gain	Nil	CGT base cost	10,000
	————		————

In effect, the donee 'takes over' the responsibility for the donor's gain until such time as he makes a disposal of the asset.

3.2 Conditions for relief

There are various conditions which must be considered before applying gift relief. We discuss them under the following headings:

- Assets which qualify for the relief
- Administration of the election

Assets which qualify for the relief include the following:

- Assets used in a trade by the donor or by his personal trading company.
- Shares and securities in an unquoted trading company (regardless of how many shares are owned).
- Shares and securities in the donor's personal trading company (quoted or unquoted).

A 'personal company' is one in which the donor holds at least 5% of the voting rights.

Note that relief is therefore only available for quoted company shares if the donor holds at least a 5% interest in the company.

Administration of the election

Gift relief requires a joint election by the donor and the donee.

This must be made within four years of the end of the year of assessment in which the gift takes place. Therefore, for a gift in 2014/15, the election must be made by 5 April 2019.

It is not possible to specify the amount of the gain to holdover in a claim. All the gain qualifying is held over if a claim is made.

Example

Jones, aged 48, gave the factory that he used in his business to his son on 16 June 2014 when it was valued at £600,000. The factory cost him £150,000 on 16 October 2001.

Calculate the chargeable gain arising and show the base cost of the factory for Jones' son, assuming gift relief is claimed.

Solution

Step 1: Calculate the gain on the gift using market value

	£
Proceeds (use market value)	600,000
Less: Cost	(150,000)
	———
Chargeable gain before reliefs	450,000
	———

Step 2: Consider whether the gift relief conditions are satisfied

- Asset used in Jones' trade.
- Factory is a qualifying asset.

Step 3: Hold over the gain against the base cost of the factory

	£
Chargeable gain before reliefs	450,000
Less: Gift relief	(450,000)
	———
Chargeable now	Nil
	———

Base cost of factory for Jones' son.

	£
Market value of factory	600,000
Less: Gain held over	(450,000)
	———
Base cost	150,000
	———

Activity 3

Matt and Ella

Matt gave a business asset to Ella on 1 February 2015. The asset originally cost Matt £21,000. On 1 February 2015 the asset had a market value of £60,000. A joint election for gift relief is made.

Which one of the following statements is correct?

A   Ella's deemed cost is £21,000

B   Ella's deemed cost is £60,000

C   Ella's deemed cost is £39,000

D   Matt has a chargeable gain of £39,000

4   Summary

The reliefs available are as follows:

	For companies	For individuals
Entrepreneurs' relief – first £10 million of gains taxed at 10%	✗	✓
Rollover relief – defer the gain against cost of the new asset	✓	✓
Gift relief – defer the gain by reducing the donee's cost	✓	✓

5 Test your knowledge

 Workbook Activity 4

Entrepreneurs' relief

Which of the following statements is correct?

A   The maximum Entrepreneurs' relief available is £10,000,000 per business disposal

B   Entrepreneurs' relief is not available in respect of a gain on a sale of shares

C   Where a gain qualifies for Entrepreneurs' relief the relief is given automatically

D   Gains qualifying for Entrepreneurs' relief are taxed at 10% even if the vendor is a higher rate taxpayer

 Workbook Activity 5

Leon

Leon is a sole trader and sold a factory in December 2014 which he had used in his business since 2004.

Leon can claim to rollover the gain on the factory against which of the following?

A   The purchase of a commercial property in January 2015 which will be let to tenants

B   The purchase of a shop in December 2014 which will be rented by his sister

C   The purchase of a new factory in May 2014 which will be used in Leon's trade

D   The purchase of a new forklift truck in December 2014 for use in Leon's trade

Workbook Activity 6

Brian

Brian bought a factory for £600,000 in March 2006. In November 2014, it was sold for £900,000. In the same month another factory was bought for £825,000.

The amount of the gain that can be rolled over is:

A   £Nil

B   £75,000

C   £225,000

D   £300,000

 Workbook Activity 7

Spares Ltd

An office building was sold by Spares Ltd on 30 April 2013. Spares Ltd has a year end of 31 December.

The dates during which the proceeds must be reinvested are:

From:

A   30 April 2012

B   30 April 2013

C   31 December 2012

D   31 December 2013

To:

A   30 April 2016

B   30 April 2017

C   31 December 2016

D   31 December 2017

Workbook Activity 8

Gift relief

Which one of the following statements is false?

A   Gift relief is available on the gift of quoted shares or securities in a trading company provided the individual holds at least 5% of the voting rights in the company

B   Gift relief is available on the gift of unquoted shares or securities in a trading company regardless of the number of shares held by the individual

C   Gift relief is only available on the assets of a trade when the trade is disposed of as a whole or after it has ceased

D   Gift relief is available on any assets used in a trade by the donor or by his personal trading company

 Workbook Activity 9

Taylor

Taylor disposed of his freehold factory on 18 July 1993 for £120,000, realising a gain of £30,000.

On 1 December 1993, he invested £115,000 of the proceeds in a warehouse for use in his business.

On 22 December 2014, he sold the warehouse for £320,000.

Required:

Compute the amount of Taylor's taxable gains which would be subject to capital gains tax as a result of the above transactions, showing the years in which they would be assessed.

Assume the annual exempt amount is £11,000 in all years.

Workbook Activity 10

Jonald

On 5 June 2014 Jonald, aged 49, gifted his 80% shareholding in Jonald Limited (with a market value of £5 million) to his son Reg.

The resulting gain for the purposes of capital gains tax was £900,000.

Required:

Assuming gift relief is claimed, compute:

(a)   the amount chargeable on Jonald in 2014/15.

(b)   Reg's base cost in respect of the shares gifted.

 Workbook Activity 11

DRV Ltd (1)

DRV Ltd prepares accounts to 31 March annually.

The company sold the freehold of a factory on 3 March 2015 for £325,000, having previously purchased it as a replacement freehold factory for £190,000 in October 1993.

The factory which it replaced was acquired in May 1989 for £65,000 and sold in December 1993 for £130,000.

Required:

Calculate the chargeable gains, assuming all available reliefs are claimed. The indexation factors are:

May 1989 – December 1993	0.234
October 1993 – March 2015	0.831

Workbook Activity 12

DRV Ltd (2)

DRV Ltd prepares accounts to 31 March annually.

The company sold the freehold of a factory on 3 March 2015 for £325,000, having previously purchased it as a replacement freehold factory for £115,000 in October 1993.

The factory which it replaced was acquired in May 1989 for £65,000 and sold in December 1993 for £130,000.

Required:

Calculate the chargeable gains, assuming all available reliefs are claimed.

The indexation factors are:

May 1989 – December 1993	0.234
October 1993 – March 2015	0.831

 Workbook Activity 13

Columbus

Columbus sold one of his factories on 30 April 2014 for £900,000. The factory had been purchased in September 1989 for £300,000.

In March 2014, Columbus purchased another factory for £700,000 and claimed rollover relief on the gain on the factory sold in April 2014.

Required:

Calculate the chargeable gain on the sale of the first factory, the amount of any rollover relief available and the base cost of the second factory.

Workbook Activity 14

Astute Ltd

Astute Ltd sold a factory on 15 February 2015 for £320,000. The factory was purchased on 24 October 2004 for £164,000, and was extended at a cost of £37,000 during March 2006.

Astute Ltd incurred legal fees of £3,600 in connection with the purchase of the factory, and legal fees of £6,200 in connection with the disposal.

Astute Ltd is considering the following alternative ways of reinvesting the proceeds from the sale of its factory:

(1)   A freehold warehouse can be purchased for £340,000.

(2)   A freehold factory building can be purchased for £300,000.

The reinvestment will take place during May 2015. All of the above buildings have been, or will be, used for business purposes.

Required:

(a)   State the conditions that must be met in order that rollover relief can be claimed.

   You are not expected to list the categories of asset that qualify for rollover relief.

(b)   Before taking account of any available rollover relief, calculate Astute Ltd's chargeable gain in respect of the disposal of the factory.

(c)   Advise Astute Ltd of the rollover relief that will be available in respect of EACH of the two alternative reinvestments.

   Your answer should include details of the base cost of the replacement asset for each alternative.

Indexation factors are as follows:

October 2004 to February 2015	0.374
March 2006 to February 2015	0.329

Workbook Activity 15

Roy and Colin

In September 2014 Roy gave his business premises to his son Colin.

At that time the premises had a market value of £500,000 and had been purchased by Roy in September 1988 for £100,000.

Roy and Colin made a joint claim for any capital gain to be held over.

Required:

Calculate the gain assessable on Roy for 2014/15, before deduction of the annual exempt amount, and the cost which will be available to Colin when computing the gain on a future disposal of the premises.

 Workbook Activity 16

Alan

On 1 August 2014 Alan sold the trade and assets of his business for £13,000,000.

The only assets of the business chargeable to capital gains tax were goodwill and a factory. The goodwill and the factory were acquired in June 2007 for £10,000 and £1,300,000 respectively.

The proceeds received on the sale of the business included £5,500,000 for goodwill and £6,000,000 for the factory.

Alan is a higher rate taxpayer and made no other disposals in 2014/15.

Required:

Calculate the capital gains tax payable by Alan for 2014/15 on the assumption that all beneficial claims are made.

Workbook Activity 17

Herbert

In 2014/15 Herbert, a higher rate taxpayer, made the following disposals:

(1)   On 1 July 2014 he sold his 25% shareholding in Osprey Ltd, a trading company for which he had worked for the last five years. Herbert acquired his shares in the company in May 2010 for £20,000. He sold the shares for £500,000.

(2)   On 1 August 2014 he sold an antique table for £8,000, incurring selling costs of £900. He had acquired the table for £2,000 in May 2007.

(3)   On 1 September 2014 he sold a painting for £20,000. He had acquired the painting for £22,000 in June 2006.

Required:

Calculate the capital gains tax payable by Herbert for 2014/15.

ANSWERS TO CHAPTER
AND WORKBOOK ACTIVITIES

Answers to Chapter and Workbook Activities

2 Principles of corporation tax

 Activity 1

The correct answer is C.

Explanation

The financial accounting period must be split into the first 12 months and then the remaining period.

Imogen Ltd therefore has the following chargeable accounting periods:

    12 months ended 30 April 2015; and

    3 months ended 31 July 2015.

Two corporation tax computations must be prepared.

 Workbook Activity 2

Period of assessment

1	False	Corporation tax is only paid by companies (Ltd or plc).
2	False	Corporation tax computations are prepared for a chargeable accounting period.
3	False	A period of account can exceed 12 months but a chargeable accounting period cannot.
4	True	

Workbook Activity 3

Harris Ltd

The correct answer is B.

Explanation

B is the correct answer because the long period of account is divided into two chargeable accounting periods as follows:

1   the first for the 12 months ended 28 February 2015

2   the second for the remaining 2 months to 30 April 2015

3   Adjusted trading profits

Activity 1

1	Capital	The purchase of a new non-current asset is capital expenditure
2	Revenue	Rates are payable every year and are revenue expenditure
3	Capital	As the asset was purchased in a damaged condition and needed to be repaired before use, it is capital expenditure
4	Capital	Legal fees in relation to a capital purchase are treated as capital expenditure
5	Revenue	Legal fees in relation to the renewal of a short lease are specifically allowed as revenue expenditure

Activity 2

Jamelia Ltd

1   The correct answer is C.

Bakers R Us Ltd

2   The correct answer is A.

Explanation

1   Fines incurred by directors are not deductible.

Parking fines incurred by employees whilst on business activity are generally deductible, but not those incurred by directors.

The other costs are deductible.

2   A is a capital cost, whereas the others are revenue costs, all of which are allowable as trading expenses, given the context.

The cost of plant and machinery will qualify for capital allowances (see Chapter 4).

 Activity 3

Brazil Ltd

Adjusted trading profit for tax purposes for year ended 30 April 2015.

	£	£
Net profits as per accounts	21,088	
Add:		
Legal fees re new lease	325	
National charity donation	25	
Depreciation	3,047	
Less: Bank deposit interest		(5,000)
	24,485	(5,000)
	(5,000)	
Adjusted trading profit	19,485	

Explanation

- Legal fees and payment in connection with unfair dismissal are allowable, as part of the cost of employing staff.

- The donation of £200 to the local charity is allowable as a business expense (small and local). Any donation to a national charity is not allowable.

Activity 4

Cashew Ltd

Adjusted trading profit for tax purposes for year ended 31 March 2015.

	£	£
Net profits as per accounts	23,988	
Add: New shop-front	1,450	
Entertaining customers	326	
Gifts	528	
Depreciation	2,120	
Less: Bank deposit interest		(4,000)
	28,412	(4,000)
	(4,000)	
Adjusted trading profit	24,412	

Explanation

- The £250 initial repainting costs in respect of the new shop are considered to be allowable, following the decision in *Odeon Theatres case.*

- Although the hampers cost less than £50 each, the cost is disallowed as the gift is of food.

- Recoveries of trade debts and movements in provisions for irrecoverable trade debts both relate to the trade and are therefore allowable.

Workbook Activity 5

Katrina Ltd

1   Deductible

2   Not deductible   This is capital expenditure as it is a new lease.

3   Not deductible   Qualifying charitable donations are not deductible in calculating the taxable trading profits.

4   Deductible

5   Not deductible   This is capital expenditure on which capital allowances may be claimed.

 Workbook Activity 6

Adjustment of profits

1   No adjustment required – allowable expense.

2   No adjustment required – allowable expense.

3   Add back – not allowable deduction from trading profits but is deductible from non-trade related interest income.

4   No adjustment required – allowable expense.

5   Add back – gift of drink.

    Note that the gift of any type of drink is not allowable (not just alcohol).

Workbook Activity 7

Tricks Ltd

Adjusted trading profits for the year ended 31 March 2015

	£
Net profit	249,250
Add: Disallowable expenses	5,900
	255,150
Less: Loan note interest receivable	(4,100)
UK dividends	(12,000)
Profit on sale of investment	(2,750)
Adjusted trading profits	236,300

The funds raised by the issue of the loan note were used for the purposes of the trade and the interest paid is therefore an allowable deduction in computing the adjusted trading profits.

Note that this alternative presentation to the two columns shown previously is also acceptable.

Workbook Activity 8

Cricket Limited

Adjusted trading profits for the year ended 31 December 2014

	£
Net profit per accounts	738,101
Add: Legal charges re new office premises	1,000
Loan to former employee written off	200
New furniture	7,600
Depreciation	30,000
Adjusted trading profit	776,901

Workbook Activity 9

Uranus Ltd

1 Running expenses, except for depreciation, are an allowable deduction. The depreciation must be disallowed but relief for capital allowances will be available.

The private use of the car by an employee of a company is irrelevant for profit adjustment purposes.

Therefore, add back £6,000.

2 Disallow all entertaining except staff entertaining.

Therefore, add back £21,000.

3 Part of this lease cost will be disallowed as the car has CO_2 emissions exceeding 130 g/km.

The disallowable portion added back is as follows:
$(15\% \times £6,000) = £900$

 Workbook Activity 10

Saturn Ltd

1 National charity donations are disallowed and treated as qualifying charitable donations. Therefore, add back £616.

2 No adjustment is required.

The write-off of a trade debt is allowable. There will be a credit in the following year's accounts, when the £5,000 is recovered, which will be taxable as part of the trading profit.

3 Trade samples, which are not for resale, are allowable.

4   Capital allowances – plant and machinery

Activity 1

ENT Ltd – Capital allowances computation

		General pool £	Special rate pool £	Total allowances £
Y/e 31 Dec 2014				
TWDV b/f		24,000		
Additions: No AIA:				
Cars:				
15 April 2014			12,600	
16 July 2014		9,200		
17 August 2014		9,400		
Disposals		(3,200)		
		39,400		
WDA @ 18%/8%		(7,092)	(1,008)	8,100
Energy saving plant	2,615			
Less FYA (100%)	(2,615)			2,615
		Nil		
TWDV c/f		32,308	11,592	
Total allowances				10,715
Y/e 31 Dec 2015				
Disposals		(7,900)	(9,400)	
		24,408	2,192	
WDA @ 18%/8%		(4,393)	(175)	4,568
TWDV c/f		20,015	2,017	
Total allowances				4,568

Activity 2

The correct answer is D.

Explanation

A WDA of (£16,000 × 18% × 9/12) = £2,160 is due.

Activity 3

Capital allowances computation

Disposal proceeds	Balancing allowance	Balancing charge	Amount £
Scrapped for no proceeds	✓		2,000
Sold for £500	✓		1,500
Sold for £2,200		✓	200

Workbook Activity 4

Plant and machinery allowances

The correct answer is B.

Explanation

The AIA is not available on any cars.

If the car is a low emission car it is entitled to a 100% first year allowance, but this is a FYA, not the AIA.

The other statements are all true.

Workbook Activity 5

Annual Investment Allowance

The correct answer is B.

Explanation

The other acquisitions will not qualify for AIA because:

A   Buildings are not plant and machinery.

C/D Cars do not attract the AIA regardless of whether they are for business or private use.

 Workbook Activity 6

Banks Ltd

The correct answer is £320.

Explanation

There is no adjustment to capital allowances as a result of private use of assets by employees. The WDA is time apportioned as the period is only three months.

3 months ended 31.3.15	£	Allowances £
Additions – no AIAs		
Car with emissions >130 g/km	16,000	
Less: WDA (8% × 3/12)	(320)	320
TWDV c/f	15,680	

Workbook Activity 7

Faraday Ltd – Capital allowances

		General pool	Special rate pool	Allowances
Year ended 31.3.15	£	£	£	£
TWDV b/f		398,100	28,060	
Additions – no AIA				
Car			48,150	
Additions – AIA				
Machinery	493,345			
Office furniture	33,610			
	———			
	526,955			
Less AIA	(500,000)			500,000
	———			
Balance of AIA exp.		26,955		
Disposal		(16,875)	(23,100)	
		———	———	
		408,180	53,110	
WDA (18%)/(8%)		(73,472)	(4,249)	77,721
Additions – FYA				
Energy saving plant	20,850			
FYA (100%)	(20,850)			20,850
	———	Nil		
		———	———	
TWDV c/f		334,708	48,861	
		———	———	
Total allowances				598,571
				———

Workbook Activity 8

Deni Ltd

Capital allowances

	£	General pool £	Allowances £
Year ended 30.9.14			
TWDV b/f		25,000	
Addition not qualifying for AIA			
Car		19,600	
Additions qualifying for AIA			
Machinery (£376,250 + £10,000)	386,250		
Less AIA (note)	(375,000)		375,000
		11,250	
Disposal		(1,750)	
		54,100	
WDA (18% × £54,100)		(9,738)	9,738
TWDV c/f		44,362	
Total allowances			384,738

Note: The maximum AIA for the year ended 30 September 2014 is £375,000 ((£250,000 × 6/12) + (£500,000 × 6/12)).

Workbook Activity 9

TEN Ltd

Capital allowances

		General pool	Allowances
Year ending 31 December 2014		£	£
TWDV b/f		16,000	
Additions not qualifying for AIA			
15 April 2014		15,000	
Disposals			
30 April 2014 (restrict to cost)		(1,600)	
		29,400	
WDA (£29,400 × 18%)		(5,292)	5,292
Additions qualifying for FYA			
Cars (2 × £9,300)	18,600		
FYA at 100%	(18,600)		18,600
		Nil	
TWDV c/f		24,108	
Total allowances			23,892
Year ending 31 December 2015			
Disposals (£7,600 + £8,000)		(15,600)	
		8,508	
WDA (18% × £8,508)		(1,531)	1,531
TWDV c/f		6,977	
Total allowances			1,531

Workbook Activity 10

Booker Ltd

Capital allowances computation

		General pool	Allowances
	£	£	£
9 months to 31.12.14			
TWDV b/f		18,150	
Additions			
Not qualifying for AIA or FYA			
Car		5,750	
Qualifying for AIA			
Plant and machinery	378,750		
Less AIA (max 9/12 × £500,000)	(375,000)		375,000
Balance of AIA qualifying expenditure		3,750	
Disposal		(4,900)	
		22,750	
WDA (18% × 9/12)		(3,071)	3,071
TWDV c/f		19,679	
Total allowances			378,071

5 Calculation of taxable total profits

 Activity 1

ABC Ltd

The correct answer is C.

Explanation

The interest received will be included in the net profit per the accounts. It therefore needs to be deducted in the adjusted trading profit computation. It is then included as non-trade interest income in the calculation of taxable total profits.

 Activity 2

GHI Ltd

1   £35,000

2   £Nil

Explanation

1   GHI Ltd would include chargeable gains of (£60,000 – £25,000) = £35,000 in taxable total profits.

2   No chargeable gains would be included in taxable total profits as the losses exceed gains by = £15,000 (£75,000 – £60,000). The excess loss will be carried forward and deducted from the next gains.

Activity 3

Laserjet Ltd (1)

Corporation tax computation – year ended 31 March 2015

	£
Trading profit (W1)	484,600
Non-trade interest (W2)	22,000
Property income	32,000
	538,600
Less: Qualifying charitable donations	(14,000)
Taxable total profits	524,600

Workings:

(W1) Trading profit

	£
Adjusted trading profit	500,600
Less: Capital allowances	(16,000)
Trading profit	484,600

Take care not to adjust a profit which has already been adjusted.

(W2) Non-trade interest

	£
Building society interest receivable	20,000
Loan note interest receivable	6,000
	26,000
Less: Loan interest payable – rental property (note)	(4,000)
Non-trade interest	22,000

Note: This interest is not an allowable deduction from property income but has to be dealt with as a 'non-trading' loan and is deductible from non-trade interest income.

Activity 4

Laserjet Ltd (2)

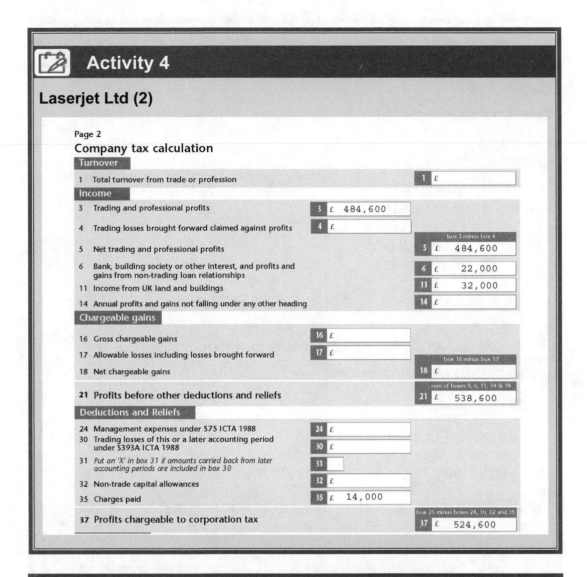

Page 2

Company tax calculation

Turnover

1	Total turnover from trade or profession		**1** £	

Income

3	Trading and professional profits	**3** £ 484,600		
4	Trading losses brought forward claimed against profits	**4** £		
			box 3 minus box 4	
5	Net trading and professional profits		**5** £ 484,600	
6	Bank, building society or other interest, and profits and gains from non-trading loan relationships		**6** £ 22,000	
11	Income from UK land and buildings		**11** £ 32,000	
14	Annual profits and gains not falling under any other heading		**14** £	

Chargeable gains

16	Gross chargeable gains	**16** £		
17	Allowable losses including losses brought forward	**17** £		
			box 16 minus box 17	
18	Net chargeable gains		**18** £	
			sum of boxes 5, 6, 11, 14 & 18	
21	Profits before other deductions and reliefs		**21** £ 538,600	

Deductions and Reliefs

24	Management expenses under S75 ICTA 1988	**24** £		
30	Trading losses of this or a later accounting period under S393A ICTA 1988	**30** £		
31	Put an 'X' in box 31 if amounts carried back from later accounting periods are included in box 30	**31**		
32	Non-trade capital allowances	**32** £		
35	Charges paid	**35** £ 14,000		
			box 21 minus boxes 24, 30, 32 and 35	
37	Profits chargeable to corporation tax		**37** £ 524,600	

 Workbook Activity 5

DEF Ltd

The correct answer is D.

Explanation

Dividends from another company are not included in taxable total profits.

Workbook Activity 6

Ballard Ltd

The correct answer is A.

Explanation

	£
Adjusted trading profits	56,000
Less: Capital allowances (W)	(18,320)
Tax adjusted trading profits	37,680
Bank interest receivable	3,000
Taxable total profits	40,680

Note: UK dividends are not chargeable to corporation tax

Working: Capital allowances

	£	Pool £	Allowances £
TWDV b/f		24,000	
Addition with AIA	14,000		
Less AIA (100%)	(14,000)		14,000
		Nil	
WDA (18% × £24,000)		(4,320)	4,320
TWDV c/f		19,680	
Total allowances			18,320

Workbook Activity 7

Pitch Ltd (1)

Taxable total profits – year ended 31 March 2015

	£
Trading profit (W)	742,113
Property income	3,500
Non-trade interest	2,400
	748,013
Less: Qualifying charitable donations	(1,000)
Taxable total profits	747,013

Working: Trading profit

	£
Adjusted trading profit	766,801
Less: Capital allowances	(24,688)
Trading profit	742,113

Workbook Activity 8

Pitch Ltd (2)

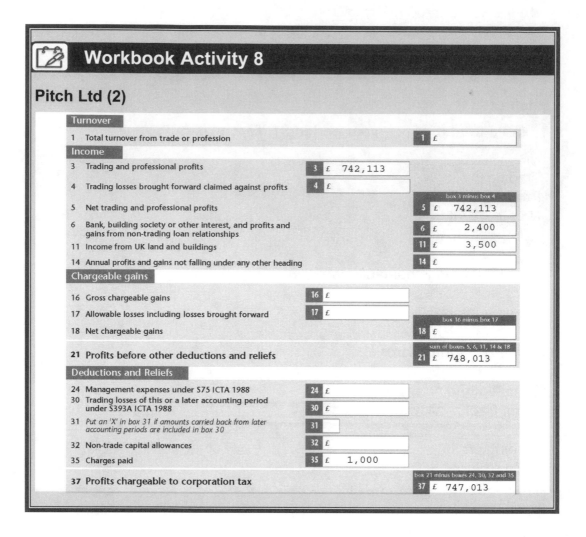

Turnover

1	Total turnover from trade or profession	**1**	£

Income

3	Trading and professional profits	**3**	£ 742,113
4	Trading losses brought forward claimed against profits	**4**	£
5	Net trading and professional profits	**5**	£ 742,113 *(box 3 minus box 4)*
6	Bank, building society or other interest, and profits and gains from non-trading loan relationships	**6**	£ 2,400
11	Income from UK land and buildings	**11**	£ 3,500
14	Annual profits and gains not falling under any other heading	**14**	£

Chargeable gains

16	Gross chargeable gains	**16**	£
17	Allowable losses including losses brought forward	**17**	£
18	Net chargeable gains	**18**	£ *(box 16 minus box 17)*
21	**Profits before other deductions and reliefs**	**21**	£ 748,013 *(sum of boxes 5, 6, 11, 14 & 18)*

Deductions and Reliefs

24	Management expenses under S75 ICTA 1988	**24**	£
30	Trading losses of this or a later accounting period under S393A ICTA 1988	**30**	£
31	*Put an 'X' in box 31 if amounts carried back from later accounting periods are included in box 30*	**31**	
32	Non-trade capital allowances	**32**	£
35	Charges paid	**35**	£ 1,000
37	**Profits chargeable to corporation tax**	**37**	£ 747,013 *(box 21 minus boxes 24, 30, 32 and 35)*

6 Calculation of corporation tax liability

Activity 1

Walton Ltd (1)

Corporation tax computation – year ended 31 March 2015

	£
Trading profit (W1 and W2)	365,724
Non-trade interest	2,900
Chargeable gains	1,538
Taxable total profits	370,162
Corporation tax liability (W3)	75,054.06

Workings :

(W1) Trading profit

	£
Adjusted trading profit (W2)	370,524
Less: Capital allowances	(4,800)
Trading profit	365,724

(W2) Adjustment of trading profit

	£
Net profit	383,499
Add: Disallowable expenses	6,344
Less: Bank interest receivable	(2,900)
UK dividends (net)	(13,365)
Profit on sale of investment	(3,054)
Adjusted trading profit	370,524

(W3) Corporation tax liability

	£
Taxable total profits (N)	370,162
Plus FII (£13,365 × $^{100}/_{90}$)	14,850
Augmented profits (A)	385,012

FY2014 applies to the year ended 31 March 2015.

'A' is above the lower limit of £300,000; marginal relief applies.

	£
£370,162 × 21%	77,734.02
Less: Marginal relief	
$^{1}/_{400}$ × (£1,500,000 − £385,012) × $\dfrac{£370,162}{£385,012}$	(2,679.96)
Corporation tax liability	75,054.06

Activity 2

Walton Ltd (2)

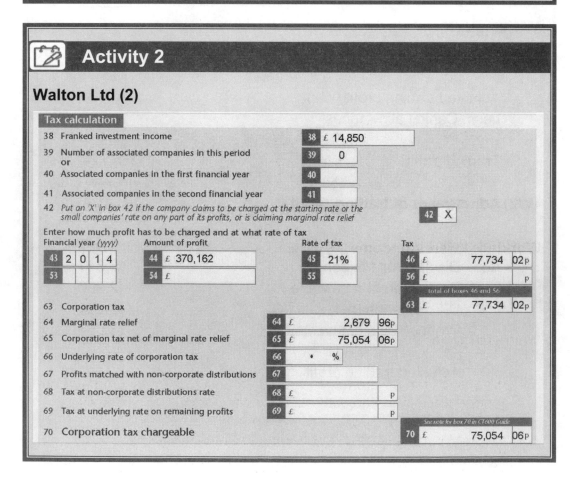

Tax calculation

38	Franked investment income	38	£ 14,850
39	Number of associated companies in this period or	39	0
40	Associated companies in the first financial year	40	
41	Associated companies in the second financial year	41	

42 Put an 'X' in box 42 if the company claims to be charged at the starting rate or the small companies' rate on any part of its profits, or is claiming marginal rate relief   42 X

Enter how much profit has to be charged and at what rate of tax

Financial year (yyyy)	Amount of profit	Rate of tax	Tax
43 2 0 1 4	44 £ 370,162	45 21%	46 £ 77,734 02p
53	54 £	55	56 £ p
			total of boxes 46 and 56

63	Corporation tax	63	£	77,734	02p
64	Marginal rate relief	64	£	2,679	96p
65	Corporation tax net of marginal rate relief	65	£	75,054	06p
66	Underlying rate of corporation tax	66	• %		
67	Profits matched with non-corporate distributions	67			
68	Tax at non-corporate distributions rate	68	£		p
69	Tax at underlying rate on remaining profits	69	£		p
70	Corporation tax chargeable	70	£	75,054	06p

See note for box 70 in CT600 Guide

Workbook Activity 3

G Ltd

Corporation tax computation – year ended 31 March 2015

	£
Trading profit	677,500
Interest income (W)	24,200
Total profits	701,700
Less Qualifying charitable donation	(1,800)
Taxable total profits	699,900

Corporation tax liability

	£
Taxable total profits (N)	699,900
Plus FII (£36,000 × $\frac{100}{90}$)	40,000
Augmented profits (A)	739,900

The FY2014 applies to the year ended 31 March 2015.

'A' is above the lower limit of £300,000 but below the upper limit of £1,500,000; therefore marginal relief applies.

	£
£699,900 × 21%	146,979.00
Less: Marginal relief	
$\frac{1}{400}$ × (£1,500,000 – £739,900) × $\frac{£699,900}{£739,900}$	(1,797.52)
Corporation tax liability	145,181.48

Working: Interest income	£
Bank interest	2,800
Loan interest	22,000
Less: Customer loan written off	(600)
Interest income	24,200

Note: Loans written off are not allowable against trading income and are added back in the adjustment of profits computation. However, they are allowable against interest income as an allowable deduction relating to a non-trading loan relationship.

Workbook Activity 4

Osmond Ltd

Corporation tax computation – year ended 31 March 2015

	£
Trading profit	510,000
Non-trade interest	8,000
Chargeable gains	7,500
Taxable total profits	525,500
Corporation tax liability (W)	108,056.24

Working: Corporation tax liability

	£
Taxable total profits (N)	525,500
Plus FII (£18,000 × $\frac{100}{90}$)	20,000
Augmented profits (A)	545,500

The FY2014 applies to the year ended 31 March 2015.

'A' is above the lower limit of £300,000 but below the upper limit of £1,500,000; therefore marginal relief applies.

	£
£525,500 × 21%	110,355.00
Less Marginal relief	
$\frac{1}{400} \times (£1,500,000 - £545,500) \times \frac{£525,500}{£545,500}$	(2,298.76)
Corporation tax liability	108,056.24

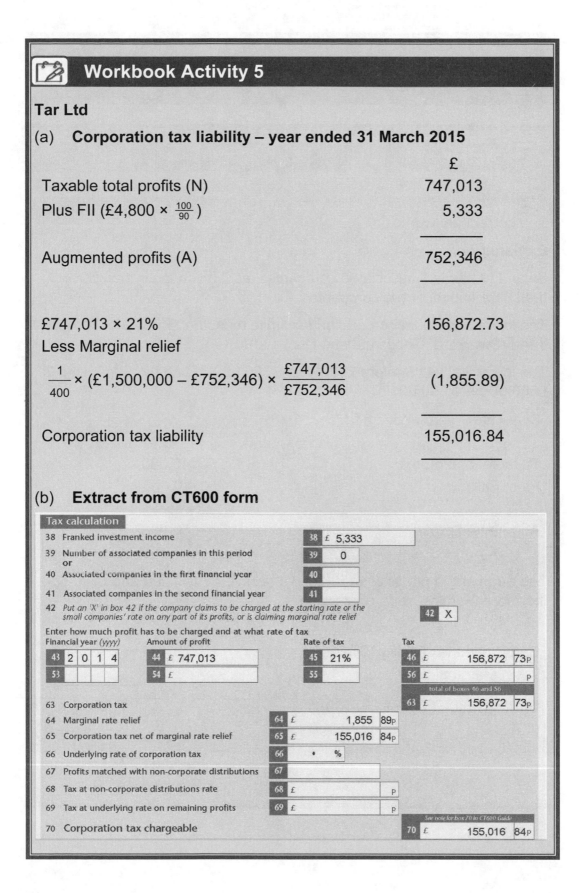

Workbook Activity 5

Tar Ltd

(a)   **Corporation tax liability – year ended 31 March 2015**

	£
Taxable total profits (N)	747,013
Plus FII (£4,800 × $\frac{100}{90}$)	5,333
Augmented profits (A)	752,346
£747,013 × 21%	156,872.73
Less Marginal relief	
$\frac{1}{400}$ × (£1,500,000 – £752,346) × $\frac{£747,013}{£752,346}$	(1,855.89)
Corporation tax liability	155,016.84

(b)   **Extract from CT600 form**

Tax calculation

38	Franked investment income	38	£ 5,333
39	Number of associated companies in this period or	39	0
40	Associated companies in the first financial year	40	
41	Associated companies in the second financial year	41	

42 *Put an 'X' in box 42 if the company claims to be charged at the starting rate or the small companies' rate on any part of its profits, or is claiming marginal rate relief*   42 **X**

Enter how much profit has to be charged and at what rate of tax

Financial year *(yyyy)*	Amount of profit	Rate of tax	Tax
43 2 0 1 4	44 £ 747,013	45 21%	46 £ 156,872 73p
53	54 £	55	56 £ p
			total of boxes 46 and 56

63	Corporation tax	63	£ 156,872 73p
64	Marginal rate relief	64	£ 1,855 89p
65	Corporation tax net of marginal rate relief	65	£ 155,016 84p
66	Underlying rate of corporation tax	66	• %
67	Profits matched with non-corporate distributions	67	
68	Tax at non-corporate distributions rate	68	£ p
69	Tax at underlying rate on remaining profits	69	£ p
			See note for box 70 in CT600 Guide
70	Corporation tax chargeable	70	£ 155,016 84p

7 Corporation tax – special scenarios

 Activity 1

Swan Ltd

The correct answer is C.

Explanation

Swan Ltd has two associated companies, as it owns more than 50% of the share capital of two companies.

The lower and upper corporation tax limits must therefore be divided by three (Swan Ltd, Goose Ltd and Duck Ltd).

The lower limit is therefore £100,000 (£300,000/3) and the upper limit is £500,000 (£1,500,000/3).

Swan Ltd – year ended 31 March 2015

	£
Taxable total profits	140,000
Plus: FII	10,000
Augmented profits	150,000

The augmented profits of £150,000 lie between £100,000 and £500,000, therefore marginal relief applies

	£
Corporation tax liability (£140,000 × 21%)	29,400.00
Less: Marginal relief	
$1/400 \times (£500,000 - £150,000) \times \dfrac{£140,000}{£150,000}$	(816.67)
	28,583.33

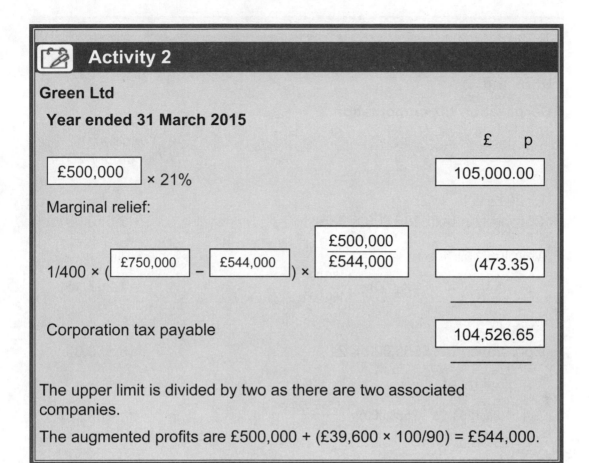

Activity 2

Green Ltd

Year ended 31 March 2015

	£	p
£500,000 × 21%		105,000.00

Marginal relief:

$1/400 \times (£750,000 - £544,000) \times \dfrac{£500,000}{£544,000}$ (473.35)

| Corporation tax payable | | 104,526.65 |

The upper limit is divided by two as there are two associated companies.

The augmented profits are £500,000 + (£39,600 × 100/90) = £544,000.

Activity 3

Rhos Ltd

Corporation tax computation

	Year ended 31 December 2014 £
FY2013 (W1, W2) Corporation tax £185,000 × 23%	42,550.00
Marginal relief:	
$\frac{3}{400} \times (£375,000 - £196,000) \times \frac{£185,000}{£196,000}$	(1,267.16)
FY2014 Corporation tax £555,000 × 21%	116,550.00
Marginal relief:	
$\frac{1}{400} \times (£1,125,000 - £588,000) \times \frac{£555,000}{£588,000}$	(1,267.16)
Corporation tax liability	156,565.68

Workings:

(W1) **Augmented profits**	£
Taxable total profits	740,000
Plus FII (£39,600 × 100/90)	44,000
Augmented profits	784,000
Marginal relief applies	

(W2) **Apportioned profits**

	FY2013 3/12 £	FY2014 9/12 £
Taxable total profits (3/12:9/12)	185,000	555,000
Augmented profits (3/12:9/12)	196,000	588,000
Apportioned upper limit (3/12:9/12)	375,000	1,125,000
Apportioned lower limit (3/12:9/12)	75,000	225,000

Activity 4

Chinny Ltd

Corporation tax computations

	Year ended 30 September 2014 £	3 months to 31 December 2014 £
Trading profit (W1)	186,550	44,182
Non-trade interest	4,420	780
Property income (W2)	8,000	2,000
Chargeable gains	–	55,000
Taxable total profits	198,970	101,962
CT liability (W3)	39,794.00	20,729.42

Workings:

(W1) Trading profit

	Year ended 30 September 2014 £	3 months to 31 December 2014 £
Adjusted trading profits (12/15:3/15)	200,000	50,000
Less: Capital allowances	(13,450)	(5,818)
Trading profit	186,550	44,182

(W2) Property income

Rent receivable for 15 months:

(£8,000 – £3,000 + £5,000) = £10,000

	Year ended 30 September 2014 £	3 months to 31 December 2014 £
Time apportioned	8,000	2,000

(W3) Corporation tax liabilities

	Year ended 30 September 2014 £	3 months to 31 December 2014 £
Taxable total profits and 'A' (as there are no dividends)	£198,970	£101,962
Financial years	FY2013 FY2014	FY2014 3 months
Lower limit: Annual	£300,000	
Three months ($£300,000 \times {}^3\!/_{12}$)		£75,000
Upper limit: Annual	£1,500,000	
Three months ($£1,500,000 \times {}^3\!/_{12}$)		£375,000
Decision	Small profits rate 20% 20%	Marginal relief applies

Calculate liabilities

	Year ended 30 September 2014 £	3 months to 31 December 2014 £
Taxable total profits	198,970	101,962
FY2013 and 2014 £198,970 × 20%	39,794.00	
FY2014 £101,962 × 21%		21,412.02
Less: Marginal relief $\frac{1}{400} \times (£375,000 - £101,962)$		(682.60)
Corporation tax liability	39,794.00	20,729.42

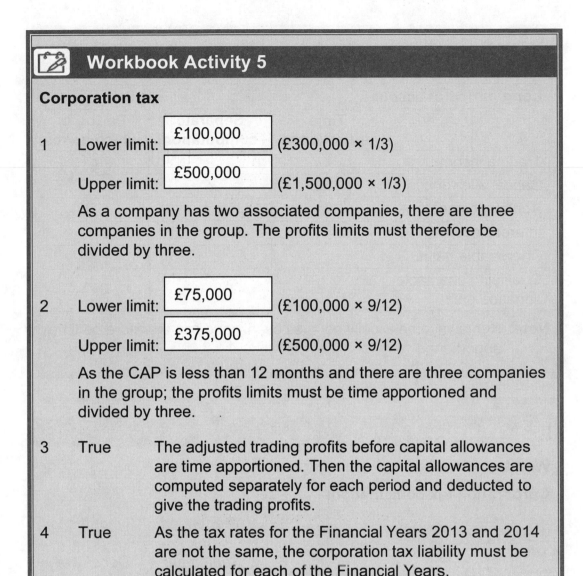

Workbook Activity 5

Corporation tax

1   Lower limit: £100,000 (£300,000 × 1/3)

    Upper limit: £500,000 (£1,500,000 × 1/3)

    As a company has two associated companies, there are three companies in the group. The profits limits must therefore be divided by three.

2   Lower limit: £75,000 (£100,000 × 9/12)

    Upper limit: £375,000 (£500,000 × 9/12)

    As the CAP is less than 12 months and there are three companies in the group; the profits limits must be time apportioned and divided by three.

3   True   The adjusted trading profits before capital allowances are time apportioned. Then the capital allowances are computed separately for each period and deducted to give the trading profits.

4   True   As the tax rates for the Financial Years 2013 and 2014 are not the same, the corporation tax liability must be calculated for each of the Financial Years.

Workbook Activity 6

Long period of account

	Time apportioned	Separate computation	Period in which arises
Trading income	✓		
Capital allowances		✓	
Rental income	✓		
Interest income			✓
Chargeable gains			✓
Qualifying charitable donation paid			✓

Note: Rental income usually accrues evenly and can therefore be time apportioned.

 Workbook Activity 7

Wolf Ltd

Corporation tax computations

	Year ended 30 September 2014 £	3 months to 31 December 2014 £
Trading profit (W1)	223,000	52,000
Property income (W2)	16,000	4,000
Chargeable gains		25,000
	———	———
Taxable total profits	239,000	81,000
	———	———
Corporation tax liability (W3)	47,800.00	16,275.00

Workings:

(W1) Trading profit

	Year ended 30 September 2014 £	3 months to 31 December 2014 £
Adjusted profits (12/15 : 3/15)	240,000	60,000
Less Capital allowances	(17,000)	(8,000)
Trading profit	223,000	52,000

(W2) Property income

	Year ended 30 September 2014 £	3 months to 31 December 2014 £
Rent receivable (12/15 : 3/15)	16,000	4,000

(W3) Corporation tax liabilities

	Year ended 30 September 2014	3 months to 31 December 2014
Taxable total profits and augmented profits (as there are no dividends)	£239,000	£81,000

	FY 2013	FY 2014	FY 2014
Lower limit			
Full limit	£300,000		
Three months (£300,000 × $\frac{3}{12}$)			£75,000
Upper limit			
Full limit	£1,500,000		
Three months (£1,500,000 × $\frac{3}{12}$)			£375,000

Corporation tax liabilities

	£ p	£ p
FY2013 and 2014		
£239,000 × 20%	47,800.00	
FY2014		
(£81,000 × 21%)		17,010.00
Less $\frac{1}{400}$ × (£375,000 – £81,000)		(735.00)
	47,800.00	16,275.00

📝 Workbook Activity 8

Unbelievable Upshots Ltd

(a) **Capital allowances computation – 9 m/e 28 February 2015**

	£	General pool £	Special rate pool £	Total allowances £
TWDV b/f		102,000	7,000	
Additions:				
Qualifying for AIA	396,250			
Less AIA				
(max. £500,000 × 9/12)	(375,000)			375,000
		21,250		
		123,250		
WDA				
(18% × 9/12)/		(16,639)		16,639
(8% × 9/12)/			(420)	420
TWDV c/f		106,611	6,580	
Total allowances				392,059

(b) **Taxable total profits – 9 m/e 28 February 2015**

	£
Adjusted trading profit	643,675
Capital allowances:	
Plant and machinery (Part (a))	(392,059)
Trading profit	251,616
Non-trading interest	13,000
Chargeable gain	30,000
Taxable total profits	294,616

(c) **Corporation tax payable – 9 m/e 28 February 2015**

	£
Taxable total profits (N)	294,616
Plus: FII (£45,000 × $\frac{100}{90}$)	50,000
Augmented profits (A)	344,616

Small profits rate limits (see note)

lower limit (£300,000 × $\frac{9}{12}$ × $\frac{1}{2}$)	£112,500
upper limit (£1,500,000 × $\frac{9}{12}$ × $\frac{1}{2}$)	£562,500

Note: The limits are adjusted due to the 9 month accounting period, and the company has one associated company.

'A' falls in between the limits, therefore marginal relief applies.

	£
FY2014 (£294,616 × 21%)	61,869.36
Less: Marginal relief	
$\frac{1}{400}$ × (£562,500 − £344,616) × $\frac{£294,616}{£344,616}$	(465.68)
	————
Corporation tax payable	61,403.68
	————

Workbook Activity 9

Unpredictably Uptown Limited
Corporation tax payable – period 30 September 2015

	12 months to 31.03.15 £	6 months to 30.09.15 £
Trading profit (W1)	660,000	330,000
Non-trade interest	9,000	3,500
	————	————
	669,000	333,500
Less Qualifying charitable donation	(20,000)	–
	————	————
Taxable total profits	649,000	333,500
Add: FII (£17,500 × $\frac{100}{90}$)	19,444	–
	————	————
Augmented profits	668,444	333,500
	————	————
Corporation tax liability (W2)	134,271.58	68,993.75
	————	————

Workings:

(1) Trading profit

			£
Apportioned	12 months to 31.03.15	¹²⁄₁₈ × £990,000	660,000
	6 months to 30.09.15	⁶⁄₁₈ × £990,000	330,000
			990,000

(2) Corporation tax liability

		Year to 31.03.15 £	6 months to 30.09.15 £
FY2014			
Lower limit	Annual / 6 months	300,000	150,000
Upper limit	Annual / 6 months	1,500,000	750,000
Decision		21% less MR	21% less MR
		£	£
(£649,000 / £333,500 × 21%)		136,290.00	70,035.00
Less Marginal relief			
1/400 × (£1,500,000 − £668,444) × £649,000/£668,444		(2,018.42)	
1/400 × (£750,000 − £333,500)			(1,041.25)
Corporation tax liability		134,271.58	68,993.75

8 Relief for company losses

 Activity 1

Banks Ltd

The correct answer is D.

Explanation

D is the correct answer. When you are asked to use the loss 'as early as possible' it means the loss is set off against profits before qualifying charitable donations in the current year and then profits before qualifying charitable donations in the preceding 12 months.

A current year claim must be made before a carry back claim, as follows:

	£
Trading loss	120,000
Less: Utilised – Current year offset	(3,000)
– Carry back claim	(52,000)
Available to carry forward	65,000

Activity 2

Coriander Ltd – Corporation tax computations

Year ended 31 December	2012 £	2013 £	2014 £
Trading profit	37,450	Nil	20,000
Less: Loss relief b/f			(20,000)[3]
			Nil
Non-trade interest	1,300	1,400	1,600
Chargeable gains (£12,000 – £5,000 b/f)	Nil		7,000
	38,750	1,400	8,600
Less: Loss relief			
– Current year		(1,400)[1]	
– Carry back	(38,750)[2]		
	Nil	Nil	8,600
Less: QCD	Wasted	Wasted	(3,000)
Taxable total profits	Nil	Nil	5,600
QCD wasted	3,000	3,000	

Loss memorandum

	£
Trading loss in the year ended 31 December 2013	81,550
(1) Current period relief	(1,400)
(2) Carry back relief – year ended 31 December 2012	(38,750)
	41,400
(3) Carry forward against trading profits – year ended 31 December 2014	(20,000)
Loss to carry forward at 31 December 2014	21,400

Activity 3

1	False	Trading losses can only be relieved by carry back after a claim for current year relief has been made.
2	False	Trading losses are deducted from other income before deducting qualifying charitable donations. Any excess QCDs remaining unrelieved are wasted.
3	True	Trading losses carried forward must be set off against the first available future trading profit from the same trade as soon as it arises.
4	False	Capital losses cannot be offset against other income. They can only be set against capital gains.

Workbook Activity 4

AB Ltd

The correct answer is D.

Explanation

Year ended	31.12.13	31.12.14
	£	£
Trading income	19,000	Nil
Interest income	2,000	1,000
Chargeable gains	4,000	4,000
	_____	_____
Total profits	25,000	5,000
Less: Loss relief – Current year		(5,000)
– 12 month carry back	(25,000)	
	_____	_____
Taxable total profits	Nil	Nil
	_____	_____

Note: Loss relief is given before qualifying charitable donations are deducted. As a result the qualifying charitable donations in 2013 are wasted.

Loss memorandum

	£
Year ended 31 December 2014	67,000
Less: Current year offset – y/e 31.12.14	(5,000)
Carry back – 12 months to y/e 31.12.13	(25,000)
Loss carried forward at 31 December 2014	37,000

Workbook Activity 5

Eldorado (Birmingham) Limited

Corporation tax computations

Year to 31 August	2013	2014	2015
	£	£	£
Trading profit	18,000	Nil	Nil
Property income	22,000	22,000	22,000
Chargeable gain	3,000	–	–
	43,000	22,000	22,000
Less Loss relief:			
– Current year		(22,000)	(6,000)
– Carry back	(43,000)		
Taxable total profits	Nil	Nil	16,000

Loss memorandum

	£		£
Loss – y/e 31.8.14	81,000	Loss – y/e 31.8.15	6,000
Offset: Current year	(22,000)	Offset: Current year	(6,000)
Carry back	(43,000)		
Losses carried forward	16,000		Nil

The losses carried forward can only be offset against future trading profits of the same trade.

Workbook Activity 6

1	True	Capital losses can only be offset against chargeable gains of the current and future periods.
2	False	Trading losses carried forward must be set off against the first available trading profit from the same trade as soon as it arises.
3	True	Trading losses can be offset against the total profits of the loss making accounting period; total profits includes income and chargeable gains.
4	False	Where trading losses have been relieved against the total profits of the loss making period, a company can choose to offset any losses remaining against the total profits of the previous 12 months but it is not obliged to do so.

Workbook Activity 7

Potter Limited

Years ended 30 September	2014 £	2015 £
Trading profit	Nil	94,000
Less: Losses b/f (£35,000 – £32,700)	–	(2,300)
	Nil	91,700
Non-trade interest	11,400	8,400
Property income	21,300	21,400
	32,700	121,500
Less: Loss relief – Current year	(32,700)	
	Nil	121,500
Less: Qualifying charitable donation	(Wasted)	(500)
Taxable total profits	Nil	121,000

Workbook Activity 8

Uncut Undergrowth Ltd

	Year ended 30.6.13 £	6 months to 31.12.13 £	Year ended 31.12.14 £
Trading profit	35,000	25,000	Nil
Non-trade interest	–	15,000	22,000
Property income	25,000	–	–
Chargeable gains (W1)	Nil	–	Nil
	60,000	40,000	22,000
Less: Loss relief			
– Current year relief			(22,000)
– Carry back relief (W2)	(30,000)	(40,000)	
	30,000	Nil	Nil
Less: Qualifying charitable donation	(1,000)	Wasted	Wasted
Taxable total profits	29,000	Nil	Nil

Balances carried forward

- There is a trading loss at 31 December 2014 to carry forward of £258,000 (W2).

- Capital losses of £10,000 available for carry forward (W1).

Workings:

(W1) **Net chargeable gains**

	£
Year ended 31 December 2014	
Chargeable gain	30,000
Losses b/f (£40,000)	(30,000)
Net chargeable gain	Nil
Losses c/f (£40,000 – £30,000)	10,000

(W2) Trading losses

	£
Loss for 12m to 31 December 2014	350,000
Current year relief	(22,000)
Carry back relief – 6 months to 31 December 2013	(40,000)
– 6 months to 30 June 2013	
(£60,000 × 6/12)	(30,000)
Carry forward at 31 December 2014	258,000

9 Payment and administration – companies

 Activity 1

Russell plc

The correct answer is C.

Explanation

C is the correct answer because even though Russell plc is liable to corporation tax at the main rate for the year ended 31 December 2014, it is large for the first time and its profits are below £10 million.

Russell plc was not paying tax at the full rate last year and therefore (given its profits do not exceed £10 m) will not have to pay instalments for the year ended 31 December 2014.

Russell plc's corporation tax liability will be due within 9 months and 1 day of the end of the accounting period (i.e. by 1 October 2015).

Activity 2

(a) **Space plc Projected corporation tax payments – y/e 31.3.2015**

Taxable total profits and augmented profits	£2,000,000
Corporation tax liability (at 21%)	£420,000.00

The accounting period will be subject to quarterly instalments as the company is large and was large in the previous year.

The liability for the year ended 31 March 2015 should be settled by four equal instalments of £105,000 (£420,000 ÷ 4).

		£ p
Instalment 1	14 October 2014	105,000.00
Instalment 2	14 January 2015	105,000.00
Instalment 3	14 April 2015	105,000.00
Instalment 4	14 July 2015	105,000.00

(b) **Administrative requirements**

(1) A return, including statutory accounts and computations, must be submitted online by 31 March 2016 (i.e. within 12 months of the accounting period end otherwise penalties will be charged).

(2) Late payments of tax will give rise to interest charges, which will be deductible from non-trade interest income.

Workbook Activity 3

Payment and administration

1 False   The due date for the payment of the corporation tax falls before the due filing date. Companies may need to estimate the payment of corporation tax that is due.

2 True   The filing date is 12 months from the end of the period of account regardless of the length of the accounting period.

3 False   The latest date that DEF Ltd can amend its return is 31 March 2017 (i.e. 12 months after the due filing date not the actual filing date).

KAPLAN PUBLISHING

4   False   The immediate penalty for late filing of £100. There are then additional penalties once the delay exceeds three months.

 Workbook Activity 4

ABC Ltd

The correct answer is A.

Explanation

ABC Ltd is a large company in the year to 31 March 2015.

It must pay its corporation tax in instalments even though it was not a large company in the year to 31 March 2014.

This is because its profits in the year to 31 March 2015 exceed £2 million (i.e. £10 million × 1/5 (four associated companies)).

The tax is due on:

14 October 2014, 14 January 2015, 14 April 2015 and 14 July 2015.

 Workbook Activity 5

Wendy Windows plc

Corporation tax liability and payment dates

	£
Corporation tax due:	
FY2013 (£2,400,000 × 2/12 × 23%)	92,000.00
FY2014 (£2,400,000 × 10/12 × 21%)	420,000.00
Corporation tax liability	512,000.00
Due date of instalments:	
14 August 2014 (£512,000.00 × ¼)	128,000.00
14 November 2014	128,000.00
14 February 2015	128,000.00
14 May 2015	128,000.00
	512,000.00

11 Taxable trade profits for unincorporated businesses

 Activity 1

Capone (1)

Adjusted trading profit for 12 months ended 30 June 2014

Expenditure charged but not allowable

Most of the required adjustments will be under this heading.

Start at the top of the statement of profit or loss and work down considering the admissibility of each item in turn and reading any relevant notes.

Do not flit from item to item at random since this is a sure way to overlook something.

If you do not know for certain whether any particular item is allowable or not, do not waste time thinking too much about it – take an informed guess; more often than not you will guess right.

Remember the main rule of admissibility – the expenditure must be 'incurred wholly and exclusively for the purposes of the trade', in this case the trade of a wine merchant.

The adjustments under this heading are as follows:

	£	Reason
Net profit per accounts	15,219	
Repairs to premises – floor alterations	1,460	Capital cost
Depreciation	4,150	Capital cost
Bad and doubtful debts		
General provision increase	3,350	An appropriation
Loan to ex-employee written off	400	Not wholly and exclusively
Sundry expenses		
Fine	250	Not wholly and exclusively
Salary – Capone	14,000	Appropriation

Notes:

(1) A company could treat the ex-employee loan write-off as a non-trade interest expense under the loan relationship rules. No such relief is available for a sole trader incurring a similar loss.

(2) It is assumed that Capone's wife's salary can be justified as a business expense.

Income credited but not taxable as trading income

It is fairly certain that all credit items will either be assessed under a different heading or will be capital items or will not be taxable.

The adjustment under this heading is as follows:

	£	Reason
Dividend income	300	Taxed under a different heading

Expenditure not charged but allowable

Where the home is used for business purposes, part of the running expenses can be allocated to the business, e.g. the business use of the private telephone.

Show £290 as adjustment on the minus side of the computation.

Income not credited but assessable

An adjustment under this heading will normally arise because goods have been taken for the proprietor's own use. Legal precedent has established that this 'sale' is to be brought to account for tax purposes at full market price, i.e. ($£455 \times {}^{100}\!/_{65}$) = £700.

The £700 will be an adjustment on the plus side of the computation.

Capone

Adjustment of profits for 12 months ended 30 June 2014

	+ £	– £
Net profit per accounts	15,219	
Repairs – alterations to flooring	1,460	
Depreciation	4,150	
Bad and doubtful debts		
General provision increase	3,350	
Loan to ex-employee written off	400	
Sundry expenses		
Fine	250	
Salary – Capone	14,000	
Dividends		300
Business calls from home telephone		290
Goods withdrawn by Capone (£455 × $\frac{100}{65}$)	700	
	39,529	590
	(590)	
Adjusted trading profit (before capital allowances)	38,939	

Activity 2

Ernest

Capital allowances computation – plant and machinery

	General pool £	Private use asset £	Allowances £
Year ended 31 March 2015			
TWDV b/f at 1 April 2014	24,000		
Additions: No AIA: Cars			
15 April 2014	16,000		
16 July 2014	9,200		
17 August 2014		9,400	
Disposals			
30 April 2014	(3,200)		
	46,000		
WDA (18%)	(8,280)	(1,692) × 70%	9,464
TWDV c/f	37,720	7,708	
Total allowances			9,464
Year ended 31 March 2016			
Disposals			
Car proceeds	(9,400)	(8,100)	
Balancing charge		(392) × 70%	(274)
	28,320		
WDA 18%	(5,098)		5,098
TWDV at 31 March 2016	23,222		
Total allowances			4,824

Activity 3

Anjula

The correct answer is B.

Explanation

B is the correct answer because:

- the equipment attracts 100% AIA

- the car attracts a WDA of 18% pro-rated up by 16/12 as the first accounting period is 16 months long

The calculation is therefore:

	£
AIA	2,500
WDA (£6,200 × 18% × 16/12)	1,488
	————
Total allowances	3,988
	————

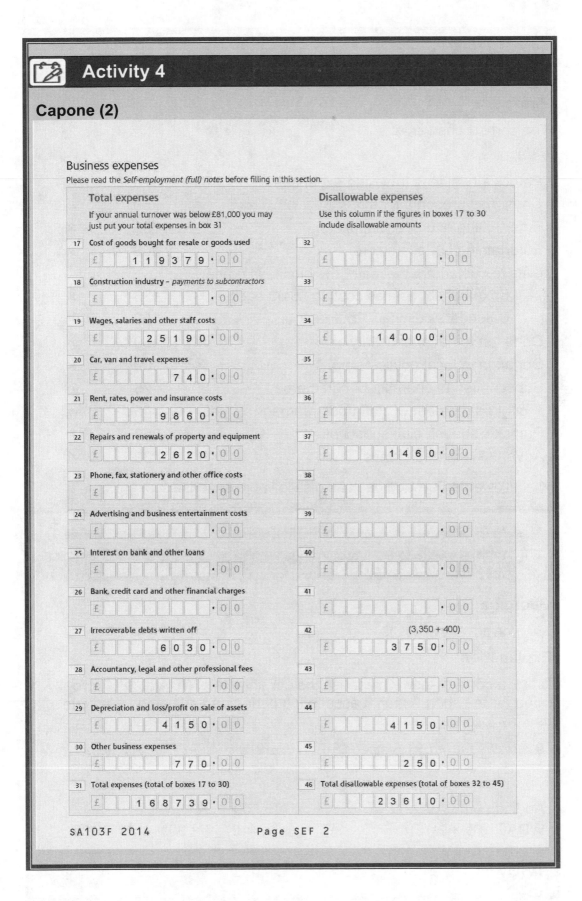

Activity 4

Capone (2)

Business expenses

Please read the *Self-employment (full) notes* before filling in this section.

Total expenses	Disallowable expenses
If your annual turnover was below £81,000 you may just put your total expenses in box 31	Use this column if the figures in boxes 17 to 30 include disallowable amounts
17 Cost of goods bought for resale or goods used £ 119379 · 0 0	**32** £ · 0 0
18 Construction industry – *payments to subcontractors* £ · 0 0	**33** £ · 0 0
19 Wages, salaries and other staff costs £ 25190 · 0 0	**34** £ 14000 · 0 0
20 Car, van and travel expenses £ 740 · 0 0	**35** £ · 0 0
21 Rent, rates, power and insurance costs £ 9860 · 0 0	**36** £ · 0 0
22 Repairs and renewals of property and equipment £ 2620 · 0 0	**37** £ 1460 · 0 0
23 Phone, fax, stationery and other office costs £ · 0 0	**38** £ · 0 0
24 Advertising and business entertainment costs £ · 0 0	**39** £ · 0 0
25 Interest on bank and other loans £ · 0 0	**40** £ · 0 0
26 Bank, credit card and other financial charges £ · 0 0	**41** £ · 0 0
27 Irrecoverable debts written off £ 6030 · 0 0	**42** (3,350 + 400) £ 3750 · 0 0
28 Accountancy, legal and other professional fees £ · 0 0	**43** £ · 0 0
29 Depreciation and loss/profit on sale of assets £ 4150 · 0 0	**44** £ 4150 · 0 0
30 Other business expenses £ 770 · 0 0	**45** £ 250 · 0 0
31 Total expenses (total of boxes 17 to 30) £ 168739 · 0 0	**46** Total disallowable expenses (total of boxes 32 to 45) £ 23610 · 0 0

SA103F 2014 Page SEF 2

Workbook Activity 5

Patrick

The correct answer is:

	£	✓ or ✗
Patrick's business travelling expenses	5,175	✓
Christmas presents for staff	250	✓
Entertaining overseas suppliers	2,750	✗
Entertaining UK customers	2,300	✗
Gifts to customers that carry the business name:		
– Boxes of chocolates costing £5.00 each	125	✗
– Calendars costing £1.50 each	150	✓
Donation to national charity	50	✗
Donation to local political party	100	✗
Subscription to chamber of commerce	25	✓
A gift to a member of staff upon marriage	45	✓
Patrick's squash club subscription	250	✗
Advertising in trade press	280	✓

✓ = allowable ✗ = add back as disallowable expense

Workbook Activity 6

Georgina

The correct answer is D.

Explanation

D is the correct answer because the car attracts a WDA at 18%, pro-rated for the short 9 month accounting period and adjusted for private use, as follows:

9 months ended 31 May 2015	Private use car		Allowances
	£		£
Addition – no AIA	10,500		
WDA (18% × 9/12)	(1,418)	× 30%	425
	———		———
TWDV c/f	9,082		

Workbook Activity 7

Adam

The correct answers are as follows:

1   A   This is fully allowable from the business point of view and, as it has already been deducted in the accounts, no adjustment is required. The employee may be assessed on the private use as a taxable benefit.

2   D   30% of the motor expenses should be added back as the private use is by the owner of the business.

3   A   This is an allowable trade expense and, as it has already been deducted in the accounts, no adjustment is required.

4   C   Bank interest is not taxed as trading profits, therefore deduct in full.

5   F   Add back the profit that would have been made had Adam paid the full selling price.

 Workbook Activity 8

Manuel Costa (1)

Adjustment of profits for 12 months ended 30 June 2014

	£
Net profit per accounts	32,205
Manuel's drawings (£300 × 52)	15,600
Manuel's NIC	116
Speeding fine	65
Motor expenses (1/3 of balance) (£2,000 – £65) × $^1/_3$	645
Legal expenses in connection with speeding offence	640
Depreciation	3,510
	52,781
Less; Capital allowances	(2,480)
Taxable trade profits	50,301

Workbook Activity 9

Manuel Costa (2)

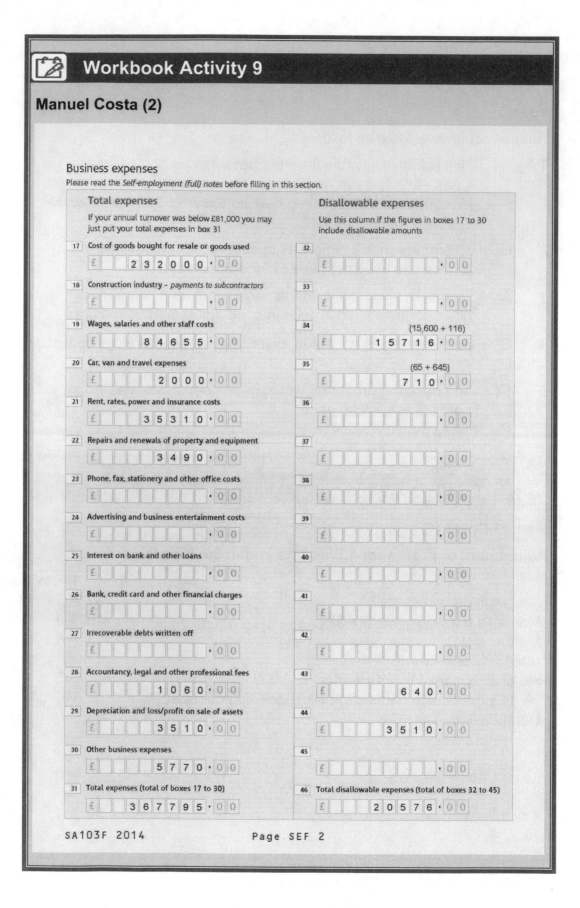

Business expenses

Please read the *Self-employment (full) notes* before filling in this section.

Total expenses	Disallowable expenses
If your annual turnover was below £81,000 you may just put your total expenses in box 31	Use this column if the figures in boxes 17 to 30 include disallowable amounts
17 Cost of goods bought for resale or goods used £ 2 3 2 0 0 0 · 0 0	**32** £ · 0 0
18 Construction industry – *payments to subcontractors* £ · 0 0	**33** £ · 0 0
19 Wages, salaries and other staff costs £ 8 4 6 5 5 · 0 0	**34** (15,600 + 116) £ 1 5 7 1 6 · 0 0
20 Car, van and travel expenses £ 2 0 0 0 · 0 0	**35** (65 + 645) £ 7 1 0 · 0 0
21 Rent, rates, power and insurance costs £ 3 5 3 1 0 · 0 0	**36** £ · 0 0
22 Repairs and renewals of property and equipment £ 3 4 9 0 · 0 0	**37** £ · 0 0
23 Phone, fax, stationery and other office costs £ · 0 0	**38** £ · 0 0
24 Advertising and business entertainment costs £ · 0 0	**39** £ · 0 0
25 Interest on bank and other loans £ · 0 0	**40** £ · 0 0
26 Bank, credit card and other financial charges £ · 0 0	**41** £ · 0 0
27 Irrecoverable debts written off £ · 0 0	**42** £ · 0 0
28 Accountancy, legal and other professional fees £ 1 0 6 0 · 0 0	**43** £ 6 4 0 · 0 0
29 Depreciation and loss/profit on sale of assets £ 3 5 1 0 · 0 0	**44** £ 3 5 1 0 · 0 0
30 Other business expenses £ 5 7 7 0 · 0 0	**45** £ · 0 0
31 Total expenses (total of boxes 17 to 30) £ 3 6 7 7 9 5 · 0 0	**46** Total disallowable expenses (total of boxes 32 to 45) £ 2 0 5 7 6 · 0 0

SA103F 2014   Page SEF 2

Workbook Activity 10

Freda Jones

Adjustment of profits for 12 months ended 31 December 2014

	£
Net profit per accounts	48,260
Goods for own use (W1)	500
Freda's drawings (£1,000 × 12)	12,000
Freda's NIC	125
Taxation (Freda's income tax)	15,590
Lease rental on expensive car (W2)	4,830
Depreciation	2,540
Motor car running expenses (½ × £2,500)	1,250
	85,095
Less Capital allowances	(1,200)
Taxable trade profits	83,895

Workings:

(W1) Goods for own use

Where goods are taken for own use, the proprietor will be taxed on the profit that would have been made, had the goods been sold at market value.

Here, the cost of the goods has already been credited to the statement of profit or loss, but an additional credit is needed to reflect the profit that would have been made.

As no information is given about profit margins, an estimate will have to be used, based on the trading account.

	£
Sales	300,000
Less: Cost of sales	(200,000)
Gross profit	100,000

Gross profit as a percentage of cost = $\frac{100,000}{200,000}$ = 50%

Gross profit on goods taken for own use = 50% × £1,000 = £500

(W2) Lease rental on high emission car

Amount to be disallowed is 15% of hire charges:

Disallowed amount = 15% × £8,400 = £1,260

The car is also used privately so in addition to the disallowable amount calculated above, the private use element of the balance must also be disallowed.

Balance of expenditure £8,400 – £1,260 = £7,140

Private use element   £7,140 × 1/2   = £3,570

Total amount disallowed:

	£
High emission element	1,260
Private use element	3,570
	4,830

Alternative calculation:

Amount allowed = (£8,400 × 85% × 50%) = £3,570

Amount to be added back = (£8,400 – £3,570) = £4,830

Workbook Activity 11

Hudson

Capital allowances computation

	General pool £	Private use asset £	Allowances £
Year ended 31 March 2015			
TWDV b/f	6,500		
Addition – No AIA		16,000	
Addition qualifying for AIA:			
– New plant	10,858		
– Second hand plant	1,000		
	11,858		
Less: AIA	(11,858)		11,858
	Nil		
WDA @ 18%	(1,170)	(2,880) × 75%	3,330
TWDV c/f	5,330	13,120	
Total allowances			15,188
7 months ended 31 Oct 2015			
Disposal proceeds	(2,450)	(14,000)	
Balancing allowance	2,880		2,880
Balancing charge		(880) × 75%	(660)
Total allowances			2,220

Note: No WDAs are given in the final period of account.

Workbook Activity 12

Ethan

Capital allowances computation

	General pool £	Private use asset £	Allowances £
Year ended 31 March 2015			
Additions not qualifying for AIA			
11.5.14	17,000		
21.6.14	8,800		
16.9.14		11,600	
	25,800		
WDA (18% × £25,800)	(4,644)		4,644
WDA (18% × 11,600) (Note 1)		(2,088)	1,462
TWDV c/f	21,156	9,512	
Total allowances			6,106
Year ended 31 March 2016			
Disposals	(10,000)	(9,700)	
	11,156	(188)	
Balancing charge (Note 2)		188	(132)
WDA (18% × £11,156)	(2,008)		2,008
TWDV c/f	9,148		
Total allowances			1,876

Notes:

(1) Business portion of WDA = (£2,088 × 70%) = £1,462

(2) Business portion of charge = (£188 × 70%) = £132

Workbook Activity 13

Raj

Capital allowances computation

	General pool	Private use asset	Allowances
	£	£	£	£
11 m/e 31 March 2015				
Additions not qualifying for AIA				
Car		16,000		
Additions qualifying for AIA				
Machinery	20,000			
Tool grinder	6,000			
	26,000			
Less AIA	(26,000)			26,000
	Nil			
WDA (8% × 11/12 × £16,000)		(1,173) × 80%		938
TWDV c/f	Nil	14,827		
Total allowances				26,938
Year ended 31 March 2016				
Additions not qualifying for AIA				
Car	11,600			
	11,600			
WDA (18% × £11,600)	(2,088)			2,088
WDA (8% × £14, 827)		(1,186) × 80%		949
TWDV c/f	9,512	13,641		
Total allowances				3,037

12 Partnership profit allocation

Activity 1

John and Kyle

Year ending 5 April 2015	Total £	John £	Kyle £
Profits split (3:2)	24,047	14,428	9,619

Activity 2

1 False The partnership is not a separate legal entity from the partners. It is the partners who pay tax on their share of the partnership profits.

2 False The profits are time apportioned to the period before and after 30 June, and then allocated using the profit sharing ratio in each period.

3 False Salaries and interest must be added back in calculating adjusted trading profit as they are not actually salaries and interest. They merely represent a method chosen by the partners of allocating profits between them.

They are taken into account in apportioning the profit between the partners, but the partners are assessed to their total share of trading profits of the partnership as trading income.

KAPLAN PUBLISHING

Activity 3

Michael, Nick and Liz (1)

	Total £	Michael £	Nick £	Liz £
y/e 30 September 2012	30,000	15,000	15,000	
y/e 30 September 2013				
1 October 2012 – 31 December 2012	9,000	4,500	4,500	
1 January 2013 – 30 September 2013	27,000	9,000	9,000	9,000
	36,000	13,500	13,500	9,000
y/e 30 September 2014				
1 October 2013 – 30 June 2014	31,875	10,625	10,625	10,625
1 July 2014 – 30 September 2014	10,625	5,313	–	5,312
	42,500	15,938	10,625	15,937
y/e 30 September 2015	40,000	20,000		20,000
Period ending 31 December 2015	17,500	8,750		8,750

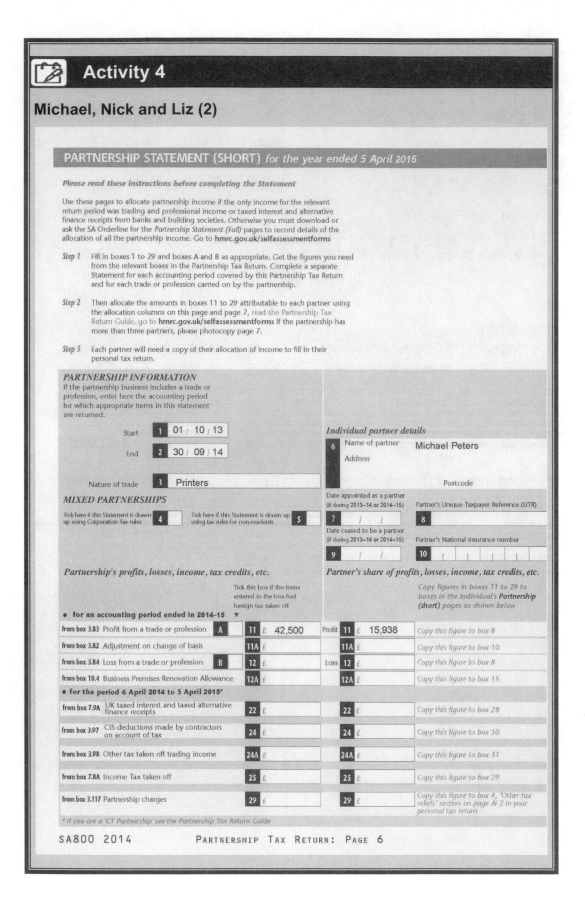

Activity 4

Michael, Nick and Liz (2)

PARTNERSHIP STATEMENT (SHORT) *for the year ended 5 April 2015*

Please read these instructions before completing the Statement

Use these pages to allocate partnership income if the only income for the relevant return period was trading and professional income or taxed interest and alternative finance receipts from banks and building societies. Otherwise you must download or ask the SA Orderline for the *Partnership Statement (Full)* pages to record details of the allocation of all the partnership income. Go to **hmrc.gov.uk/selfassessmentforms**

Step 1   Fill in boxes 1 to 29 and boxes A and B as appropriate. Get the figures you need from the relevant boxes in the Partnership Tax Return. Complete a separate Statement for each accounting period covered by this Partnership Tax Return and for each trade or profession carried on by the partnership.

Step 2   Then allocate the amounts in boxes 11 to 29 attributable to each partner using the allocation columns on this page and page 7, read the Partnership Tax Return Guide, go to **hmrc.gov.uk/selfassessmentforms** If the partnership has more than three partners, please photocopy page 7.

Step 3   Each partner will need a copy of their allocation of income to fill in their personal tax return.

PARTNERSHIP INFORMATION
If the partnership business includes a trade or profession, enter here the accounting period for which appropriate items in this statement are returned.

Start **1** 01 / 10 / 13

End **2** 30 / 09 / 14

Nature of trade **3** Printers

MIXED PARTNERSHIPS

Tick here if this Statement is drawn up using Corporation Tax rules **4**

Tick here if this Statement is drawn up using tax rules for non-residents **5**

Individual partner details

6 Name of partner   Michael Peters

Address

Postcode

Date appointed as a partner (if during 2013–14 or 2014–15) **7** / /

Partner's Unique Taxpayer Reference (UTR) **8**

Date ceased to be a partner (if during 2013–14 or 2014–15) **9** / /

Partner's National Insurance number **10**

Partnership's profits, losses, income, tax credits, etc.

Tick this box if the items entered in the box had foreign tax taken off ▼

Partner's share of profits, losses, income, tax credits, etc.

*Copy figures in boxes 11 to 29 to boxes in the individual's **Partnership (short)** pages as shown below*

• for an accounting period ended in 2014–15					
from box 3.83 Profit from a trade or profession **A**	**11** £ 42,500	Profit **11** £ 15,938	*Copy this figure to box 8*
from box 3.82 Adjustment on change of basis	**11A** £	**11A** £	*Copy this figure to box 10*
from box 3.84 Loss from a trade or profession **B**	**12** £	Loss **12** £	*Copy this figure to box 8*
from box 10.4 Business Premises Renovation Allowance	**12A** £	**12A** £	*Copy this figure to box 15*
• for the period 6 April 2014 to 5 April 2015*					
from box 7.9A UK taxed interest and taxed alternative finance receipts	**22** £	**22** £	*Copy this figure to box 28*
from box 3.97 CIS deductions made by contractors on account of tax	**24** £	**24** £	*Copy this figure to box 30*
from box 3.98 Other tax taken off trading income	**24A** £	**24A** £	*Copy this figure to box 31*
from box 7.8A Income Tax taken off	**25** £	**25** £	*Copy this figure to box 29*
from box 3.117 Partnership charges	**29** £	**29** £	*Copy this figure to box 4, 'Other tax reliefs' section on page Ai 2 in your personal tax return*

* if you are a 'CT Partnership' see the Partnership Tax Return Guide

SA800 2014   PARTNERSHIP TAX RETURN: PAGE 6

Workbook Activity 5

Lindsay, Tricia and Kate (1)

The correct answers are as follows:

First period to: 31 July 2014

(1)   C

(2)   A

(3)   B

Second period to: 31 March 2015

(4)   D

(5)   D

(6)   C

(7)   B

Explanation:

The split of partnership profits will be as follows:

	Total £	Lindsay £	Tricia £	Kate £
Year ending 31 March 2015				
1 April 2014 – 31 July 2014 (4m)	50,000	30,000	20,000	
1 Aug 2014 – 31 March 2015 (8m)	100,000	44,445	33,333	22,222
	150,000	74,445	53,333	22,222

Workbook Activity 6

Anne, Betty, Chloe and Diana

		Anne £	Betty £	Chloe £	Diana £
Year ended 31.12.13					
01.01.13 – 30.06.13	$^6/_{12}$ × £60,000	15,000	15,000		
01.07.13 – 31.12.13	$^6/_{12}$ × £60,000	15,000		15,000	
		30,000	15,000	15,000	
Year ended 31.12.14					
01.01.14 – 31.03.14	$^3/_{12}$ × £72,000	9,000		9,000	
01.04.14 – 31.12.14	$^9/_{12}$ × £72,000	18,000		18,000	18,000
		27,000		27,000	18,000

Workbook Activity 7

Bert and Harold

Allocation of taxable trade profits

The profit-sharing ratio was changed on 1 July 2014 which is 9 months into the accounting period. The profits will therefore be time-apportioned for allocation as follows:

Old ratio £16,500 × $^{9}/_{12}$ = £12,375

New ratio £16,500 × $^{3}/_{12}$ = £4,125

Allocation of taxable trade profits

	Total £	Bert £	Harold £
1.10.13 to 30.6.14			
Salaries ($^{9}/_{12}$)	3,750	2,250	1,500
Balance (3:2)	8,625	5,175	3,450
	12,375	7,425	4,950
1.7.14 to 30.9.14			
Salaries ($^{3}/_{12}$)	2,500	1,500	1,000
Balance (2:1)	1,625	1,083	542
	4,125	2,583	1,542
Total allocation	16,500	10,008	6,492

Workbook Activity 8

Peter and Nathan Flannery

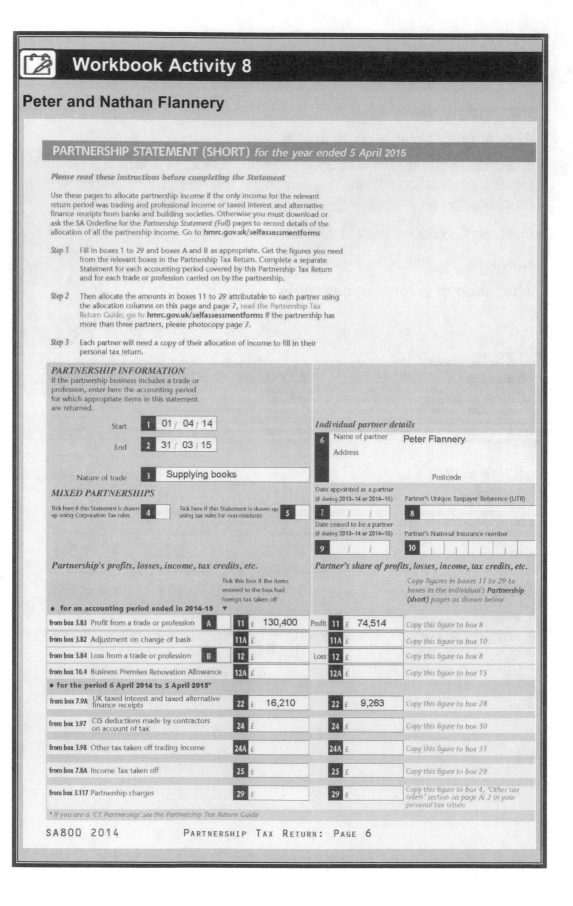

PARTNERSHIP STATEMENT (SHORT) *for the year ended 5 April 2015*

Please read these instructions before completing the Statement

Use these pages to allocate partnership income if the only income for the relevant return period was trading and professional income or taxed interest and alternative finance receipts from banks and building societies. Otherwise you must download or ask the SA Orderline for the *Partnership Statement (Full)* pages to record details of the allocation of all the partnership income. Go to hmrc.gov.uk/selfassessmentforms

Step 1 Fill in boxes 1 to 29 and boxes A and B as appropriate. Get the figures you need from the relevant boxes in the Partnership Tax Return. Complete a separate Statement for each accounting period covered by this Partnership Tax Return and for each trade or profession carried on by the partnership.

Step 2 Then allocate the amounts in boxes 11 to 29 attributable to each partner using the allocation columns on this page and page 7, read the Partnership Tax Return Guide, go to hmrc.gov.uk/selfassessmentforms If the partnership has more than three partners, please photocopy page 7.

Step 3 Each partner will need a copy of their allocation of income to fill in their personal tax return.

PARTNERSHIP INFORMATION
If the partnership business includes a trade or profession, enter here the accounting period for which appropriate items in this statement are returned.

Start **1** 01 / 04 / 14

End **2** 31 / 03 / 15

Nature of trade **3** Supplying books

MIXED PARTNERSHIPS

Tick here if this Statement is drawn up using Corporation Tax rules **4**

Tick here if this Statement is drawn up using tax rules for non-residents **5**

Individual partner details

6 Name of partner Peter Flannery

Address

Postcode

Date appointed as a partner (if during 2013–14 or 2014–15) **7** / /

Partner's Unique Taxpayer Reference (UTR) **8**

Date ceased to be a partner (if during 2013–14 or 2014–15) **9** / /

Partner's National Insurance number **10**

Partnership's profits, losses, income, tax credits, etc.

Tick this box if the items entered in the box had foreign tax taken off

Partner's share of profits, losses, income, tax credits, etc.

Copy figures in boxes 11 to 29 to boxes in the individual's **Partnership (short)** pages as shown below

● **for an accounting period ended in 2014–15** ▼

from box 3.83 Profit from a trade or profession	**A**	**11** £ 130,400	Profit **11** £ 74,514	Copy this figure to box 8
from box 3.82 Adjustment on change of basis		**11A** £	**11A** £	Copy this figure to box 10
from box 3.84 Loss from a trade or profession	**B**	**12** £	Loss **12** £	Copy this figure to box 8
from box 10.4 Business Premises Renovation Allowance		**12A** £	**12A** £	Copy this figure to box 15

● **for the period 6 April 2014 to 5 April 2015***

from box 7.9A UK taxed interest and taxed alternative finance receipts	**22** £ 16,210	**22** £ 9,263	Copy this figure to box 28
from box 3.97 CIS deductions made by contractors on account of tax	**24** £	**24** £	Copy this figure to box 30
from box 3.98 Other tax taken off trading income	**24A** £	**24A** £	Copy this figure to box 31
from box 7.8A Income Tax taken off	**25** £	**25** £	Copy this figure to box 29
from box 3.117 Partnership charges	**29** £	**29** £	Copy this figure to box 4, 'Other tax reliefs' section on page Ai 2 in your personal tax return

* if you are a 'CT Partnership' see the Partnership Tax Return Guide

SA800 2014   PARTNERSHIP TAX RETURN: PAGE 6

Workbook Activity 9

Lindsay, Tricia and Kate (2)

PARTNERSHIP STATEMENT (SHORT) *for the year ended 5 April 2015*

Please read these instructions before completing the Statement

Use these pages to allocate partnership income if the only income for the relevant return period was trading and professional income or taxed interest and alternative finance receipts from banks and building societies. Otherwise you must download or ask the SA Orderline for the *Partnership Statement (Full)* pages to record details of the allocation of all the partnership income. Go to **hmrc.gov.uk/selfassessmentforms**

Step 1   Fill in boxes 1 to 29 and boxes A and B as appropriate. Get the figures you need from the relevant boxes in the Partnership Tax Return. Complete a separate Statement for each accounting period covered by this Partnership Tax Return and for each trade or profession carried on by the partnership.

Step 2   Then allocate the amounts in boxes 11 to 29 attributable to each partner using the allocation columns on this page and page 7, read the Partnership Tax Return Guide, go to **hmrc.gov.uk/selfassessmentforms** If the partnership has more than three partners, please photocopy page 7.

Step 3   Each partner will need a copy of their allocation of income to fill in their personal tax return.

PARTNERSHIP INFORMATION
If the partnership business includes a trade or profession, enter here the accounting period for which appropriate items in this statement are returned.

Start   **1**   01/ 04/ 14

End   **2**   31/ 03/ 15

Nature of trade   **3**   Dry cleaning

MIXED PARTNERSHIPS

Tick here if this Statement is drawn up using Corporation Tax rules **4**

Tick here if this Statement is drawn up using tax rules for non-residents **5**

Individual partner details

6   Name of partner   Lindsay

Address

Postcode

Date appointed as a partner (if during 2013–14 or 2014–15)

7   / /

Partner's Unique Taxpayer Reference (UTR)

8

Date ceased to be a partner (if during 2013–14 or 2014–15)

9   / /

Partner's National Insurance number

10

Partnership's profits, losses, income, tax credits, etc.

Partner's share of profits, losses, income, tax credits, etc.

Tick this box if the items entered in the box had foreign tax taken off

Copy figures in boxes 11 to 29 to boxes in the individual's **Partnership (short)** pages as shown below

● **for an accounting period ended in 2014–15** ▼

				Partner's share	
from box 3.83 Profit from a trade or profession	**A**	**11** £ 150,000	Profit **11** £ 74,445		Copy this figure to box 8
from box 3.82 Adjustment on change of basis		**11A** £	**11A** £		Copy this figure to box 10
from box 3.84 Loss from a trade or profession	**B**	**12** £	Loss **12** £		Copy this figure to box 8
from box 10.4 Business Premises Renovation Allowance		**12A** £	**12A** £		Copy this figure to box 15

● **for the period 6 April 2014 to 5 April 2015***

from box 7.9A UK taxed interest and taxed alternative finance receipts	**22** £	**22** £	Copy this figure to box 28
from box 3.97 CIS deductions made by contractors on account of tax	**24** £	**24** £	Copy this figure to box 30
from box 3.98 Other tax taken off trading income	**24A** £	**24A** £	Copy this figure to box 31
from box 7.8A Income Tax taken off	**25** £	**25** £	Copy this figure to box 29
from box 3.117 Partnership charges	**29** £	**29** £	Copy this figure to box 4, 'Other tax reliefs' section on page Ai 2 in your personal tax return

* if you are a 'CT Partnership' see the Partnership Tax Return Guide

SA800 2014   PARTNERSHIP TAX RETURN: PAGE 6

13 Basis periods

 Activity 1

Jane

1   The correct answer is B.

Explanation

1 November 2011 (the date of commencement of trade) falls in the 2011/12 tax year.

2   The correct answer is C.

Explanation

The taxable profits in the first tax year are always the actual profits arising in the tax year.

Therefore the taxable profits are:

5 months ended 5 April 2012 (5/6 × £12,000)   £10,000
                                                    _____

3   The correct answer is B.

Explanation

As the accounting period ending in the second tax year (2012/13) is less than 12 months long, the taxable period will be the first 12 months of trade.

Therefore the taxable profits are:

	£
6 months ended 30 April 2012	12,000
6 months ended 31 October 2012 (6/12 × £27,000)	13,500
	_____
	25,500
	_____

4   The correct answer is C.

Explanation

In the third tax year of trade (2013/14) the taxable trading profits are the profits for the 12 months ending on the accounting date falling in the tax year.

Therefore the taxable profits are the profits for the year ended 30 April 2013.

5   The correct answer is £23,500.

Explanation

There are two periods which are taxed twice.

Therefore the overlap profits are:

	£
5 months ended 5 April 2012 (5/6 × £12,000)	10,000
6 months ended 31 October 2012 (6/12 × £27,000)	13,500
	————
	23,500
	————

6   The correct answer is D.

 Activity 2

Robert and Jack

(a)   **Robert**

Year of assessment	Basis period	Assessment £
2012/13	1 May 2012 – 5 April 2013	
	£20,250 + (£29,700 × $^{6}/_{12}$)	35,100
2013/14	Year ending 30 September 2013	29,700
2014/15	Year ending 30 September 2014	36,450
2015/16	Year ending 30 September 2015	28,350

Overlap profits are:

1 Oct 2012 – 5 April 2013 (£29,700 × $^{6}/_{12}$)	£14,850

(b) **Jack**

Year of assessment	Basis period	Assessment £
2011/12	1 January 2012 – 5 April 2012 (£37,800 × $\frac{3}{16}$)	7,087
2012/13	Year ending 5 April 2013 (£37,800 × $\frac{12}{16}$)	28,350
2013/14	Year ending 30 April 2013 (£37,800 × $\frac{12}{16}$)	28,350
2014/15	Year ending 30 April 2014	26,325
2015/16	Year ending 30 April 2015	28,350

Overlap profits are:

1 May 2012 – 5 April 2013 (£37,800 × $\frac{11}{16}$)   £25,987

 Activity 3

Adam, Ben and Catrina

The correct answer is D.

Explanation

The partnership continues despite Adam's resignation. Only Adam has to consider the closing rules to calculate his trading income assessments for 2014/15 (i.e. his final year).

The remaining partners continue to be assessed on a current year basis.

Workbook Activity 4

Xavier

The correct answer is C.

Explanation

C is the correct answer because Xavier commenced trading in 2013/14, the assessment for which is calculated as the profits between 1 January 2014 and 5 April 2014.

There is no set of accounts ending in the second tax year, 2014/15, and therefore Xavier will be taxed on the basis of profits arising between 6 April 2014 and 5 April 2015.

 Workbook Activity 5

Mario

The correct answer is B.

Explanation

The statement is false because there are no accounts ending in 2014/15 and therefore Mario will be assessed on the basis of profits arising between 6 April 2014 and 5 April 2015.

Workbook Activity 6

Rupert

The correct answer is B.

Explanation

Assessable trading profits:

Year of assessment	Basis period	Assessment £
2013/14	Actual basis – 1 July 2013 to 5 April 2014 9/22 × £33,000	13,500
2014/15	Actual basis – 6 April 2014 to 5 April 2015 12/22 × £33,000	18,000
2015/16	12 months to 30 April 2015 12/22 × £33,000	18,000

There are overlap profits for the period 1 May 2014 to 5 April 2015 of £16,500 (£33,000 × $\frac{11}{22}$).

 Workbook Activity 7

Katrina

The correct answer is C.

Explanation

Assessable trading profits

Year of assessment	Basis period	Assessment £
2013/14	Year ended 30 June 2013	30,000
2014/15	1 July 2013 – 28 February 2015 (£27,000 + £20,000 – £12,000)	35,000

Workbook Activity 8

James

Year of assessment	Basis period		Assessment £
2010/11	1 January 2011 to 5 April 2011	(£75,600 × $\frac{3}{16}$)	14,175
2011/12	Actual basis (6 April 2011 to 5 April 2012)	(£75,600 × $\frac{12}{16}$)	56,700
2012/13	12 months to 30 April 2012	(£75,600 × $\frac{12}{16}$)	56,700
2013/14	Year ended 30 April 2013		52,650
2014/15	Year ended 30 April 2014		56,900
Overlap	1 May 2011 to 5 April 2012 (£75,600 × $\frac{11}{16}$)		51,975

Workbook Activity 9

Avril

Year of assessment	Basis period	Assessment £
2011/12	(01.01.12 – 05.04.12) (3 months) £80,000 × $\frac{3}{6}$	40,000
2012/13	Accounting period is less than 12 months therefore use first 12 months Period ended 30.06.12 (6 months) Year ended 30.06.13 (£100,000 × $\frac{6}{12}$)	80,000 50,000
		130,000
2013/14	Current year basis to 30.06.13	100,000
2014/15	Current year basis to 30.06.14	110,000
Overlap	(01.01.12 – 05.04.12) £40,000 Plus (01.07.12 – 31.12.12) £50,000	90,000

Workbook Activity 10

Benny

Year of assessment	Basis period	Assessment £
2012/13	(01.07.12 – 05.04.13) (9 months)	
	Period ended 31.12.12 (6 months)	14,000
	Year ended 31.12.13 (3 months)	
	(£36,000 × ³⁄₁₂)	9,000
		23,000
2013/14	Current year basis to 31.12.13	36,000
2014/15	Current year basis to 31.12.14	28,000
Overlap	(01.01.13 – 05.04.13) (£36,000 × ³⁄₁₂)	9,000

Workbook Activity 11

Elle

(a) **Cessation on 31 May 2015**

Year of assessment	Basis period	Assessment £
2013/14	Current year basis to 31.05.13	22,000
2014/15	Current year basis to 31.05.14	26,000
2015/16	Current year basis to 31.05.15	27,000
	Less: Overlap profits	(5,000)
		22,000

(b) **Cessation on 31 January 2015**

Year of assessment	Basis period	Assessment £
2013/14	Current year basis to 31.05.13	22,000
2014/15	Year to 31.05.14	26,000
	Plus: Period to 31.01.15 (cessation)	22,500
	Less: Overlap profits	(5,000)
		43,500

Workbook Activity 12

Bernadette

Year of assessment	Basis period	Assessment £
2011/12	(1 October 2011 – 5 April 2012)	
	($^6\!/_{12}$ × £21,280)	10,640
2012/13	Year ended 30 September 2012	21,280
2013/14	Year ended 30 September 2013	24,688
2014/15	Year ended 30 September 2014	28,816
2015/16	Year ended 30 September 2015	30,304
	Plus period to cessation on 28 February 2016	16,792
	Less: Overlap profits (W)	(10,640)
		36,456

Working:

Overlap profits (1 Oct 2011 to 5 April 2012) (£21,280 × 6/12) = £10,640

Workbook Activity 13

Bay

Year of assessment	Basis period	Assessment £
2010/11	1 January 2011 – 5 April 2011 ($^3/_{12}$ × £15,144) (W)	3,786
2011/12	Year ended 31 December 2011	15,144
2012/13	Year ended 31 December 2012	13,961
2013/14	Year ended 31 December 2013	13,618
2014/15	10 months to 31 October 2014	16,714
	Less Overlap relief (W)	(3,786)
		12,928

Workings:

Overlap profits (1 Jan 2011 to 5 April 2011) ($^3/_{12}$ × £15,144) = £3,786

Adjusted profits after capital allowances

	Trading profit £	Capital allowances £	£
Year to 31 December 2011	19,487	(4,343)	15,144
Year to 31 December 2012	17,840	(3,879)	13,961
Year to 31 December 2013	16,928	(3,310)	13,618
10 months to 31 October 2014	18,040	(1,326)	16,714

Workbook Activity 14

Ranjit

Year of assessment	Basis period	Assessment £
2012/13	01.11.12 – 05.04.13 (5 months of the 11-month period to 30.09.13) ($£2,306 × \frac{5}{11}$)	1,048
2013/14	Accounting period less than 12 months so: First 12 months 11 months to 30.09.13 plus 1 month to 31.10.13 ($£3,845 × \frac{1}{12}$)	2,306 320
		2,626
2014/15	Year ended 30.09.14	3,845
2015/16	Year ended 30.09.15	9,137

Overlap profits = (£1,048 + £320) = £1,368

Workings: Adjusted trading profits after capital allowances

	Trading profit £	Capital allowances £	£
Period ending 30.09.13	6,106	(3,800)	2,306
Year ended 30.09.14	8,845	(5,000)	3,845
Year ended 30.09.15	19,087	(9,950)	9,137

Workbook Activity 15

Period of assessment

1 False This is not true in the opening and closing years.

2 True The taxable trade profits of 2013/14 will be those of the period to 5 April 2014, and for 2014/15 will be those of the year to 5 April 2015, and so on. There are no overlap periods.

3 False The opening year rules apply to individuals joining a partnership as if they had commenced a new trade.

Workbook Activity 16

John and Edward

The correct answer is A.

Explanation

A is the correct answer because profits are allocated to Joe in his first year of assessment as follows:

	John £	Edward £	Joe £
1.4.14 – 31.12.14 (£60,000 × 9/12) – split evenly	22,500	22,500	
1.1.15 – 31.3.15 (£60,000 × 3/12) – split 3:2:1	7,500	5,000	2,500
	30,000	27,500	2,500

 Workbook Activity 17

Richard and Brenda

The correct answer is B.

Explanation

This is the fourth year of trading for Richard and Brenda, so they are assessed on the normal current year basis.

It is the second year for Michael, his assessment is therefore based on his first 12 months of trading.

The basis period for Michael will be:

2014/15   01.10.13 – 30.09.14 (1st 12 months)

The profits assessable on Michael will be:

(9/12 × £50,000/3) + (3/12 × £60,000/3) = £17,500

14 Trading losses for individuals

Activity 1

Caroline

Income tax computations

	2012/13 £	2013/14 £	2014/15 £
Taxable trade profits	10,500	Nil	350
Less: Loss relief b/f	–	–	(350)[3]
	10,500	Nil	Nil
Employment income	2,000	2,000	2,000
Interest	220	8,715	8,700
Total income	12,720	10,715	10,700
Less: Loss relief			
– preceding year	(12,720)[1]		
– current year		(10,715)[2]	
Net income after reliefs	Nil	Nil	10,700

Notes:

1 Relief against total income can be in any order.

2 The question says offset the loss as early as possible, therefore the claim is made against 2012/13 first, then 2013/14.

3 The remaining loss is then carried forward to 2014/15 and set against the first available trading profits.

Loss memorandum

		£
Loss in 2013/14 – year ended 31 December 2013		25,000
Less: Claim 2012/13 (preceding year)	(1)	(12,720)
		12,280
Less: Claim 2013/14 (year of loss)	(2)	(10,715)
		1,565
Less: Carry forward claim 2014/15	(3)	(350)
Loss carried forward		1,215

 Activity 2

1 False   Loss relief claims cannot be restricted to preserve the personal allowance.

2 True

3 False   Each partner can choose independently what loss relief to claim.

 Workbook Activity 3

Sole trader losses

The correct answer is C.

Explanation

Once a loss has been carried forward it must be set against future profits of the same trade. It cannot be set against total income in the future.

The taxpayer can choose whether to offset a trading loss against total income in the current year and/or the preceding year. It is not necessary to make these claims in any particular order.

Workbook Activity 4

Belinda

The correct answer is C.

Explanation

The trading loss can be carried forward and set against future trading profits, but the loss is incurred in 2014/15 and will therefore be available to carry forward to 2015/16, not 2014/15.

The trading loss can be set against total income of 2014/15 and/or 2013/14. There is no need for the claim for 2014/15 to be made before that of 2013/14 or vice versa.

 Workbook Activity 5

Bourbon

(a) **Alternative means of loss relief**

   (i)   Carry forward for set off against the next available taxable trading income from the same business until the loss is fully relieved.

   (ii) Claim against the total income of:
      – the tax year of loss; and/or
      – the preceding tax year.

(b) **Advice on relief**

From the following computations it can be seen that the best method of obtaining relief is for Bourbon to claim relief against total income for 2013/14 to obtain relief as early as possible.

A claim against total income should be made also in 2014/15 for the balance of the loss, as there will still be enough income remaining after the loss claim to use up the personal allowance of £10,000.

	2013/14 £	2014/15 £	2015/16 £
Trading profits	12,200	Nil	12,750
Less: Loss relief b/f	–	–	–
	12,200	Nil	12,750
Interest	7,250	15,250	5,250
	19,450	15,250	18,000
Less: Loss relief			
– Current year		(4,600)	
– Carry back	(19,450)		
Net income after reliefs	Nil	10,650	18,000

15 Payment and administration – individuals

Activity 1

1 A
2 C
3 B
4 D

KAPLAN PUBLISHING

Activity 2

Self assessment

(a) (i)   31 January following the tax year to which the return relates (i.e. 31 January 2016 for 2014/15).

(ii) 31 October following the tax year to which the return relates (i.e. 31 October 2015 for 2014/15).

(b) (i)   (1)   31 January in the tax year (i.e. 31 January 2015).

(2)   31 July following the tax year (i.e. 31 July 2015).

(3)   31 January following the tax year (i.e. 31 January 2016).

(ii) Payments one and two are equal amounts each amounting to half the income tax and Class 4 NIC payable in respect of the preceding income tax year.

Payment three is the balancing figure (i.e. it is the amount of the final tax and Class 4 NIC liability for the year, less any tax deducted at source, less payments one and two).

(c) (i)   There will be an immediate penalty of £100.

A further penalty of £10 per day for a maximum of 90 days will be charged once the return is more than three months late.

(ii) As well as the penalties listed above, there will be a further penalty of 5% of the tax due (minimum £300) once the return is more than six months late.

Once the return is more than 12 months late there will be a further penalty equal to a percentage of the tax due (minimum £300). The percentage is determined by the reason for the delay.

No deliberate withholding of information	5%
Deliberate withholding	70%
Deliberate withholding with concealment	100%

Activity 3

1   James must notify HMRC by 5 October 2015.

2   Isabel will be charged interest from the due date of 31 July 2015 until 14 September 2015, the day before payment.

3   The latest date for opening a compliance check (enquiry) is 18 January 2017; one year after Mike filed the return.

 Workbook Activity 4

Payments on account

1   31 January 2015

2   31 July 2015

3   31 January 2016

4   31 January 2016

 Workbook Activity 5

Period of assessment

1   False   The records must be retained until 31 January 2021.

2   True

3   False   The penalties start at 0% for a genuine mistake.

4   True

KAPLAN PUBLISHING

Workbook Activity 6

Kazuo

The correct answer is A.

Explanation

The payment on account is calculated as follows:

	£
2013/14 income tax liability	18,700
Less: Collected at source	(2,000)
Income tax payable under self assessment	16,700
First payment on account for 2014/15 (£16,700 ÷ 2)	8,350

 Workbook Activity 7

Income tax self assessment

(a)   The date by which a return must be filed depends on the filing method used.

A paper return must be filed by 31 October 2015 for the tax year 2014/15 (i.e. 31 October following the end of the tax year).

An electronic return must be filed by 31 January 2016 for the tax year 2014/15 (i.e. 31 January following the end of the tax year).

(b)   Notification is due by 5 October 2015 if a new source arises in 2014/15 and a tax return has not been issued.

(c)   If a tax return is submitted late, a £100 fixed penalty is charged.

If it is still outstanding after 3 months, a further £10 per day is charged for a maximum of 90 days.

If it is still outstanding after 6 months, a further penalty equal to 5% of the tax due is charged.

If the return is still outstanding after 12 months, a penalty of up to 100% of the tax outstanding is charged.

(d)   The penalty for submitting an incorrect tax return is a percentage of the revenue lost.

The percentage ranges from 0% (where the taxpayer has simply made a mistake) to 100% (where the taxpayer has deliberately understated the return and concealed the error).

(e)   The penalty for failing to maintain adequate records is up to £3,000.

16   National Insurance contributions payable by self employed individuals

Activity 1

1   £38,135   (£80,000 − £41,865)

2   £1,983.96 (£30,000 − £7,956) × 9%

3   Anne's NICs for 2014/15 are:

- Class 4 − £Nil, taxable profits less than £7,956;

- Class 2 − £143.00 (£2.75 per week for 52 weeks), as accounts profits exceed £5,885.

4   The correct answer is D.

Explanation

Taxpayers are only required to pay Class 2 NICs if their accounting profits for the tax year exceed £5,885, but they can be liable to both Classes 2 and 4.

Class 4 NICs are based on the taxable trading profits, **not** the amount of income a taxpayer withdraws from the business.

Workbook Activity 2

Naomi

Naomi must pay Class 2 NICs of £2.75 per week. In all cases her accounts profits exceed her taxable profits, therefore they exceed the small earnings limit of £5,885.

She is liable to pay Class 4 NICs as follows:

		£
(a)	Profits do not exceed lower limit, no Class 4 NIC	Nil
(b)	Class 4 NICs (£24,500 – £7,956) × 9%	1,488.96
(c)	Class 4 NICs (£41,865 – £7,956) × 9% + (£44,500 – £41,865) × 2%	3,104.51

 Workbook Activity 3

Adrian

The correct answer is C.

Explanation

The relevant amount for income tax is   £7,300
The relevant amount for Class 4 NIC is   £700

Payments on account will be due for 2014/15 as follows:

	£
31 January 2015 (£7,300 + £700 = £8,000 × ½)	4,000
31 July 2015	4,000

No payment on account of capital gains tax is ever required.

17 Introduction to chargeable gains

Activity 1

1	Chargeable	Even though Bill receives no actual payment for the property, a gift is still a chargeable disposal.
2	Exempt	As ABC Ltd is a building company, the proceeds will be dealt with as trading income.
3	Exempt	A racehorse is a wasting chattel (i.e. life of 50 years or less).
4	Chargeable	The painting is a non-wasting chattel which was sold for more than £6,000. It is not a wasting chattel as it will have a life of more than 50 years.

Workbook Activity 2

1	Exempt	Motor cars are exempt regardless of the use of the asset, cost or sale proceeds.
2	Exempt	A racehorse is a wasting chattel.
3	Chargeable	The painting is a non-wasting chattel that was bought for less than £6,000 but sold for more than £6,000. It would only be exempt if it had also been sold for less than £6,000.
4	Chargeable	The land, although bought and sold for less than £6,000, is not moveable property and therefore not a chattel.

KAPLAN PUBLISHING

18 Gains and losses for companies

Activity 1

Bubbles Ltd

The amount to include in taxable total profits will be £7,000 (£13,000 – £4,000 – £2,000 b/f).

Activity 2

JHN Ltd

Chargeable gains

	£
Plant (W1)	1,688
Building (W2)	(1,000)
Car – exempt	Nil
Memorabilia (W3)	5,168
Land (W4)	Nil
Total chargeable gains	5,856

Workings:

(W1) Plant

	£
Proceeds	15,000
Less: Cost	(8,000)
Unindexed gain	7,000
Less: Indexation allowance (£8,000 × 0.664)	(5,312)
Chargeable gain	1,688

(W2) Building

	£
Proceeds	26,500
Less: Cost	(27,500)
Allowable loss	(1,000)

No indexation is available to increase the loss.

(W3) Memorabilia

	£
Proceeds	19,000
Less: Cost	(7,000)
Unindexed gain	12,000
Less: Indexation allowance (£7,000 × 0.976)	(6,832)
Chargeable gain	5,168

(W4) Land

	£
Proceeds	25,000
Less: Cost	(15,000)
Unindexed gain	10,000
Less: Indexation allowance (£15,000 × 1.075) (restricted)	(10,000)
	Nil

The IA is restricted because indexation cannot create an allowable loss.

Activity 3

Linda Ltd

The correct answer is B.

Explanation

The gain is calculated as shown below.

	£	£
Disposal proceeds		420,000
Less: Incidental costs of disposal		(6,200)
Net proceeds		413,800
Less: Acquisition cost	194,000	
Incidental costs of acquisition	3,600	
		(197,600)
Enhancement expenditure		(58,000)
		158,200
Less: Indexation allowance		
Cost (£197,600 × 0.487)		(96,231)
Extension (£58,000 × 0.441)		(25,578)
Chargeable gain		36,391

The expenditure incurred in May 2005 for repairing the roof does not enhance the cost of the factory and is therefore not an allowable deduction in this gain computation.

The repair is a revenue expense which is allowable against the company's trading profits.

Activity 4

Smith Ltd

The correct answer is £13,054.

Explanation

The gain is calculated as shown below.

	£
Sale proceeds for 3 acres	15,000
Less: Cost of 3 acres	
£4,500 × (£15,000/(£15,000 + £25,000))	(1,688)
Unindexed gain	13,312
Less: Indexation allowance (£1,688 × 0.153)	(258)
Chargeable gain	13,054

KAPLAN PUBLISHING

Activity 5

Chattel disposals

ABC Ltd

The chargeable gain cannot exceed:

5/3 × (£6,500 − £6,000) = £833.

Therefore the chargeable gain will be restricted to £833.

DEF Ltd

The allowable loss will be restricted to (£6,000 − £7,500) = £1,500.

GHI Ltd

	£
Proceeds	14,000
Less: Cost	(5,000)
	9,000
Less: Indexation allowance (£5,000 × 0.291)	(1,455)
Gain	7,545
Chargeable gain cannot exceed: (5/3 × (£14,000 − £6,000)	13,333
Chargeable gain	7,545

Workbook Activity 6

RBQ Ltd

	£
Shop (W1)	3,208
Painting (W2)	(5,000)
Car – exempt	Nil
Land (W3)	19,622
Total net chargeable gains	17,830

Workings:

(W1) **Shop**

	£
Proceeds	15,000
Less: Cost	(8,000)
Unindexed gain	7,000
Less: Indexation allowance (£8,000 × 0.474)	(3,792)
Chargeable gain	3,208

(W2) **Painting**

	£
Proceeds	25,000
Less: Cost	(30,000)
Allowable loss	(5,000)

No indexation is available to increase the cost

(W3) **Land**

	£
Proceeds	29,000
Less: Cost	(6,000)
Unindexed gain	23,000
Less: Indexation allowance (£6,000 × 0.563)	(3,378)
Chargeable gain	19,622

Workbook Activity 7

Jackson Ltd

		£	£
(a)	**Land**		
	Sales proceeds	27,000	
	Less: Cost	(14,000)	
		———	
	Unindexed gain	13,000	
	Less: Indexation allowance		
	(£14,000 × 0.669)	(9,366)	
		———	
	Chargeable gain		3,634

		£	£
(b)	**Factory**		
	Sale proceeds	100,000	
	Less Legal fees	(1,200)	
		———	
		98,800	
	Less Cost (March 1995)	(10,500)	
	Extension (April 1999)	(3,000)	
	Extension (June 2002)	(4,600)	
		———	
	Unindexed gain	80,700	
	Less Indexation allowance		
	Cost (£10,500 × 0.718)	(7,539)	
	Extension (£3,000 × 0.534)	(1,602)	
	Extension (£4,600 × 0.438)	(2,015)	
		———	
	Chargeable gain		69,544

(c)	**Racehorse** – exempt asset	Nil
	(wasting chattel)	

✍ Workbook Activity 8

Chattel disposals

Alphabet Ltd

The gain will be restricted to 5/3 × (£7,500 − £6,000) = £2,500.

Delta Ltd

The allowable loss will be restricted to (£6,000 − £8,500) = £2,500.

Golf Ltd

	£
Proceeds	17,000
Less: Cost	(4,000)
	13,000
Less: Indexation allowance (£4,000 × 0.244)	(976)
Gain	12,024
Chargeable gain cannot exceed: 5/3 × (£17,000 − £6,000)	18,333
Chargeable gain	12,024

KAPLAN PUBLISHING

19 Shares and securities – disposals by companies

Activity 1

FDC Ltd

Share pool working	Note	Number	Cost £	Indexed cost £
Purchase 1 June 1991	1	4,000	8,000	8,000
Indexed rise to July 2000	2			
£8,000 × 0.269				2,152
Purchase – July 2000		1,800	9,750	9,750
		5,800	17,750	19,902
Indexed rise to March 2015				
£19.902 × 0.523				10,409
		5,800	17,750	30,311
Sale of 2,000 shares	3	(2,000)		
$\frac{2,000}{5,800}$ × £17,750/£30,311			(6,121)	(10,452)
Carried forward		3,800	11,629	19,859

Notes:

(1) Any entry in the cost column must also be made in the indexed cost column.

(2) Indexation must be added before the purchase in July 2000 is added to the pool.

(3) Use apportionment to allocate cost and indexed cost.

Gain on share pool shares

	£
Sale proceeds	20,571
Less: Cost	(6,121)
Unindexed gain	14,450
Less: Indexation allowance (£10,452 – £6,121)	(4,331)
Chargeable gain	10,119

Note: In the assessment it is not acceptable just to deduct the indexed cost from the proceeds.

This shortcut can only be used if the final result is a gain (not a loss). This is because the indexation allowance cannot increase a loss and has to be therefore separately identifiable.

Activity 2

Scarlet Ltd

Share pool	Number	Cost £	Indexed cost £
Balance at 5 May 2002	2,500	3,900	4,385
4 April 2003 Bonus issue (1 for 2)	1,250	–	–
	3,750	3,900	4,385
Indexed rise to January 2004 £4,385 × 0.039			171
19 January 2004			4,556
Rights issue (1 for 3) × 140p	1,250	1,750	1,750
	5,000	5,650	6,306
Indexed rise to September 2014 £6,306 × 0.405			2,554
	5,000	5,650	8,860
Cost of sale $\frac{1,500}{5,000}$ × £5,650/£8,860	(1,500)	(1,695)	(2,658)
Pool balance c/f	3,500	3,955	6,202

KAPLAN PUBLISHING

Gain on the disposal of shares

	£
Proceeds	4,725
Less: Cost	(1,695)
Unindexed gain	3,030
Less: Indexation allowance (£2,658 – £1,695)	(963)
Chargeable gain	2,067

Workbook Activity 3

Share disposals for companies

1   True

2   False   You do not apply an indexed rise as you do not need to add or deduct anything to or from the cost column.

3   False   The rights shares relate to the underlying shares.

4   True

Workbook Activity 4

Jerry Ltd

	£
Disposal – September 1997	
Proceeds	9,000
Less: Cost (W)	(4,000)
Unindexed gain	5,000
Less: Indexation (£5,933 – £4,000)	(1,933)
Chargeable gain	3,067

Disposal – March 2015

Proceeds	14,500
Less: Cost (W)	(4,043)
Unindexed gain	10,457
Less: Indexation (£9,452 – £4,043)	(5,409)
Chargeable gain	5,048

Share pool working

	Number of shares	Unindexed cost £	Indexed cost £
1 July 1993 Balance	4,100	8,200	10,744
September 1997			
(i) Indexed rise (0.132 × £10,744)			1,418
			12,162
(ii) Disposal			
(2,000/4,100) × £8,200 and £12,162	(2,000)	(4,000)	(5,933)
	2,100	4,200	6,229
January 1999			
(i) Indexed rise (0.026 × £6,229)			162
(ii) Acquisition	200	450	450
	2,300	4,650	6,841
March 2015			
(i) Indexed rise (0.589 × £6,841)			4,029
			10,870
(ii) Disposal			
(2,000/2,300) × £4,650 and £10,870	(2,000)	(4,043)	(9,452)
	300	607	1,418

Workbook Activity 5

Purple Ltd

Disposal – 8 August 2014

(Sale of 500 shares purchased in previous 9 days)

	£
Sale proceeds (500/5,000 × £15,000)	1,500
Less: Cost	(1,410)
Unindexed gain	90
Less: Indexation allowance	Nil
Chargeable gain	90

Disposal – 8 August 2014 (Sale of 4,500 shares from the pool)

	£
Sale proceeds (£15,000 – £1,500)	13,500
Less: Cost	(5,250)
Unindexed gain	8,250
Less: Indexation allowance (£9,229 – £5,250)	(3,979)
Chargeable gain	4,271

Total gains (£90 + £4,271) = £4,361

Note that no indexation allowance is given for disposals matched with shares purchased on the same day or the previous 9 days.

Share pool working

	Number	Cost	Indexed cost
		£	£
Balance at 9 June 1996	3,000	4,000	5,010
12 August 2001			
Bonus issue (1 for 3)	1,000	Nil	Nil
	4,000	4,000	5,010
Indexed rise to May 2006 (£5,010 × 0.292)			1,463
7 May 2006 Rights issue (1 for 2 × 150p)	2,000	3,000	3,000
	6,000	7,000	9,473
Indexed rise to August 2014 (£9,473 × 0.299)			2,832
			12,305
8 August 2014 Sale $\frac{4,500}{6,000}$ × £7,000/£12,305	(4,500)	(5,250)	(9,229)
Pool c/f	1,500	1,750	3,076

KAPLAN PUBLISHING

Workbook Activity 6

Chrome Ltd

	£
Disposal – October 2014	
Proceeds	17,760
Less: Cost (W)	(16,080)
Unindexed gain	1,680
Less: Indexation (£20,336 – £16,080)	
Restricted, indexation allowance cannot create a loss	(1,680)
Chargeable gain	Nil

Share pool working

	Number of shares	Unindexed cost £	Indexed cost £
May 2005			
(i) Acquisition	3,200	9,600	9,600
June 2009			
(i) Indexed rise (0.111 × £9,600)			1,066
(ii) Rights issue (3,200/4 × £2.60)	800	2,080	2,080
	4,000	11,680	12,746
January 2011			
(i) Indexed rise (0.073 × £12,746)			930
(ii) Acquisition	2,100	4,400	4,400
	6,100	16,080	18,076
October 2014			
(i) Indexed rise (0.125 × £18,076)			2,260
			20,336
(ii) Disposal	(6,100)	(16,080)	(20,336)
	Nil	Nil	Nil

20 Gains and losses for individuals

Activity 1

The correct answer is A.

Explanation

Taxable gains are defined as net chargeable gains after the deduction of the annual exempt amount, as follows:

	£
Total chargeable gains (£60,000 + £12,000)	72,000
Less Capital loss	(4,000)
	————
Net chargeable gains	68,000
Less Annual exempt amount	(11,000)
	————
Taxable gain	57,000
	————

Activity 2

False – The transaction is between husband and wife and therefore takes place on a no gain/no loss basis.

Workbook Activity 3

1	Yes	A chargeable disposal of a chargeable asset by a chargeable person
2	No	A motor car is not a chargeable asset.
3	Yes	Gifts are chargeable disposals.
4	No	A chattel sold at a gain where the proceeds are less than £6,000 is exempt.
5	Yes	The proceeds (i.e. the value) exceed £6,000.

Workbook Activity 4

1	True	
2	False	Capital losses cannot be set against anything except gains.
3	True	Once trade losses have been set against total income for the year, they can be treated like a capital loss of the year and deducted from capital gains.
4	False	Current year losses must be relieved in full but brought forward losses are only utilised to the extent that they reduce net gains to the level of the annual exempt amount.
5	False	Higher rate taxpayers pay 28% capital gains tax.

Workbook Activity 5

Mary

1   The correct answer is B.

2   The correct answer is C.

Explanation

1   Net chargeable gains for 2014/15 are £9,400 (£12,400 – £3,000). As this is less than the annual exempt amount, the loss brought forward of £4,000 is carried forward to 2015/16.

2   If Mary had only made the chargeable gain of £12,400 in 2014/15, losses brought forward of £1,400 would have been offset to reduce the gain to the level of the annual exempt amount. The balance of the capital losses of £2,600 (£4,000 – £1,400) would have been carried forward.

Workbook Activity 6

Bert

The correct answer is £3,000.

Explanation

Bert's net gains for 2014/15 are £8,300.

The capital losses brought forward of £3,000 will be carried forward to 2015/16 as the net gains for 2014/15 are less than the annual exempt amount of £11,000.

Workbook Activity 7

Misha

The correct answer is £3,734.00.

	£
Chargeable gains (£17,000 + £11,300)	28,300
Less: Annual exempt amount	(11,000)
Taxable gains	17,300
£11,100 (£31,865 – £20,765) × 18%	1,998.00
£6,200 (£17,300 – £11,100) × 28%	1,736.00
Capital gains tax liability	3,734.00

Workbook Activity 8

John

	£	£
Cottage		
Proceeds	73,600	
Less: Cost	(29,000)	
		44,600
Investment property		
Proceeds	26,000	
Less: Cost	(30,000)	
		(4,000)

	£	£
Total net gains b/f		40,600
Land		
Proceeds	60,000	
Less: Cost		
£50,000 × $\dfrac{60,000}{60,000 + 250,000}$	(9,677)	
	———	50,323
		———
Net chargeable gains		90,923
Less: Annual exempt amount		(11,000)
		———
Taxable gains		79,923
		———
CGT (at 28%)		22,378.44

21 Shares and securities – disposals by individuals

 Activity 1

Petra

The correct answer is A.

Explanation

A is the correct answer because the share identification rules match shares in the following priority

1   Shares acquired on the same day as the disposal – not applicable here.

2   Shares acquired in the following 30 days – 50 shares acquired on 5 January 2015.

3   Shares in the share pool (all acquisitions up to date of disposal).

Activity 2

Ken

10 October 2014 disposal of 2,000 shares identified with:

		£
(a)	Shares acquired on the same day	400
(b)	Shares from share pool	1,600
		2,000

Sale proceeds are £33,000 for 2,000 shares = £16.50 each

(a) **10 October 2014 acquisition**

	£	£
Sale proceeds (400 × £16.50)	6,600	
Less: Cost	(6,000)	
Chargeable gain		600

(b) **Share pool**

	£	£
Sale proceeds (1,600 × £16.50)	26,400	
Less: Cost (W)	(4,000)	
Chargeable gain		22,400
Total chargeable gains		23,000

Workings: Share pool

	Number	Cost
		£
February 1998 purchase	1,800	3,100
September 2007 purchase	1,200	4,400
	3,000	7,500
October 2014 disposal	(1,600)	(4,000)
Pool balance c/f	1,400	3,500

Activity 3

Mr Jones

	£
Sale proceeds	36,000
Less: Cost (W)	(10,414)
Chargeable gain	25,586

Workings: Share pool	*Number*	*Cost*
		£
June 1991 purchase	4,200	11,600
August 2005 rights issue ($\frac{1}{3} \times 4,200$) = 1,400 × £5.60	1,400	7,840
	5,600	19,440
October 2014 disposal $\frac{3,000}{5,600} \times £19,440$	(3,000)	(10,414)
Pool balance c/f	2,600	9,026

Workbook Activity 4

Ben

The correct answer is C.

Explanation

C is the correct answer because the share identification rules match shares in the following priority

1 Shares acquired on the same day as the disposal – not applicable here.

2 Shares acquired in the following 30 days – 500 shares acquired on 5 September 2014.

3 Shares in the share pool.

Workbook Activity 5

Tony

	£
Sale proceeds (9,000 × £14)	126,000
Less: Cost (W)	(50,625)
Chargeable gain	75,375

Workings: Share pool

	Number	Cost £
August 2003 purchase (15,000 × £6)	15,000	90,000
January 2006 bonus issue	1,000	
	16,000	90,000
November 2014 disposal $\frac{9,000}{16,000} \times £90,000$	(9,000)	(50,625)
Pool balance c/f	7,000	39,375

Workbook Activity 6

Conrad

	£
Proceeds	8,580
Less: Cost (W)	(3,928)
Chargeable gain	4,652

Working: Share pool

		Shares number	Cost £
July 2010	purchase	1,750	2,625
May 2011	purchase	200	640
		1,950	3,265
June 2012 (1 for 10)	rights issue @ £3.40	195	663
		2,145	3,928
Nov 2014	sale	(2,145)	(3,928)
		Nil	Nil

Workbook Activity 7

David

The correct answer is D.

Explanation

Working: Share pool		Shares number	Cost £
October 2001	purchase	2,000	4,000
March 2007	purchase	1,000	3,000
		3,000	7,000
February 2009 (1 for 5)	rights issue @ £4.00	600	2,400
		3,600	9,400
September 2014	sale	(400)	(1,044)
		3,200	8,356

Workbook Activity 8

Irving

September 2014 disposal of 1,500 shares identified with:

		£
(a)	Shares acquired in the next 30 days	700
(b)	Shares from share pool	800
		1,500

Net sale proceeds = £5,550 for 1,500 shares = £3.70 each

(a) 4 October 2014 acquisition

	£	£
Sale proceeds (700 × £3.70)	2,590	
Less: Cost	(2,450)	
Chargeable gain		140

(b) Share pool

	£	£
Sale proceeds (800 × £3.70)	2,960	
Less: Cost (W)	(2,048)	
Chargeable gain		912
Total chargeable gains		1,052

Workings: Share pool

	Number	Cost £
June 2009 purchase	4,800	15,360
April 2013 bonus issue (4,800/4)	1,200	
	6,000	15,360
October 2014 disposal	(800)	(2,048)
Pool balance c/f	5,200	13,312

22 Chargeable gains – reliefs

 Activity 1

Oliver

The correct answer is A.

Explanation

The gain is calculated as follows:

	£
Gain on disposal of business assets	600,000
Less: Capital losses (£22,000 – £9,300)	(12,700)
Annual exempt amount	(11,000)
Chargeable gain	576,300

The capital losses are offset against the gain on the sale of the antique table in preference to the gain on the sale of the business as this is more tax efficient.

 Activity 2

Karim

The correct answer is C.

Explanation

The gain on the sale of the original building can be rolled over against the cost of the new building as follows:

	£
Gain on sale of building	190,000
Less: Rollover relief	(155,000)
Chargeable gain = proceeds not reinvested (£450,000 – £415,000)	35,000

Activity 3

Matt and Ella

The correct answer is A.

Explanation

The gain is calculated as follows:

	£
Market value	60,000
Less: Cost	(21,000)
Chargeable gain before reliefs	39,000
Less: Gift relief	(39,000)
Chargeable gain	Nil

Base cost to Ella:

	£
Deemed cost (MV)	60,000
Less: Gift relief	(39,000)
Base cost	21,000

 Workbook Activity 4

Entrepreneurs' relief

The correct answer is D.

Explanation

The maximum Entrepreneurs' relief is £10,000,000 per lifetime not per disposal.

The relief must be claimed within 12 months of the 31 January following the end of the tax year in which the disposal occurs.

Workbook Activity 5

Leon

The correct answer is C.

Explanation

C is the correct answer because rollover relief is available against qualifying assets purchased within 12 months before and 3 years after the sale of the original factory.

However, property let out to tenants does not qualify for rollover relief, nor does moveable (rather than fixed) plant and machinery (i.e. the forklift truck).

 Workbook Activity 6

Brian

The correct answer is C.

Explanation

The rollover relief is restricted because the proceeds have not been fully reinvested.

The chargeable gain now will be calculated as follows:

	£
Proceeds	900,000
Less: Cost	(600,000)
	———
	300,000
Less: Rollover relief (balancing figure)	(225,000)
	———
Chargeable gain (£900,000 − £825,000)	75,000
	———

Workbook Activity 7

Spares Ltd

The correct answers are both A.

Explanation

A business or company has from 12 months before the disposal to 3 years after the disposal to reinvest the proceeds.

 Workbook Activity 8

Gift relief

The correct answer is C.

Explanation

C is the correct answer because gift relief is available on:

- quoted shares or securities in a trading company provided the individual holds at least 5% of the voting rights in the company

- unquoted shares regardless of the number of shares held, and

- any assets used in a trade by the donor or by his personal trading company.

It is Entrepreneurs' relief that is only available on the assets of a trade when the trade is disposed of as a whole or after it has ceased.

Workbook Activity 9

Taylor

Disposal of freehold factory (18 July 1993)

£115,000 has been reinvested in a business asset (warehouse) within three years and therefore part of the gain may be rolled over.

The £5,000 (£120,000 – £115,000) proceeds not reinvested is taxed in 1993/94, but will be covered by the annual exempt amount.

The gain rolled over is £25,000 (£30,000 – £5,000).

Disposal of warehouse (22 December 2014)

	£	£
Proceeds		320,000
Less: Cost	115,000	
Gain rolled over	(25,000)	
	————	
Base cost of warehouse		(90,000)
		————
Capital gain		230,000
Less: Annual exempt amount		(11,000)
		————
Taxable gain in 2014/15		219,000
		————

 Workbook Activity 10

Jonald

(a) **Amount chargeable on Jonald in 2014/15**

Gain eligible to be held over = £900,000

The gain assessable in 2014/15 is therefore £Nil.

(b) **Reg's base cost for shares gifted**

Market value at date of gift less gain held over
= (£5,000,000 – £900,000) = £4,100,000

Workbook Activity 11

DRV Ltd (1)

Sale of original freehold factory (purchased May 1989)

	£
Sale proceeds (December 1993)	130,000
Less: Cost	(65,000)
	———
Unindexed gain	65,000
Less: Indexation allowance	
(May 1989 – December 1993) (0.234 × £65,000)	(15,210)
	———
Chargeable gain before relief	49,790
Less: Rollover relief upon purchase of replacement	
factory in October 1993	(49,790)
	———
Chargeable gain – year ended 31 March 1993	Nil
	———

Sale of replacement factory

	£	£
Sale proceeds (March 2015)		325,000
Cost (October 1993)	190,000	
Less: Rolled over gain	(49,790)	
	———	(140,210)
		———
Unindexed gain		184,790
Less: Indexation allowance		
(October 1993 – March 2015) (0.831 × £140,210)		(116,515)
		———
Chargeable gain (Note)		68,275
		———

Note: DRV Ltd may be able to roll this gain over if it makes a further qualifying purchase in the qualifying time period.

Workbook Activity 12

DRV Ltd (2)

Sale of original freehold factory (purchased May 1989)

	£
Sale proceeds (December 1993)	130,000
Less: Cost	(65,000)
Unindexed gain	65,000
Less: Indexation allowance	
(May 1989 – December 1993) (0.234 × £65,000)	(15,210)
Indexed gain (as above)	49,790
Less: Rollover relief (balancing figure)	(34,790)
Chargeable gain – year ended 31 March 1994 (Note)	15,000

Note: Not all of the sale proceeds are reinvested.

Therefore, the chargeable gain arising now is the sale proceeds not reinvested = £15,000 (£130,000 – £115,000).

Sale of replacement factory

	£	£
Sale proceeds (March 2015)		325,000
Cost	115,000	
Less: Rolled over gain	(34,790)	
		(80,210)
Unindexed gain		244,790
Less: Indexation allowance		
(October 1993 – March 2015) (0.831 × £80,210)		(66,655)
Chargeable gain		178,135

Workbook Activity 13

Columbus

Disposal of first factory

	£
Proceeds	900,000
Less: Cost	(300,000)
Chargeable gain before reliefs	600,000

Gain taxable in 2014/15:
Lower of
(1) Sale proceeds not reinvested
(£900,000 – £700,000) — 200,000
(2) Chargeable gain before reliefs — 600,000

Therefore a gain of £200,000 is taxable in 2014/15

Rollover relief is therefore:
(£600,000 – £200,000) — 400,000

Base cost of second factory

	£
Cost of second factory	700,000
Less: Gain rolled over	(400,000)
Base cost	300,000

 Workbook Activity 14

Astute Ltd

(a) **Conditions for rollover relief**

(i) The reinvestment must be within the period starting 12 months before the disposal and ending 36 months after the date of disposal of the original asset.

(ii) The original asset and the replacement asset must be qualifying business assets used for a trading purpose by the taxpayer.

(iii) The replacement asset must be brought into use by the taxpayer for a trading purpose on acquisition.

(b) **Disposal of the factory – 15 February 2015**

	£
Proceeds (£320,000 – £6,200)	313,800
Less Cost (October 2004)	(164,000)
Legal fees of purchase	(3,600)
Extension (March 2006)	(37,000)
Unindexed gain	109,200
Less Indexation allowance	
on cost: (£164,000 + £3,600) × 0.374	(62,682)
on extension: (£37,000 × 0.329)	(12,173)
Chargeable gain	34,345

(c) **Alternative reinvestments**

(1) *Freehold warehouse costing £340,000*

As the full sale proceeds will have been reinvested, the company can claim to rollover the gain in full.

The base cost of the warehouse will be £305,655 (£340,000 – £34,345).

(2) *Freehold factory building costing £300,000*

As less than the full proceeds will have been reinvested, only part of the gain can be rolled over.

The proceeds not reinvested of £20,000 (£320,000 – £300,000) results in a gain of £20,000 remaining chargeable (see notes).

The balance of £14,345 (£34,345 – £20,000) is rolled over.

The base cost of the factory building becomes £285,655 (£300,000 – £14,345).

Note: HMRC allow the 'proceeds not reinvested' to be calculated as the difference between the **net** sale proceeds (i.e. after selling costs) and the purchase cost (including purchase expenses) of the replacement asset.

In (c) (2) this would mean only £13,800 (£313,800 – £300,000) of the gain remaining chargeable. However, you may not be expected to know this and would not be penalised either way.

Workbook Activity 15

Roy and Colin

Roy

	£
Deemed disposal proceeds	500,000
Less: Cost	(100,000)
	————
Chargeable gain before reliefs	400,000
	————

If a joint claim for gift relief is made, there will be no chargeable gain arising on Roy in 2014/15.

Colin

The cost available to Colin when computing the gain on a future disposal of the building is (£500,000 – £400,000) = £100,000.

 Workbook Activity 16

Alan

	£	£
Goodwill		
Proceeds	5,500,000	
Less: Cost	(10,000)	
	————	5,490,000
Factory		
Proceeds	6,000,000	
Less: Cost	(1,300,000)	
	————	4,700,000
		————
Total chargeable gains		10,190,000
Less: Annual exempt amount		(11,000)
		————
		10,179,000
		————
Qualifying gains (£10,000,000 × 10%)		1,000,000.00
Remaining gains (£179,000 × 28%)		50,120.00
		————
Capital gains tax payable		1,050,120.00
		————

Workbook Activity 17

Herbert

	Not qualifying for ER £	Qualifying for ER £
Shares		
Proceeds		500,000
Less: Cost		(20,000)
Chargeable gain		480,000
Table		
Proceeds	8,000	
Less: Selling costs	(900)	
Net proceeds	7,100	
Less: Cost	(2,000)	
Chargeable gain	5,100	
Chargeable gain restricted to 5/3 × (£8,000 – £6,000)	3,333	
Painting		
Proceeds	20,000	
Less: Cost	(22,000)	
Allowable loss	(2,000)	
Total net chargeable gains on non-qualifying assets (£3,333 – £2,000)	1,333	
Less: Annual exempt amount	(1,333)	(9,667)
Taxable gains	Nil	470,333
Capital gains tax payable (£470,333 × 10%)		47,033.30

MOCK ASSESSMENT
AQ 2013

1 Mock Assessment Questions

You should attempt and aim to complete EVERY task.

Each task is independent. You will not need to refer to your answers to previous tasks.

Read every task carefully to make sure you understand what is required.

Where the date is relevant, it is given in the task data.

Both minus signs and brackets can be used to indicate negative numbers UNLESS task instructions say otherwise.

You must use a full stop to indicate a decimal point.

Task 1 (12 marks)

(a) For each item, tick whether the following items are capital or revenue expenditure for tax purposes for a trading company.

	Capital	Revenue
Stationery		
Legal costs on purchase of a second hand building		
Repairs to the building to make it useable		
Computer software which will be replaced in two years		

(b) Tick the appropriate box to show how the following items should be dealt with when calculating adjusted profit for a sole trader. All items have been charged or credited (as appropriate) in arriving at net profit of £190,000.

	Increase net profit	Decrease net profit	No adjustment needed
Staff salaries			
Profit on the sale of a capital asset			
Decrease in general bad debt provision			
Legal fees for an unsuccessful appeal against a business rating assessment			
Costs of installing new machinery			
Food hampers given to staff as Christmas gifts			
Boxes of chocolates given to customers who spent over £250			
Leasing costs for car for sales person. The car has CO_2 emissions of 120 g/km			

Task 2 (14 marks)

Armin is a sole trader who prepares annual accounts to 31 March 2015. His capital allowance information is as follows:

	£
Tax written down value at 1 April 2014	
General pool	74,000
Armin's car	8,200

Armin's car originally cost £14,000, has CO_2 emissions of 120 g/km and 60% business use.

During the year ended 31 March 2015, Armin makes the following additions and disposals.

Additions:

Car for employee – CO_2 emissions 92 g/km (private use 40%)	12,000
Plant and machinery	37,000
New car for Armin – CO_2 emissions 170 g/km	22,000

Disposals:

Armin's old car	10,000

Using the following grid, calculate the total capital allowances and show the balances to carry forward to the next accounting period.

Task 3   **(12 marks)**

(a) Wasim ceased to trade on 31 January 2015. His previous tax adjusted trading profits were as follows:

	£
Year ended 30 September 2012	70,000
Year ended 30 September 2013	81,000
Year ended 30 September 2014	56,000
Period ended 31 January 2015	13,000

His overlap profits from the commencement of his business were £8,000. Wasim has calculated that if this amount was inflated to today's value it would be £11,200.

Calculate the taxable profits and state the tax year and basis period for the last three tax years of trading.

Tax year	Basis period	Profit £

(b) David, George and Nick are in partnership sharing profits equally. On 1 August 2014 they changed their profit sharing arrangements so that David received a salary of £24,000. The balance of profits was to be shared 2:3:1 for David, George and Nick.

For the year ended 31 March 2015, their tax adjusted trading profit was £180,000.

Show the division of profit between the partners.

	Total £	David £	George £	Nick £
Period to				
Salary				
Balance				
Period to				
Salary				
Balance				
Total				

Task 4 (12 marks)

(a) Sirtis Ltd has prepared accounts for the 15 months to 30 June 2015.

    (i) **How will this period be split for tax purposes?**

        A   3 months to 30 June 2014: Year ended 30 June 2015

        B   9 months to 31 December 2014: 6 months to 30 June 2015

        C   10 months to 31 January 2015: 5 months to 30 June 2015

        D   12 months to 31 March 2015: 3 months to 30 June 2015

    (ii) The tax adjusted trading profit before capital allowances is £450,000.

    How will this be split between the two periods?

    (iii) Sirtis Ltd has a tax written down value of £70,000 on their capital allowances pool at the beginning of the 15 month period. There are no additions or disposals during the 15 month period.

    What are the capital allowances for each period?

(b) XYZ plc has the following information for the nine months to 31 March 2015:

	£
Taxable total profits	400,000
Dividends received (net)	64,800

The company has one associated company

Complete the following computation.

                                        £

[   ] × 21%   [   ]

Marginal relief:

1/400 × ([   ] – [   ]) × [   ]   [   ]

Corporation tax payable   [   ]

Due date for paying this corporation tax   [   ]

Task 5 (4 marks)

Your answers for parts (a) and (b) should be to the nearest penny. If your answer is zero enter 0.

(a) A 40 year old taxpayer has business profits of £60,000 for 2014/15.

How much Class 4 NIC is due on these profits? £ [   ]

(b) A 67 year old taxpayer has business profits per their accounts of £8,000 for 2014/15.

How much Class 2 NIC is due for 2014/15? £ [   ]

(c) **Which one of the following statements is correct?**

A Class 2 and 4 NIC is paid with income tax through the payment on account system.

B Joseph is a sole trader whose 65th birthday is on 7 April 2014. He has taxable business profits of £35,000 for 2014/15 but he pays no NIC for 2014/15.

C Class 4 NIC is paid on a trader's taxable trading profits less any trading losses brought forward.

D Class 2 NIC is a tax allowable expense for a self employed trader.

Task 6 (6 marks)

Mark the following statements as true or false.

	True	False
When a partnership makes a trading loss, all the partners must claim the same methods of loss relief.		
When a company makes a trading loss, it can choose not to offset the loss in the current year but instead offset it first in the previous 12 months.		
When a sole trader makes a trading loss, they can choose not to offset the loss in the current year but instead offset it first in the previous tax year.		
A company wishing to offset a trading loss in the current year must submit an election within nine months and one day after the end of the year.		
When a company carries back a trading loss, it can only deduct it from previous periods' trade profits.		

Task 7 (10 marks)

Zahera is a client of your firm. You have agreed the following income tax liabilities in recent years.

	2012/13 £	2013/14 £
Income tax liability	16,350	17,550
Tax deducted at source and tax credits	(9,280)	(7,420)
Income tax payable	7,070	10,130
Class 4 NIC	2,500	2,370
Capital gains tax	1,670	1,965
	11,240	14,465

Zahera does not understand the tax payment system and wants you to explain:

(a) **how her tax liabilities for 2013/14 are paid**

(b) **the effect of making a payment late.**

Task 8 (6 marks)

A company has the following information for the year ended 31 March 2015.

	£
Trade profits	427,345
Rental income	16,525
Chargeable gains for the year	39,342
Interest received from Government stocks	10,000
Interest paid on loan to buy investment property	4,500
Qualifying charitable donations	2,750

The company has the following losses brought forward:	
Trading loss	140,000
Capital loss	8,100

Complete the form CT600 below as far as the information given permits.

Company tax calculation

Turnover

1	Total turnover from trade or profession	**1** £

Income

3	Trading and professional profits	**3** £
4	Trading losses brought forward claimed against profits	**4** £
5	Net trading and professional profits	box 3 minus box 4 **5** £
6	Bank, building society or other interest, and profits and gains from non-trading loan relationships	**6** £
11	Income from UK land and buildings	**11** £
14	Annual profits and gains not falling under any other heading	**14** £

Chargeable gains

16	Gross chargeable gains	**16** £
17	Allowable losses including losses brought forward	**17** £
18	Net chargeable gains	box 16 minus box 17 **18** £
21	Profits before other deductions and reliefs	sum of boxes 5, 6, 11, 14 & 18 **21** £

Deductions and Reliefs

24	Management expenses under S75 ICTA 1988	**24** £
30	Trading losses of this or a later accounting period under S393A ICTA 1988	**30** £
31	Put an 'X' in box 31 if amounts carried back from later accounting periods are included in box 30	**31**
32	Non-trade capital allowances	**32** £
35	Charges paid	**35** £
37	Profits chargeable to corporation tax	box 21 minus boxes 24, 30, 32 and 35 **37** £

Task 9

(8 marks)

(a) **For each of the following assets, tick the appropriate box to show whether the item is chargeable or exempt for capital gains tax.**

	Chargeable	Exempt
Half of a racehorse owned jointly with a friend		
£10,000 of 5% Treasury Stock		
Car used by Joe in his business		

(b) Obscure Ltd purchased ten acres of land in December 2006 for £120,000. On 15 March 2015 it sold two acres out of the ten acres for £80,000 incurring £3,420 of legal costs. On 15 March 2015 the remaining eight acres were worth £240,000.

The indexation factor is:

December 2006 – March 2015   0.281

Complete the following computation. Use brackets to indicate numbers to be deducted.

	£
Proceeds	
Selling costs	
Cost	
Unindexed gain	
Indexation allowance	
Indexed Gain/Loss	

Task 10 (10 marks)

Immense plc bought 40,000 shares in Smith plc for £2.20 each in August 2008. There was a bonus issue of 1 for 1 in February 2011 and a rights issue of 1 for 4 at £2.11 each in September 2013. Immense plc took up all its rights. Immense plc sold 75,000 shares in February 2015 for £350,000.

Indexation factors were:

August 2008 – February 2011	0.065
August 2008 – September 2013	0.160
February 2011 – September 2013	0.089
September 2013 – February 2015	0.029

Using the grid below calculate the gain made on this disposal and show the balance of shares carried forward.

Task 11 (6 marks)

(a) **Tick the correct box to show whether the following statements about capital gains are true or false.**

	True	*False*
A company can offset a capital loss against its total income of the same accounting period.		
Opera Ltd sells a painting for £12,000. This painting had hung on the wall of the boardroom. This is an exempt disposal.		
An individual taxpayer cannot carry their unused annual exempt amount forward for one year.		

(b) Overs Ltd made a capital gain on the sale of a factory building of £124,300. The building was sold for £500,000 in March 2015. In January 2013, Overs Ltd had bought a new factory building for £481,500.

How much of the gain of £124,300 can be rolled over into the purchase of the new factory?

(c) **Which of the following statements about Entrepreneurs' relief is correct? Select one answer only.**

A The first £10 million of gains on each qualifying disposal is charged at 10%.

B Manuel has owned 10% of the shares in ABC Ltd, a trading company, for 20 years. He does not work for the company. If he sells his shares in ABC Ltd he will be able to claim Entrepreneurs' relief.

C Jonah bought a sole trader business, ran it for nine months and then sold it making a gain of £500,000. Jonah will be able to claim Entrepreneurs' relief on this disposal.

D Abigail bought a sole trader business which she ran successfully for 10 years. Due to illness she ceased to trade in June 2014. She was unable to sell her business until July 2015. Abigail will be able to claim Entrepreneurs' relief on this disposal.

2 Mock Assessment Answers

Task 1

(a) Capital or revenue

	Capital	Revenue
Stationery		✓
Legal costs on purchase of a second hand building	✓	
Repairs to the building to make it useable	✓	
Computer software which will be replaced in two years	✓	

(b) Treatment in adjustment of profits computation

	Increase net profit	Decrease net profit	No adjustment needed
Staff salaries			✓
Profit on the sale of a capital asset		✓	
Decrease in general bad debt provision		✓	
Legal fees for an unsuccessful appeal against a business rating assessment			✓
Costs of installing new machinery	✓		
Food hampers given to staff as Christmas gifts			✓
Boxes of chocolates given to customers who spent over £250	✓		
Leasing costs for car for sales person. The car has CO_2 emissions of 120 g/km			✓

Task 2

Capital allowances computation – year ended 31 March 2015

	AIA/FYA	Pool	Armin's car (1)	(2)	Total
	£	£	£	£	£
Tax WDV b/f		74,000	8,200		
Additions – no AIA or FYA				22,000	
Additions with AIA	37,000				
Less: AIA	(37,000)				37,000
	———	Nil			
Disposals			(10,000)		
			———		
			(1,800)		
BC			1,800	× 60%	(1,080)
			———		
		74,000		22,000	
WDA at 18%		(13,320)			13,320
WDA at 8%				(1,760)	
				× 60%	1,056
Addition with FYA	12,000				
FYA 100%	(12,000)				12,000
	———	Nil			
Tax WDV c/f		60,680		20,240	
					62,296

Note: In the assessment you do not need to enter lines marking totals and subtotals.

Task 3

(a) **Taxable profits**

Wasim ceases to trade in 2014/15

Tax year	Basis period	Profit £
2012/13	Year ended 30.9.2012	70,000
2013/14	Year ended 30.9.2013	81,000
2014/15	1.10.2013 – 31.1.2015	61,000

Working:

£56,000 + £13,000 – £8,000 overlap = £61,000

The figure to use for overlap profits brought forward is the original figure with no adjustment for inflation.

(b) **Division of profits between partners**

	Total £	David £	George £	Nick £
Period to 31.7.2014				
Salary	0	0	0	0
(4/12 of £180,000)	60,000	20,000	20,000	20,000
Period to 31.3.2015				
(8/12 of £180,000)= £120,000				
Salary (8m)	16,000	16,000		
Balance 2:3:1	104,000	34,667	52,000	17,333
	180,000	70,667	72,000	37,333

Task 4

(a) **Long period of account**

(i) The answer is D.

When a company prepares accounts for a period exceeding 12 months the profits must be split into a 12 month period and a balance period, in this case 3 months.

(ii) Profits before capital allowances are time apportioned.

12/15 £360,000	3/15 £90,000

(iii) Capital allowances are calculated for each period separately. For the second period the WDA must be time apportioned.

£70,000 × 18% = £12,600	(£70,000 – £12,600) × 18% × 3/12 = £2,583

(b) **Short period of account – XYZ plc**

	£ pp
£400,000 × 21%	84,000.00
Marginal relief:	
1/400 (£562,500 – £472,000) × £400,000/£472,000	(191.74)
Corporation tax payable	83,808.26

Due date   1 January 2016

Workings:

(1) The upper limit for small profits marginal relief for a 9 month accounting period with one associated company is:

£1,500,000 ÷ 2 × 9/12 = £562,500

	£
(2) Taxable total profits	400,000
Add: FII (£64,800 × 100/90)	72,000
Augmented profits	472,000

(3) Dividends from associated companies are ignored in the calculation of FII.

Task 5

(a) **Class 4 NICs**

£3,414.51

Working:	£
(£41,865 – £7,956) × 9%	3,051.81
(£60,000 – £41,865) × 2%	362.70
	3,414.51

(b) **Class 2 NICs**

No Class 2 NIC is due as the taxpayer is over retirement age.

(c) **NICs**

The answer is C.

A is incorrect because Class 2 is not paid through the payments on account system.

B is incorrect because in order to be exempt from Class 4NIC, Joseph must be 65 or more at the start of the tax year on 6 April.

D is incorrect because the trader's own NIC is never an allowable expense.

Task 6

Losses

	True	False
When a partnership makes a trading loss, all the partners must claim the same methods of loss relief.		✓
When a company makes a trading loss, it can choose not to offset the loss in the current year but instead offset it first in the previous 12 months.		✓
When a sole trader makes a trading loss, they can choose not to offset the loss in the current year but instead offset it first in the previous tax year.	✓	
A company wishing to offset a trading loss in the current year must submit an election within nine months and one day after the end of the year.		✓
When a company carries back a trading loss, it can only deduct it from previous periods' trade profits.		✓

Task 7

(a) **Payment of 2013/14 tax liabilities**

Payments on account must be made for income tax and class 4 NIC on 31 January 2014 and 31 July 2014. These payments are 50% of the income tax and class 4 NIC payable for 2012/13. Any balance of tax due, together with all the 2013/14 capital gains tax, is paid on 31 January 2015. This gives a payment schedule as follows:

Date		Amount £
31 January 2014	First payment on account 50% × (£7,070 + £2,500)	4,785
31 July 2014	Second payment on account	4,785
31 January 2015	Balancing payment (£10,130 + £2,370 – £9,570)	2,930
	2013/14 CGT	1,965
	Total	4,895

The whole process starts again with the first payment on account of £6,250 (50% × (£10,130 + £2,370) for 2014/15, also due on 31 January 2015.

(b) **Effect of late payments**

Any tax paid late attracts an interest charge from the due date until the amount is paid.

In addition, if the tax of £4,895 due on 31 January 2015 is paid more than 30 days late there will be a penalty equal to 5% of the tax due. Further 5% penalties will be due if the tax is still outstanding after 6 and 12 months after 31 January.

Task 8

CT600 Form

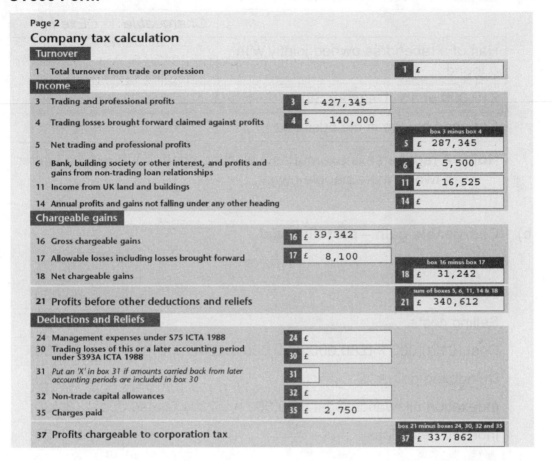

Page 2

Company tax calculation

Turnover

1	Total turnover from trade or profession	**1** £

Income

3	Trading and professional profits	**3** £ 427,345	
4	Trading losses brought forward claimed against profits	**4** £ 140,000	
5	Net trading and professional profits		**5** £ 287,345 (box 3 minus box 4)
6	Bank, building society or other interest, and profits and gains from non-trading loan relationships		**6** £ 5,500
11	Income from UK land and buildings		**11** £ 16,525
14	Annual profits and gains not falling under any other heading		**14** £

Chargeable gains

16	Gross chargeable gains	**16** £ 39,342	
17	Allowable losses including losses brought forward	**17** £ 8,100	
18	Net chargeable gains		**18** £ 31,242 (box 16 minus box 17)
21	Profits before other deductions and reliefs		**21** £ 340,612 (sum of boxes 5, 6, 11, 14 & 18)

Deductions and Reliefs

24	Management expenses under S75 ICTA 1988	**24** £	
30	Trading losses of this or a later accounting period under S393A ICTA 1988	**30** £	
31	Put an 'X' in box 31 if amounts carried back from later accounting periods are included in box 30	**31**	
32	Non-trade capital allowances	**32** £	
35	Charges paid	**35** £ 2,750	
37	Profits chargeable to corporation tax		**37** £ 337,862 (box 21 minus boxes 24, 30, 32 and 35)

Task 9

(a) Chargeable or exempt assets

	Chargeable	Exempt
Half of a racehorse owned jointly with a friend		✓
£10,000 of 5% Treasury Stock		✓
Car used by Joe in his business		✓

Note: A racehorse is exempt as a wasting chattel. It does not matter if two or more people own it.

(b) Chargeable gain – part disposal

	£
Proceeds	80,000
Selling costs	(3,420)
Cost (£120,000 × (£80,000/(£80,000 + £240,000)))	(30,000)
Unindexed gain	46,580
Indexation allowance Cost (£30,000 × 0.281)	(8,430)
Indexed gain / loss	38,150

Task 10

Chargeable gain – Share disposal

Gain calculation		£	
Proceeds		350,000	
Less: Cost (W)		(97,650)	
Less Indexation (W)			
(£111,348 – £97,650)		(13,698)	
		————	
Chargeable gain		238,652	
		————	
Working: Share pool			
	Number	Cost	Indexed cost
8/08 Purchase	40,000	88,000	88,000
2/11 Bonus issue 1 for 1	40,000	Nil	Nil
Indexed rise to 9/13			
£88,000 × 0.160			14,080
9/13 Rights issue 1 for 4	20,000	42,200	42,200
	————	————	————
	100,000	130,200	144,280
Indexed rise to 2/15			
£144,280 × 0.029			4,184
			————
			148,464
2/15 Disposal	(75,000)	[1] (97,650)	[2] (111,348)
	————	————	————
Balance c/f	25,000	32,550	37,116
	————	————	————
[1] 75,000/100,000 × £130,200			
[2] 75,000/100,000 × £148,464			

In the assessment you do not need to enter lines marking totals and subtotals.

Task 11

(a) True or False

	True	False
A company can offset a capital loss against its total income of the same accounting period. (Capital losses can only be offset against capital gains)		✓
Opera Ltd sells a painting for £12,000. This painting had hung on the wall of the boardroom. This is an exempt disposal.		✓
An individual taxpayer cannot carry their unused annual exempt amount forward for one year.	✓	

(b) Rollover relief

The answer is Nil.

None of the gain can be rolled over because the purchase of the new factory building is more than 12 months before the disposal of the old factory.

(c) Entrepreneurs' relief

The answer is D.

Abigail's disposal qualifies as it is within 3 years of the cessation of her business.

A is incorrect because the £10 million is a cumulative lifetime limit covering all disposals, not each disposal.

B is incorrect because Entrepreneurs' relief would only be available if Manuel worked for the company.

C is incorrect because qualifying assets must be owned for at least 12 months before disposal.

INDEX